BULLETPROOF
PRESENTATIONS

No One Will Ever
Shoot Holes in
Your Ideas Again!

By

G. Michael Campbell

CAREER
PRESS

Bulletproof Presentations
Edited By Jodi Brandon
Typeset By Eileen Dow Munson
Cover design by Johnson Design
Printed in the U.S.A. by Book-mart Press

To order this title, please call toll-free 1-800-CAREER-1 (NJ and Canada: 201-848-0310) to order using VISA or MasterCard, or for further information on books from Career Press.

The Career Press, Inc., 3 Tice Road, PO Box 687
Franklin Lakes, NJ 07417
www.careerpress.com

Library of Congress Cataloging-in-Publication Data

Campbell, G. Michael, 1948-
    Bulletproof presentations : no one will ever shoot holes in you ideas again! / by G. Michael Campbell.
        p. cm.
    Includes index.
    ISBN 1-56414-590-5 (pbk.)

    HF5718.22 .C36 2002
    658.4'52—dc21

                                                      2001054390

To my wife, Molly,
for all the patience and love
over the years
as I pursued my dreams.

———

To my sunshine team:
Heather, Megan, and Courtney.

To my book team:
Tammy Herrera, Denise Sparks,
Jodi Brandon, Stacey A. Farkas, and Mike Snell.

Special thanks to Janet Elliott of El Paso Energy for the
inspiration for the title and to Shalandra Sollat and Richard
Bretscheider of Microsoft for their help.

CONTENTS

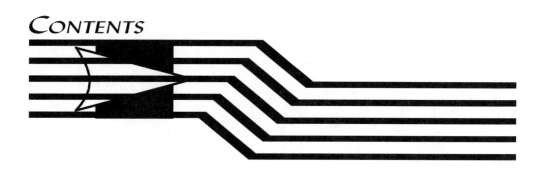

INTRODUCTION

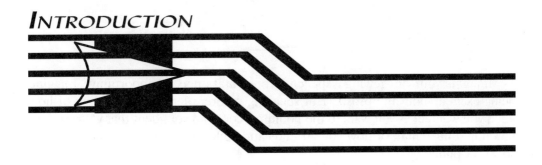

U.S. News & World Report first reported Americans' fear of speaking in 1978. Since then, several follow-up studies have confirmed the fact: Americans fear speaking before a group more than they do death itself (death came in third!). **The number-one fear among Americans is speaking in public.**

The fear of getting up and talking to others hurts the careers of many Americans because, as the Harvard Business Review reports, the number-one skill among all the criteria for advancement and promotion for professionals is their ability to communicate effectively. Clearly, making an effective presentation, whether to your peers, your boss, the customer, the general public, or the media, may play a major role in your career advancement. **The number-one skill for advancement and promotion for professionals is their ability to communicate their ideas effectively.**

Fortunately, anyone can learn to talk in any situation effectively. In fact, this book will show you how, as it leads you through a step-by-step program that can turn even the shakiest speaker into a cool, confident presenter. It will make both you and your ideas bulletproof! The good news is that you can learn to be a cool, confident speaker!

Consider this

Everyone has the equal ability to become unequal. Think about that for a minute! All people are created with an equal ability to grow and change. Not everyone is created with the same talents, gifts, or abilities. Each of us is unique in some special way. Our personalities are as diverse as the number of stars in the sky. Yet there is one constant: By using our talents to the fullest, we can stand out from the crowd.

"The distribution of talents in this world should not be our concern," says noted psychologist Alan Loy McGinnis. "Our responsibility is to take the talents we have and ardently parley them to the highest possible achievement."

Thomas Edison was almost deaf. Yet he did not spend his time attempting to learn how to hear. Instead he focused on his ability to think, organize, and create. His accomplishments speak well for his decision to build on the qualities he possessed. "If we did all the things we were capable of doing," reflected Edison," we would literally astound ourselves."

Figure out what talents you can use for your presentation, and prepare to astound yourself!

———

Imagine yourself viewing a speech or presentation as an opportunity. Imagine being excited about the prospect of speaking before a large group. Think of how good you will feel as you walk to the podium—cool and confident that your presentation is solid. Think of how your friends and colleagues will envy your ability to speak in public.

And with the Worksheets provided at this end of the book, you will be able to repeat that success over and over again!

Consider this

According to Max De Pree, chairman of the board of Herman Miller, Inc., "There may be no single thing more important in our efforts to achieve meaningful work and fulfilling relationships than to learn to practice the art of communication."

———

Here is a list of the benefits you will receive from reading, and the tools and techniques you will learn to use, as you work your way through this book.

1. This is a proven, tested process for developing a bulletproof presentation. I have taught this method to hundreds of people from all walks of life, from executives to sales reps to technical people in businesses large and small. I know it works, because people have told me of the successes they have had in using this approach.

2. The book contains a series of tools for developing all the correct elements of a bulletproof presentation. One thing you will want to do is continue to make solid, bulletproof presentations each time you are called on. The elements of any presentation are the same and the Worksheets in the Appendix will help you to repeat your success every time you make a presentation.

3. You will receive guidelines for selecting and using visual aids to enhance the presentation. The way in which you use and develop your visual aids will have a dramatic impact on your listeners. The ideas you are presenting are the "meat" of your presentation, but the visual aids will be the "sparkle" and polish that will set you apart as a speaker.

4. You will learn about the latest techniques for effectively delivering a bulletproof presentation, including body language and voice. The way you deliver the presentation will show your confidence and grasp of the subject. It will give the audience confidence in you, and they will want to listen to you!

5. Most speakers are very concerned about handling questions during a presentation. They know that the respect a speaker receives from the audience is often swayed by how effectively the speaker answers the difficult questions that come up. I will provide you with some valuable and tested models for handling questions during a presentation. You will sound confident and logical, even if the audience members don't agree with you!

6. Finally, you will receive several suggestions for handling stage fright successfully. This is the biggest problem most speakers have—speaking while their voice is quavering and their knees are shaking. There are things you can do to manage fear, and I will share them with you.

7. Just by buying this book, you are acknowledging a need to learn more about how successful presentations are developed and delivered. As you continue through this book, you will learn all the tricks and techniques the professionals use that make them look so good.

I recognize there are different types of presentations that you may be giving. **Presentations can range from one-on-one sales presentations to team presentations, from technical presentations to quick sound bite presentations at trade shows.** Over the course of the chapters, you will learn how to apply the techniques in this book, and they might be used in any of these particular settings.

Consider this

Motivational guru Anthony Robbins wrote in his book, *Unlimited Power*, that "the way we communicate with others and with ourselves ultimately determines the quality of our lives."

Why do we make presentations? Most organizations thrive because of the exchange of information critical to their success. Whether it be a formal or informal presentation, the basic idea of a presentation is to allow the speaker to tell others about something they need or want to know.

To give bulletproof presentations, you must make sure the audience can hear and understand you. **You must be able to demonstrate to the members of your audience that your ideas are important to them and you must be able to answer their questions when they ask them with clear and concise answers.** When a presenter mumbles or evades answering a question, people will stop listening. Then they will get upset because they believe you are wasting their time.

At the end of each chapter, you will find a review of the main points (called "Bulletproof Advice") and an activity that will assist you in building your presentation. Coupled with the Worksheets in the Appendix, you will be able to construct a bulletproof presentation.

Using bulletproof presentations, you will be convincing in your ideas, confident in your manner, and clear in the delivery of your material!

Consider this

As I write this book, cyclists from all over the world are competing in the grueling Tour de France bicycle race. In an edition of the *National Geographic* magazine titled "An Annual Madness," Gilbert Duclos-Lassalle describes the arduous event. The bicycle race covers approximately 2,000 miles, including France's most difficult, mountainous terrain. Physical needs such as eating and drinking are literally done "on the fly." Temperatures can be extreme as the cyclists attempt to win this prestigious event.

What kind of trophy or prize could motivate people to train for up to 60 miles a day, every day, to prepare for the event? The prize is a special winner's jersey! Duclos-Lassalle sums up each participant's inspiration this way: "To sweep through the Arc de Triomphe on the last day. To be able to say that you finished the Tour de France."

Presenters are often motivated by the challenge itself. Self-discipline, preparation, and the desire to be successful serve as a catalyst for achievement. The very thought of "crossing the finish line" successfully makes all the pain and suffering worthwhile.

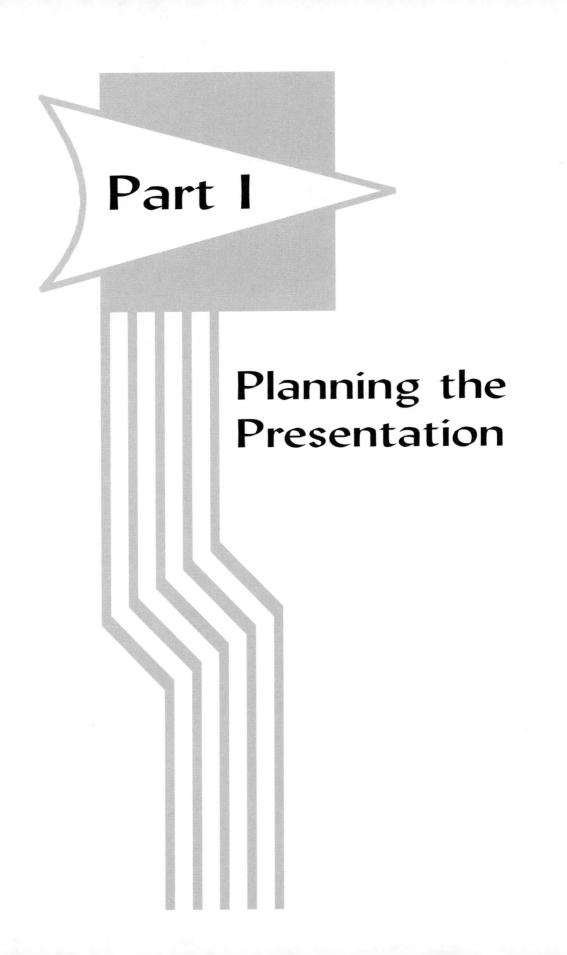

Part I

Planning the Presentation

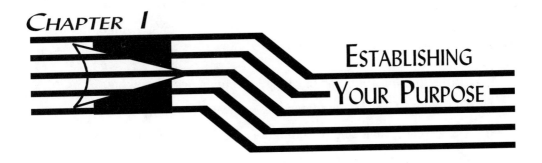

CHAPTER 1

ESTABLISHING YOUR PURPOSE

In this chapter, I want to convince you that understanding your purpose in making your presentation is the first step to developing a Bulletproof Presentation. If you cannot state your purpose clearly and simply, your audience will not understand your purpose either.

Consider this

Motivational expert George Shinn once stated, "Action is indeed therapy. It erases doubts and fears, anxieties, and worries. It capitalizes on failures and mistakes and turns them into positive influences. It exercises the mind for problem-solving and for creativity. It develops poise under pressure and uses wisdom and experience to consider alternatives and to provide a back-up plan. It calls forth the best in all of us, and it becomes the password to success."

This is just as true for presentations. Don't procrastinate! Begin to take action as soon as you know you must make a presentation, and continue that action until you actually make the Bulletproof Presentation.

Writers have a term they call "writers' block." What it usually means to writers is that they are having trouble getting started. They have thoughts swirling around in their heads, but they cannot seem to get them on paper. One of the best ways to prevent the presentation equivalent to writers' block is to just get started—and start with your purpose.

Consider this

The purpose of any presentation should be simple and direct. David Belasco, writer and theatrical giant, said that the idea for every play he ever produced could be written as one simple sentence on the back of a business card. Could your presentation pass David Belasco's test?

In my years of training and coaching people to make Bulletproof Presentations, it still amazes me how many times people will believe their objective is "give someone else information." The myth persists. And I suppose that if the presentation is simply a report during a staff meeting, or similar situation, then perhaps it is simply informative.

By establishing your purpose as the first step in building a Bulletproof Presentation, you will be able to achieve one or more of the five basic objectives of any presentation:

1. Instruction: informing or teaching your audience something.

2. Inspiration: inspiring or motivating your audience to act.

3. Advocating: convincing or selling a point of view to your audience.

4. Stimulation: stimulating discussion and debate among the audience.

5. Gratification: entertaining or amusing your audience.

Most presentations are given with the intent of influencing someone else's thoughts, ideas, or actions. When the objective is to exert that kind of influence, then these other types of presentations are really persuasive in nature. To be really effective, a business presentation must allow the audience members to think, know, and do what you (the presenter) want them to think and know and do, or to give you a clear "no" because they understood what you said and just disagree. At least you had a fair hearing!

Most presentations are really persuasive in nature.

However, people really believe that if they lay out all the facts properly, the idea (project, budget, you pick the term) will sell itself. That is one reason they feel so frustrated by the lack of success. The problem is that **facts alone are not persuasive.**

Consider this

Alfred Marshall, a 19-century economist, once wrote, "Facts never speak for themselves." Think about that for a moment. When was the last time you saw two people who had seen the same event describe it very differently? It happens all the time. Police officers will tell you that if 10 people saw an accident, they are likely to get 10 different descriptions of what happened.

———

Facts, by themselves, are not really worth very much. What makes them valuable and interesting is when someone clarifies them, analyzes them, interprets them or presents them.

When you have all the facts, your work is just beginning. The audience members are waiting to see how you use them before making up their minds about how successful your presentation was.

The reason that is true is simple, but important—facts appeal only to the logical part of the individual, and not the emotional side. Once you realize that most of the time you are trying to get someone to think, act, or feel, a certain way, then you will be much better prepared to build a persuasive presentation. Most of the time, you are trying to influence someone's thoughts, actions, or feelings.

Often, the reason facts alone do not work is because of preconceived notions that the audience may have prior to listening to your presentation. You must factor those notions into your purpose and give the audience members reason to change their minds.

For example, suppose you have been asked to lead a highly respected department in a mature business. (By "mature business," I mean a business that has been around for more than 100 years and has a long, historical way of doing things.) Until now, the people you are supervising have not been encouraged to take any initiative. All they are used to doing is following orders—and not asking questions. You want to change this attitude and encourage an entrepreneurial spirit from top to bottom within the department. What might their preconceptions be?

A few possibilities might be:

➤ Take initiative? I can't do that! My responsibility is to do what I'm told!

➤ Take initiative? I can't do that! Then I would have to take responsibility for any mistakes and I can no longer just blame the boss.

➤ Take initiative? This must be some kind of trick, because they have never asked us to do this before!

➤ Take initiative? The new boss probably knows exactly what he wants and the safest thing to do is just "go through the motions" and wait until this thing blows over.

Most of the time, you are trying to influence someone's thoughts, actions, or feelings.

The general tone and style of your presentation can reinforce its purpose. If you are truly trying to just pass information, then you will need to present the information logically in a consistent and well-structured way (we will cover this in more detail in Chapter 8). If your main purpose is to entertain, then you will need to include some funny stories and anecdotes. If you want to inspire the audience, then the content must be very positive and presented in a way that audience members can respond to emotionally and personally. Also remember that usually the audience will want to know *why* you are talking about this subject and *why* you believe your approach is the one that is best for them.

I want to challenge you to establish a specific purpose for any presentation you give.

Ask yourself the following in your own mind to help establish a clear purpose:

1. What do you want your audience to know after hearing your presentation?

2. What do you want your audience to do after hearing your presentation?

3. What do you want your audience to feel after hearing your presentation?

Now that you have established the reason for your presentation, you must put that reason into a specific statement. For example:

➤ **I want my audience to understand the reasons for recycling newspapers and to commit to recycling.**

➤ **I want my audience to understand the characteristics of shared services and how they are different than corporate support services.**

➤ **I want my audience to believe that drug testing by employers is necessary in certain industries.**

However, there are certain guidelines you should follow in establishing your purpose. Use these guidelines to help you. Establish an objective that will be:

➤ **R**ealistic.

➤ **A**chievable.

➤ **M**easurable.

These three terms really work together in answering this question: **Can the audience, or the listener, actually accomplish my objective?**

For example, if I am in a sales presentation, and my objective is to get the listener to buy, I must be sure the listener has the authority to buy. In the case where my listener cannot buy, I need to shift my objective. Perhaps my objective will be to persuade this person to take me to the person who *can* buy. The objective is now realistic and achievable. This type of purpose also allows me to measure my success in a concrete way.

I want to stress how very important it is that the purpose allows you to "RAM" that objective home with the listeners.

**The purpose will tell you what information you need
and what information you will not need.**

If you are like most people, you will have far more information than you can realistically use. The purpose will help you decide, because you can always ask yourself:

1. **Will this help me accomplish my purpose?**

2. **Do I need this information to "RAM" the point home?**

If the answer is yes, then you use it. If it is maybe or no, then you probably will not use that information.

The best way to begin your preparation for any presentation is to establish your purpose. **Write your purpose in one sentence that is clear and simple.**

Examples of purposes that might be the keystone for certain presentations might be:

➤ The audience should be able to list, demonstrate, or define.

➤ The audience will buy my product or service.

➤ The audience will believe in this new approach.

Beware of purpose statements that are too generic. For example, if I say that my purpose is "to help the audience understand" something, how will I know that they do? Will I give them a test?

No matter what you choose as your purpose statement, it should always answer these questions:

1. Why am I giving this presentation?

2. How will I know if I have succeeded?

Consider this

I was called in to work with a team that had to prepare a presentation for a large defense contract that the company really wanted to win. It was for millions of dollars over three years with a possible two-year extension. After I saw the first run-through of the presentation, it appeared listless and very uninspiring. I talked with the project manager and asked him about the team and its approach. His response spoke volumes: "We really don't have our best players available to put on this project, so we put what we had together." It confirmed for me a basic tenet of a Bulletproof Presentation: If you are trying to put across an idea, but you don't believe in it yourself, you are in for a very rough road.

When you or your team is merely going through the motions, rather than really believing passionately that you are the best, it is time to pull the plug on the presentation—or get someone else to do it who can believe. Sincerity and conviction are essential if you are going to be successful, even if your delivery is not as polished as you would like.

Take the positive approach

Often, when deciding your purpose, you can probably "frame" the issue in either a positive or negative way. Framing is a term psychologists use to describe how people approach a problem or situation—the old adage about whether the glass is half empty or half full. Probably we all have an intuitive sense that a positive approach is more successful. However, there is some research that confirms our suspicions.

We all have an intuitive sense that a positive approach is more successful.

For example, if my purpose is to get the customer to purchase training services, I could say they want to hire us because "the employees cannot speak in public" (negative frame) or I could say they want to hire us "to improve the skills of the employees in public speaking" (positive frame).

Several years ago, some researchers conducted a study to determine if a positive or negative approach was more persuasive with voters during a presidential campaign. The idea of the research was to determine how voters responded to controversial problems when the problem was framed in a positive or negative way.

When the presidential candidate used a negative approach, they framed the issue with these characteristics:

➤ A stable explanation that says this problem will last forever if we don't do something.

➤ A global explanation that says this problem will affect everything we do.

➤ An internal explanation that says we are the problem.

The positive approach to framing the problem had these characteristics:

➤ An unstable explanation that describes the problem is only temporary.

➤ A specific explanation to this problem and only it affects this situation.

➤ An external explanation that says the problem is because of the situation we are in.

Based on the research conclusions, the more optimistic approach was more persuasive with voters and therefore more effective.

That research should support a purpose statement that is positive (optimistic) over one that is negative (pessimistic).

With that in mind, here are some guidelines to remember as you establish your purpose and plan the presentation:

1. Don't complain about how unfair a problem might be; instead, focus on how your solution will solve the problem.

2. Remain positive and point out specific problems that are only temporary and resist any temptation to fix blame.

3. If you do need to admit to a problem, make it very specific and explain it in a way that will help the audience understand.

Preparing your presentation

Now think about your presentation. As you draft your presentation, consider the following:

1. Can you establish the purpose with one clear, simple statement?

2. Does it meet the RAM (realistic, achievable, measurable) test?

3. Do you have a clear deliverable to produce? A deliverable can be a report, a product, or a written procedure. It is something that can be physically "given" to the audience.

The key thought here is this:
Don't ever think you are just delivering information!

You are always in a persuasive mode in that the listeners are making judgments about how well informed and well prepared you are. You are always sending a message about yourself and the way you work when you make a presentation. Don't underestimate the value of "winning a few points" when you are making a presentation, even if that presentation is relatively informal and casual.

Activity: Establishing Your Purpose

1. Think of a presentation that you must prepare for (or one that would be typical of your presentations).

2. For that presentation, complete the following sentence: "The purpose of my presentation is _____."

3. Ask yourself if the purpose is realistic, achievable, and measurable.

4. Adjust the sentence in #2 if needed.

Bulletproof advice

➤ **Facts alone are not persuasive.**

- Most of the time in making a presentation, you are trying to influence someone else's thoughts, actions, or feelings.

➤ **Make the purpose for your presentation very specific.**

- The more specific you make the purpose of your presentation, the more clearly it will help you determine the information you need and how successful you were in achieving the goals of the presentation.

➤ **Make sure any purpose you establish is realistic, achievable, and measurable.**

- Write out the purpose of your presentation by completing the sentence, "The purpose of my presentation is _____."

➤ **Take the positive approach in the way that you frame the issues or problems.**

- Based on research, the more optimistic the approach, the more successful it will be in persuading and influencing people.

➤ **Only occasionally are you delivering just information.**

- There are occasions when you are simply providing information, but they are probably the exception rather than the rule. And even in those instances where you are only delivering information, don't underestimate the value of winning a few points along the way by developing a Bulletproof Presentation.

CHAPTER 2

DECIDING ON YOUR OVERRIDING THEME

In this chapter, we want to tie the purpose that you established in Chapter 1 to the major theme you want to establish in your presentation.

Consider this

I have heard numerous times from people who attend presentations that their hope is that they can come away with *one* good idea they can put to use. Research shows that they are usually disappointed: 49 percent of all presentations are regarded as failures—in other words, devoid of any ideas the members of the audience could use.

So if you can give your audience at least one idea that each person feels he or she can use, you will not only have delivered a Bulletproof Presentation, you will be hailed as a great presenter! You will be seen as someone who actually took the time to give them something useful.

———

Many books on presentations will mention the concept of establishing your objective, or purpose, but very few mention the concept of the overriding theme.

The overriding theme, which I refer to in my training as the "OT," is best explained this way: **If your audience didn't remember anything else about your presentation, they would remember this.**

As an example, consider Dr. Martin Luther King's "I Have a Dream" speech. Very few people have heard that entire speech. Fewer still remember all the things that Dr. King referred to in the speech. But almost everyone will be able to tell you Dr. King's overriding theme.

The problem most presenters will have in their presentation seems to be the enormous amount of material they want to cover within the allotted time.

And that is true—from the presenter's point of view! However, research into the listening habits of people presents a different problem: getting them to remember what you have said.

Given the amount of time you will spend developing and practicing your presentation, **what is more important: that you make sure you cover everything, or that the people you are speaking to remember what you said?**

I would much rather cover less ground and have the audience remember what I said.

That is the reason for thinking about an overriding theme. It will help you to imagine what you want to leave the audience with and then build a presentation that can give it to them!

Also, in helping to understand how to establish the overriding theme during the presentation, you need to understand the *Four Rules for Communication.*

➤ **Rule of Frequency.**

➤ **Rule of Primary.**

➤ **Rule of Recency.**

➤ **Rule of Emotion.**

These four rules will demonstrate *how* audiences remember, and *what* they remember from any presentation. Here are more details about these four laws.

➤ **Rule of Frequency:**
  Listeners will remember ideas or information they have heard more frequently.

  This rule is why you will hear speakers repeat ideas or themes throughout their presentation. When we talk later about the elements that you must include in your introduction, body, and conclusion, this rule will be very prominent. This rule also explains why an overriding theme is so crucial: If you can keep that central thought in front of the audience throughout the presentation, they could remember it much easier.

➤ **Rule of Primary:**
  Listeners will remember ideas or information they heard first during a speech or presentation.

  The Rule of Primary tells us that our introduction is very important because it will be one part of the presentation that the audience will remember very well.

➤ **The Rule of Recency:**
  Listeners will remember the last ideas or information they hear.

  The Rule of Recency reminds us as presenters that the conclusion is very important to our presentation. Very often, the success or failure of a presentation will be determined in the conclusion. The reason? The Rule of Recency.

➤ **The Rule of Emotion:**
Listeners will remember the ideas and information that touched
their hearts.

Any time you can weave strong emotions into your presentation, try
to do that. Great speakers often cause our emotions to swing from
heartwarming stories to terrible tragedies. And we remember them as
being very powerful at the time. Such is the Rule of Emotion.

As you think about your overriding theme, keep in mind these four rules.
Along with your purpose statement (from Chapter 1), these two elements will
help you define and refine all the information that you have at your disposal for a
presentation. Use them as guides for what should be used, and not used, in your
presentation.

Defining the Overriding Theme

In doing training and various presentations over the years, I have conducted
an exercise where I ask the audience to listen carefully to a list of words without
writing any of the words until I have completed the list. After I finish reading the
words, I ask the audience to write down as many words as they can remember. I
then predict certain keys words to illustrate the Rules for Communication. I have
correctly predicted the words hundreds of times. Here's why it works.

I repeat one word three times and inevitably everyone gets that word. In fact,
they usually laugh because it seems so obvious. I explain it is obvious because it
follows the Rule of Frequency. If I want you to remember something, I need to
say if more than once.

Then I predict the first word on my list, and nearly everyone has it on his or
her paper. I explain that this follows the Rule of Primary. The introduction is
critical to the success of any presentation because people remember it so well.

The next word I predict is the final word in my list. Sure enough, about 75
percent of the people have it. I explain how this relates to the Rule of Recency.
It also illustrates how important a good conclusion is to any presentation. People
will remember the last thing you say to them.

Finally, I predict a final word in my list that always strikes an emotional
chord. Again, about 75 percent of the audience will have the word. It demonstrates the Rule of Emotion. When I am trying to be persuasive, I will generally
strike some sort of emotional note with a listener. It may be fear, uncertainty,
or joy, but I must remember how powerful emotions are in the way people
make decisions. If I neglect this important element, I may be unsuccessful and
not even realize why.

> **In fact, a presenter who ignores any of these rules does so at**
> **his or her own peril. They are quite formidable and rarely is a**
> **presentation bulletproof if they have not been followed.**

Activity: Preparing your presentation

1. Now think about your presentation or one that is typical of presentations you give.

2. What do you want them to remember if they don't remember anything else?

3. Write out your overriding theme.

Bulletproof advice

➤ **Use the overriding theme to help you decide what you want the audience to remember—even if they forget everything else.**

  - The Overriding Theme will help you sort through the enormous amount of information that you could use in your presentation and focus on the information that will help you establish the Overriding Theme.

➤ **Presenters who remember the Four Rules of Communication are far more successful in the minds of the audience.**

  - Use the Rules of Frequency, Primary, Recency, and Emotion to guide you in the development of the presentation.

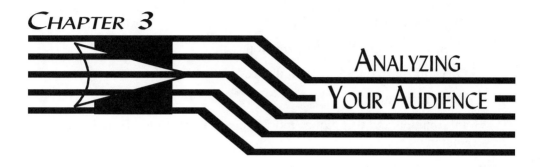

Chapter 3

Analyzing
Your Audience

In this chapter, I want to convince you to change, or tailor your presentation to the audience. This can be one of the key elements of success in making a presentation.

Consider this

Great teachers can be a real inspiration to us in making an outstanding presentation. Whenever I have asked people what they remember about their

favorite teachers from childhood, they tell me a variety of things, such as the clothes they wore or their mannerisms or habits. But one theme consistently comes up: that their favorite teachers always took a real interest in them as individuals. They were sensitive to their needs and fears even in sometimes-crowded classrooms. Great presenters do the same thing when they analyze their audience carefully. The presentation makes each individual in the audience feel as though the presenter is speaking to him or her and their needs and concerns. When that happens, the audience will remember that speaker and have a special regard for his or her abilities.

All of us have suffered through presentations that were either clearly too elementary or too difficult for us to enjoy and relate to easily. I want you to consider the following:

→ The key individuals.

→ Their relationship to each other.

→ Their level of knowledge on this topic.

→ Objections or concerns the audience might have.

→ Their motivation.

→ Information and techniques most likely to be accepted by the audience.

→ What the audience hopes to gain from listening to this presentation.

→ Hidden agendas.

→ Environmental factors (anything in the audience that may cause you to alter your message).

All of these elements need to be considered when you begin planning the Bullet-proof Presentation. **Connecting with the audience is crucial to the success of any presentation, and analyzing the audience will ensure the best chance for success.**

Consider this

You can never know too much about your audience! The more you know, the better off you will be in anticipating the audience's concerns and objections. The more you concentrate on its problems, the less time you have to focus on your problems.

─────

The key individuals

You will need to keep in mind the key individuals you will be speaking to. You need to ask yourself these questions:

➤ Who plans to attend?

➤ Who really cares about the topic I am presenting?

➤ What are their responsibilities?

➤ Who will be attending that really understands the topic I am presenting?
  ■ Can I preview my presentation with that person in advance?

➤ Who will be attending that will not understand the topic I am presenting?
  ■ Can I preview my presentation with that person in advance?

➤ What is his or her relationship to the ideas I am trying to present?

➤ Who created things the way they are today?

➤ Who has won a promotion because of their contributions to the way things are today?

➤ Who might look bad if things change from the way they are now?

➤ Why are they attending?

➤ Who is likely to dislike my ideas? What will they dislike about them?

➤ Who loses power if things change?

➤ Who loses access to power if things change?

➤ Who is most affected by my ideas? How will they be hurt/helped? If I assume they will be hurt, how will they be hurt? If they will be helped, how will they be helped?

Try to get as many names and job titles as possible. The more you can know about the audience and exactly what they do, the better you will be able to adapt your subject to their expertise and experience.

Identify any key listeners. A key listener is a person who will be making a decision about the ideas you are presenting. It could also be that this person will influence the decision that others will make. You will want to key into the way he or she makes decisions and the way he or she likes to receive information.

What do I mean by that? In making decisions, what is your key listener's approach to information? **Some people will tend to focus on ideas within your message. Others will tend to focus on the specific facts within the message.**

The other element to consider is the key individual's approach to outcomes.

Some people are very results-oriented; they focus on the "what" of your message. Other individuals are much more people-oriented in their focus. They will be concerned with how people will react to the information you are presenting. One manager always asked me the same question after a presentation: "Who will be mad at me if I do it?" ("It," in this case, refers to accepting the recommendation of the presenter.) Clearly a results-oriented, people-oriented type of person. Whenever I made a presentation to her, I had to tailor the message to answer that question.

Does the listener focus on:

➤ Ideas?

➤ Specifics?

➤ Results?

➤ People?

Listeners sometimes won't tell you what their concerns are. You often have to figure them out by talking to other people who may know those people better. If you ever have a feeling that you are missing someone's concerns, make sure you talk to others who can give you guidance and insights into the key individuals.

That "hidden agenda" can be a killer! Tailoring your presentation to these two distinct approaches (results-oriented and people-oriented) will help you to be far more successful in making your presentation bulletproof. (You'll read more about that later in the chapter.)

Pre-sell certain key people

Before you even begin the presentation, you may want to consider asking for a meeting before the presentation and selling your ideas to key listeners. You will want to get suggestions from them and listen to their questions and concerns.

Consider this

Machiavelli wrote in *The Prince* that "there is nothing more difficult to take in hand, more perilous to conduct, or more uncertain in its success, than to take the lead in the introduction of a new order of things, because the innovator has for enemies all those who have done well under the old conditions and lukewarm defenders in those who may do well under the new."

———

The idea here is to get key influencers to help you shape your ideas. If they hear those ideas during the presentation, they are far more likely to support you.

Do not try to sell someone who you know will be against your ideas. However, you can talk with him or her to get his or her opinions on the downside of your ideas. Usually, others will have the similar concerns. You will then be prepared to address those issues during your presentation.

The idea is to get stronger, clearer ideas in the presentation. Do not risk having these key listeners develop a negative position too early.

Their relationship to each other

This presumes that more than one person will be present, but it also means the presenter must understand the relationships among the various people. If one is the supervisor of the others, that is important to consider.

Many presenters make assumptions about the people in the audience and make poor choices as a result. For example, they hear that the CEO will be at the session and decide to gear the presentation to that person. Why? Because they think this is the most important person at the presentation. It's a reasonable, but perhaps incorrect, assumption. **Always be aware of the relationship among your listeners.**

However, another person may be the more likely decision-maker. Why is that true? Because he or she possesses special technical information or expertise, the CEO probably will rely on him or her and his or her judgment. The decision-maker will certainly rely on them to supply input into any decisions.

Another important reason to consider relationships is the very real risk that you will alienate other people in the room who have influence on the decision. You are discounting them and their ideas. Remember: Even the president of the United States has advisors.

Address everyone present no matter what the mix of people. This is important to consider because of the next element.

Finally, always consider who will be impacted by the ideas you are proposing. If you are suggesting anything that will make someone look silly, foolish, or outdated, you will have an enemy out there!

Their level of knowledge on this topic

Particularly when you are presenting material that is technical (or financial) in nature, you must be aware of how much knowledge each of the listeners has coming into the presentation. **Some people will have knowledge and expertise matching yours; others' levels could be both above and below yours.**

Consider this

> Remember that your audience needs to understand your point, and you must help them get there. Consider the Wright brothers. Their efforts to get their new flying machine off the ground were met with continual failure. Finally one December day at Kitty Hawk, Orville achieved a historical milestone. He did what no one had ever done before, and the moment deserved celebration. The two brothers quickly wired their sister Katherine, "We did it. We have actually flown in the air 120 feet. Will be home for Christmas." Excited about her brothers' achievement, Katherine delivered the message to the local news-paper editor. He glanced at the wired message and said, "This is nice news for the family—having both boys home for Christmas."

What happens when you either speak above the heads of the audience or below their understanding? Needless to say, either is bad news for you. In either case, the listeners will be bored, angry, or both, and they'll feel that listening to you was a waste of their time. And rightly so! **If you speak over their heads, you will be seen as haughty, and if you talk beneath their knowledge, you will be seen as either condescending or stupid!**

Targeting your talk to the lowest common denominator may not be the best approach. I have been at presentations where the decision-maker is the least knowledgeable person in the room. It would be a mistake, in most cases, to target this person for the presentation. **In all likelihood, the decision-maker will rely on the expert knowledge of the people around him or her to give an analysis of the technical merits of your presentation.**

Decision-makers are more likely to judge you on how you present the material, handle questions, and interact with their subordinates.

If you are giving a technical presentation, remember that several people in the audience may not understand all the details. However, they will understand information that concerns potential risks or other business implications.

Here are a few guidelines to follow:

➤ Focus on the business outcomes that result from the technical facts.

➤ Explain technical facts in nontechnical terms.

➤ Use visual aids to help explain any technical information.

➤ Use action verbs that clearly explain and describe a series of events or facts.

Objections or concerns the audience might have

During any presentation, but particularly during a persuasive presentation, you will need to be prepared to address any concerns or objections the listeners may have. **Some presenters try to duck the listeners' concerns. That is the quickest way to get crucified.**

As part of your audience analysis, you must take this into consideration. Sit down and brainstorm any and all of the questions that you could be asked. Even if they seem silly, do not cross them off.

Try to identify any weaknesses that could be exposed in your presentation. While you are doing this exercise, list all the potential risks to your ideas. Then list any assumptions you are using in your logic. Ask yourself how your ideas would change if the assumptions changed. You may think your idea is perfect, but others may disagree! What you are trying to do is decide, first of all, if you will address these concerns, and then how to address them. If you are not going to address these concerns immediately in your presentation, you must at least know what they are. I can assure you, they will be asked during the question period if you have not prepared—it's Murphy's Law!

> **Prepare backup material on any**
> **objections or concerns, even if you may not use it**
> **during the presentation.**

It could be handy during the question period later.

Their motivation

Try to find out why the listeners have come to your presentation.

Their level of interest will be affected by how they got there. For example, try to find out if people want to be there or have been ordered to be there. Sometimes people were sent to a meeting because someone else more senior did not want to attend.

Also, if you are presenting at a convention, try to assess whether people are attending because they have a genuine interest in your topic or because it was a great opportunity to go to San Diego!

Remember: **In presenting new ideas or approaches to a problem, you will need to show benefits that will appeal to this audience.** A benefit is something that the decision-maker receives from your suggestion. If can be reduced costs, more profit, improved customer service, or better quality.

> **Talk to the decision-makers about the benefits to them**
> **and the organization and, whenever possible,**
> **quantify them in dollars or other tangible measures.**

Information and techniques most likely to be accepted by the audience

When analyzing your audience, you will need to use information, data, and other techniques to give evidence that will support your argument. Keep in mind what sources of information and techniques will be acceptable to this group.

Consider this

In an article about the challenges facing leaders in a rapidly changing business world, the *Royal Bank of Canada* newsletter from Toronto stated, "Someone once described management as a 'Chinese baseball game.' In this mythical sport, both the ball and the bases are in motion. As soon as the ball is hit, the defending players can pick up the base bags and move them anywhere in fair territory. The batters never know in advance where they must run to be safe."

The point is this: Once you have settled on your presentation and begin to rehearse it, do not keep changing it, or "moving the bases." Otherwise, you will never feel comfortable knowing where you are going and the material that will get you there.

———

Developing new ideas to "fit" an audience can be a similar challenge. You must know where the "bases" are and target your message to cover as many as possible.

Keep in mind what sources of information and techniques will be acceptable to this group.

For example, using data from the oil industry to convince an audience of aerospace engineers may or may not convince them that what you say is true. What does the audience hope to gain from the presentation?

What the audience hopes to gain from listening to this presentation

Most people do not come to any presentation because they have extra time to kill. They hope to gain some information, knowledge, or insights from the speaker that will help them in some tangible way.

Put yourself in the shoes of the audience members and ask the question: What's in it for me?

The best presenters always make sure that the listeners come away with something they have gained as a result of listening. It is an essential part of your audience analysis.

In putting together your facts, remember that people will begin to think about the following:

➤ What will this cost us?

➤ How many resources will we need to devote to this to make it work?

➤ How do we know we will receive the benefits of this idea?

➤ What are the risks that we will need to plan for if we go forward?

➤ Are those risks too high or acceptable?

➤ What commitment will I have to make if I approve this idea?

All of these concerns are critical to consider as you determine what information to include and what information to hold "just in case."

Hidden agendas

What you are looking for in this exercise is the ability to guard against hidden agendas. A hidden agenda is a purpose someone has that he or she does not want others to know about.

Hidden agendas are very dangerous to the presenter. People will seem to be arguing about facts or information that does not seem significant. If you can uncover this hidden agenda in your preparation, then the arguments will make sense to you and you can respond accordingly. What you are trying to do is keep your presentation on target.

Although these are less tangible at times, they are no less important in completing the analysis of your audience.

Environmental factors

You will want to consider other factors in analyzing your audience. Environmental factors are anything in the audience or situation that may cause a presenter to alter his or her message. Following are some examples.

Gender

Is your audience primarily one gender? You will want any examples to apply to the audience. That is especially true if the audience is mixed. For example, sports metaphors are often received coolly by women, but might be very appropriate for a male-only audience.

Age

Try to find out the age range of the audience so you can determine various life experiences audience members may have had. For example, you might have to explain the impact of President Kennedy's assassination in far more detail to those who were born in the late 1970s or early 1980s. However, an audience of 50-year-olds might relate quite easily.

Education level

The audience's education level should influence your vocabulary and language choices. For example, the lower the level of education in the audience, the more concrete you will need to be in your language and examples. However, that does not mean to "talk down" to your audience; it merely means to choose words that are appropriate for your audience.

Political or religious affiliation

The political party of the audience may tell you how liberal or conservative audience members are and what types of examples and topics will appeal to them. For example, a conservative Republican audience would probably react negatively to the topic of gun control. Another example might be talking to a group of Southern Baptists about the health benefits of dancing.

Occupation

Use examples that will relate to the occupation of the audience if appropriate. Insurance brokers will need different examples than an audience primarily made up of nurses.

Income level

Knowing something about your audience's income level may help you if you need to adapt a presentation with a financial focus. For example, if you were seeking to persuade an audience to invest in an expensive insurance plan, that would be very difficult for low- to moderate-income audiences, but it might sell well to middle- or upper-income people.

Heritage and geography

If you have an audience that contains a large number of immigrants whose first language is not English, you will need to carefully consider the vocabulary you use. You may also use a number of visual aids to help people follow along easily.

Also consider the geographic region of the United States. Examples about cattle ranching will probably do well in Texas or Colorado, but fair poorly in New York or Massachusetts.

Be careful! All of these assumptions are just a good first guess. Just because the audience has a good mix of men and women, for example, does not mean that they are all mothers and fathers. Be careful about assumptions and check them out as you plan your presentation. That is the only sure way to make your presentation bulletproof!

Never underestimate the environmental factors in a presentation. When you are in a business situation giving a presentation, you are constantly being assessed as to your level of contribution and how clearly you can think and analyze information!

Consider this

> While being interviewed on CNN's *Larry King Live*, Donald Trump lowered the boom on King.
>
> King's interview with the real-estate tycoon was just under way when Trump asked, "Do you mind if I sit back a little? Because your breath is very bad. It really is. Has anyone ever told you this before?"
>
> King responded, "No."
>
> "Okay, then I won't bother."
>
> A confused King continued, "That is how you get the edge. See, that little thing you threw at me right then—that no one has ever told me."
>
> "Has nobody ever told you that? You are kidding?"
>
> "Nobody."
>
> "Okay, Larry, your breath is great!" conceded Trump.
>
> According to the network producers, Donald Trump was just demonstrating how he gets the edge in negotiations. Sounds like a really unpleasant approach. Consider the words of Lord Chesterfield when he said, "People hate those who make them feel their own inferiority."

Activity: Audience checklist

For your presentation, or one that is typical of presentations you give, answer the following questions:

❑ Who plans to attend?

❑ Who really cares about the topic I am presenting?

❑ What are their responsibilities?

❑ Who will be attending that really understands the topic I am presenting? Can I preview my presentation with that person in advance?

❑ Who will be attending that will not understand the topic I am presenting? Can I preview my presentation with that person in advance?

❑ What is their relationship to the ideas I am trying to present?

❑ Who created things the way they are today?

❑ Who has won a promotion because of their contributions to the way things are today?

❑ Who might look bad if things change from the way they are now?

❑ Why are they attending?

❑ Who is likely to dislike my ideas? What will they dislike about them?

❑ Who loses power if things change?

❑ Who loses access to power if things change?

❑ Who is most affected by my ideas? How will they be hurt/helped? If I assume they will be hurt, how will they be hurt? If they will be helped, how will they be helped?

Bulletproof advice

➤ **To be successful in preparing a Bulletproof Presentation, you must connect with the audience.**

   ▪ Doing a good job of analyzing the audience will help ensure the best chance for success.

➤ **Keep in mind the key individuals who you will be speaking to during the presentation.**

   ▪ Find out as much about them as you can. You can never know too much about your audience, their relationships, and who will influence whom.

➤ **Be sure to consider the audience's objections or concerns.**

   ▪ Don't try to duck listeners' concerns or you will lose credibility with them. Spot any potential weaknesses in your presentation in advance and come prepared to answer any of those concerns.

➤ **Always put yourself in the shoes of the audience members and ask,** *What's in it for me?*

   ▪ Listeners come away from the best presentations with something they have gained as a result of listening to the presentation.

CHAPTER 4

ANALYZING THE SITUATION

Understanding all aspects of the situation where you will be presenting is a crucial step in planning a Bulletproof Presentation.

Consider this

Take the time to get acquainted with the room you are speaking in before you get there. The first time I spoke to an audience as part of an after-dinner presentation, I made the mistake of not checking out the room in advance. It turned out to be a mistake that made my presentation very difficult. The room was long and narrow, and people at the far end of the table had difficulty seeing the visuals I had prepared. When I set up, I discovered there was no electrical outlet for my overhead projector. I found myself in an awkward situation waiting for someone at the restaurant to find an extension cord. Finally, I had not arranged for the timing of the coffee service and the wait staff began to pour and stand in front of people as I was trying to establish my overriding theme and the agenda.

Needless to say, the presentation was not bulletproof! However, I learned my lesson and have never put myself in that position since. Experience is the best teacher, but, believe me, I would not like to learn that lesson more than once!

How to prepare the room

It's amazing how many good speeches have been ruined by a non-functioning microphone, miserable lighting, or a poor ventilating system.

You may have prepared a wise and witty speech, but if the audience can't hear or see you, who cares? And if the audience is suffering from an air-conditioning system that doesn't work, you might as well wrap it up early and head home.

Check out the room before you speak. If you can't go in person, ask someone else to look at it. Or telephone the person who invited you to speak. Ask some basic questions:

➤ *Does the room have windows?* Even more importantly, do the windows have heavy drapes? You'll need to close them if you show any slides.

You'll also need to close the drapes if you're speaking in a hotel or motel conference room that looks onto a swimming pool. There's *no way* you can compete with beautiful, young bodies in scanty bathing wear, so shut those drapes before the audience arrives and save yourself a lot of frustration during the speech.

➤ *Is there a lectern?* Does it have a light? Is it plugged in and ready to go? Is a spare bulb handy? Does the lectern have a shelf underneath where you can keep a glass of water, a handkerchief, and a few cough drops? Can the lectern be adjusted to the proper height? If you're short, is there a box to stand on?

Move everything into place *before* you arrive at the lectern to speak.

➤ *Can you be heard without a microphone?* If so, don't use one.

➤ *Is the public address system good?* Test it and ask an assistant to listen to you. Must you stoop or lean to reach the microphone? It should be pointed at your chin. Can you be heard in all corners of the room? Is the volume correct? Do you get feedback? Where do you turn the microphone on and off?

➤ *How is the lighting?* Do a "test run" with the house lights. Do they create a glare when you look at the audience? In general, the light level on you should be about the same as the light level on the audience. Does a crystal chandelier hanging over your head create a glare for the audience? Remove the bulbs. Will the spotlight appear where it should? Adjust it.

➤ *What about the seating?* After they've taken off their coats and seated themselves and gotten comfortable, people hate to be asked to move. Perhaps it reminds them of school days. Be sure to arrange the seating to your advantage *before* the audience arrives.

Will people be seated at round dining tables, with some of their backs to you? If so, allow time for them to shuffle their seats before you start to speak.

It's too difficult to maintain eye contact when listeners are scattered around a large room. If you expect a small crowd, try to remove some of the chairs before the audience arrives. Do anything you can to avoid "gaps" in the audience where energy can dissipate.

If you'll speak in a large auditorium, have the rear seats roped off. This forces the audience to sit closer to you. This roped-off area is also great for latecomers, who can slip in without disturbing the rest of the audience.

If only a few people show up, move your lectern from the stage to floor level to create more intimacy. The closer you are to your listeners, and the closer your listeners are to each other, the more successful you will be.

➤ *Is there good ventilation?* Can the air-conditioning system handle large crowds? Can the heat be regulated?

Hotels are notoriously stuffy. One time I had to give a speech at a big hotel in Houston, and when I arrived I found the room temperature had been set at 80 degrees. I immediately pushed the thermostat way back, and by the time the audience arrived the room was comfortable.

➤ *How many doors lead into the room?* Can you lock the doors at the front of the room to prevent intruders from upstaging you? Can you have assistants posted at the rear doors to ensure quiet entrances from latecomers and quiet exits from people who must leave before you finish?

➤ *Is music being "piped" into the room?* If so, turn it off immediately. Do not rely on hotel staff to do so when it's your time to speak.

➤ *Is the room soundproof?* This becomes a critical issue when you speak in a hotel room. Who knows what will be happening in the room next to yours: a raucous bachelor party, a pep rally, or an enthusiastic sales pitch. What audience members would concentrate on, say, cogeneration if they could listen to the excitement happening next door?

Don't take any chances. If possible, make an unannounced visit to the hotel to check things out for yourself. Hotel managers always say their conference rooms are "nice and quiet." You're better off checking for yourself.

If you find that sound carries through the walls, speak to the manager. Ask to have the adjacent rooms empty during your speech. If the hotel is booked solid, they won't be able to accommodate this request, but it doesn't hurt to ask.

Above all, get the name and telephone number of a maintenance person who can step right in and replace a fuse or a light bulb or adjust the air conditioner. Keep this person's name and number handy at all times.

Remember: When you are the giving the presentation, you are in charge! Insist on not only knowing what the room looks like, but how it will be arranged and its size, seating, and lighting. Any time you give a presentation, it is your responsibility to make *all* the arrangements. Always arrive well ahead of your audience, so you can make any necessary changes more easily.

Why are they here?

You will want to analyze why people have come. We just looked at the audience analysis in Chapter 3, and you may be thinking that this question belongs there. However, it is important to answer this question relative to the situation.

Are they here to be entertained, to receive important information, or as part of a standard agenda for regular meetings?

All of these things will influence how formal your presentation needs to be. For example, if the presentation is part of a departmental staff meeting, it can be far more informal than a presentation attended by a customer who is considering the purchase of additional services.

Large vs. small groups

The number of listeners you will have in the presentation can influence how you deliver it. Essentially, it will influence how formal you will need to be in the presentation. The larger the audience, the more formal it is.

So how "big" is big? I would say that any time your audience exceeds 30 people, I would think of the presentation as a "large" presentation. Other people will tell you that a number more than 100 is what they would consider large.

Whatever number you choose, if you cannot see each of the members of the audience as an individual, then the presentation is a large one regardless of the exact number.

When you present to a small audience, you may often sit down during the presentation, for example, around a conference room table. It often allows you to have more casual conversations with members of the audience without raising your voice very much.

**Small groups will tend to invite more
questions during the presentation than large ones.**

However, if the subject is a sensitive one for the audience, then you should err on the side of being more, and not less, formal.

For large audiences, you will need to be formal in your presentation. What does that mean?

**A formal presentation means the presenter
stands in front of an audience and uses visual aids and
a set agenda that includes questions and answers,
usually at the end, so that the speaker is not interrupted.**

One-to-one presentations

One-to-one presentations can be formal or informal, depending on the relationship of the two people and the sensitivity of the topic.

If the presentation is to a senior executive, where a good deal of money could be at stake, the presentation will need to be formal. You will need charts, graphs, pictures, and so on, to illustrate your key points.

It could be a sales presentation where the presenter is introducing a new company or product line to a customer. Again, a formal presentation would include everything outlined in this book.

Other situations may call for less formal presentations. **Backup material is still important, and the need for clarity and organization is no different.** However, it may be that the presentation can take on the characteristics of a discussion, with key ideas and evidence brought out at the appropriate times.

Environmental factors

Particularly in competitive situations, you will need to consider the agenda you have been given.

Consider any environmental factors. Environmental factors are any conditions that may cause you to alter or change your message.

You will also need to gather information on what is currently happening within the organization that can impact the audience's evaluation of your ideas.

There may be some business conditions that will either make your ideas more or less appealing. You will want to know about these conditions before you make your presentation.

They can be complex conditions such as deadlines, current priorities, available resources, or organizational risk.

For example, would your idea be familiar to the audience, but not particularly valued? If so, then you will need to make sure the benefits are very appealing to the audience. If the ideas you present have the potential to make someone look bad, even if he or she is not in the audience, you will need to figure out a way to present the ideas so it does not look like someone has not been doing his or her job.

Environmental conditions

You may need to consider the politics of the situation, including others who may also be speaking.

You can analyze who will precede you and who will follow you on the agenda. Although you cannot know exactly what the others will say during their presentations, you will probably have a pretty good idea if you know your topic and theirs.

There are advantages to being first, last, or in the middle. However, the strategies for each of those positions will be different.

If you are speaking at a difficult time (for example, just before or just after lunch), you will need to be highly energetic to keep the interest of the audience. Otherwise, the audience will get restless and/or sleepy. Consider getting the audience involved by asking people questions or having them do a quick activity that gets everyone talking.

For example, I have used puzzles or word riddles (always where they fit and make sense) to get the audience involved.

Some other logistics of the situation should also be considered, such as:

➤ The time of day.

➤ The amount of time allotted to the presentation.

➤ The location and facilities.

Are you an Insider or an Outsider?

Often you will need to consider whether you are an Insider or Outsider with the audience.

An Insider is usually considered a peer or colleague of the audience. Insiders know the audience, and the audience knows them. Remember, however, that if you are significantly higher or lower than others in the audience within your organization's hierarchy, you are an Outsider—even though you may feel you should be treated as an Insider.

As an Outsider, you need to establish your credentials with the audience to gain credibility.

You are being evaluated from the first moment the audience lays eyes on you. You create an immediate impression, and you want it to be favorable. **Your presentation style needs to be formal, clear, and informative if you want a Bulletproof Presentation!**

The time of day

As you can imagine, there are times of day that are better than others for a presenter. We can probably all remember the times we have been subjected to a boring presentation just before lunch or at the end of a long day.

The best times for presentations
are mid-morning and mid-afternoon.

The worst times are just before and just after lunch. People are sleepy, and if you find yourself in front of an audience then you'd better make it lively. And *don't turn out the lights* to show slides or overheads for very long or the audience will be asleep!

The allocated time

Often speakers will find they don't get as much time as they had originally planned. They are usually part of a larger meeting or session, and these have a way of veering off schedule. At these times, it is good to remember the four rules we learned about earlier. **The Rule of Primary and the Rule of Recency tell us not to cut the Introduction or the Conclusion.**

When you are preparing, if you are at all worried about losing time, think of material in the middle that you can cut without damaging your overall message.

I know that you are thinking that you cannot cut anything, but you may be forced to. In that case, it is better to be prepared in advance.

The location and facilities

Often, the setting of the room can be a big challenge for any speaker.

If the room is too big or too small or the lighting is poor, your listeners will be uncomfortable. Also, the room temperature can be very distracting if it is too hot or too cold. So what should you do?

I always try to go to the location in advance of the presentation to look it over if I am not familiar with the room. The location will set much of the mood for your presentation.

An informal gathering in a sunny room at a restaurant will have a much different effect on the audience than a sterile hotel conference hall. If it means arriving early and then waiting for a while (before giving my presentation), I will do that, too! Try to note as many details as possible, including the atmosphere and the size of the room. What you look for are things such as the position of the screen or projector if you are using your laptop. You want to make sure you understand where people will be seated and where you will need to stand, so that the audience can see the screen or any other materials or props you will use in your presentation.

There is nothing more annoying
to an audience than having its vision blocked by the speaker.

If you need to make changes, talk with the organizer of the meeting or gathering and get the staff to change the seating arrangements to a more favorable setting. Don't forget to consider the lighting as well. Check out locations of doors, power outlets, light switches, and refreshments. See if you can adjust the temperature if it gets too warm or too cold. Remember: If the group is large, it will generate considerable heat, so be careful about turning the temperature up if you feel cool when you first get there.

There are a number of ways to set up the room. Classroom style with tables and chairs for your audience to take notes, often works better for presentations with a lot of visuals.

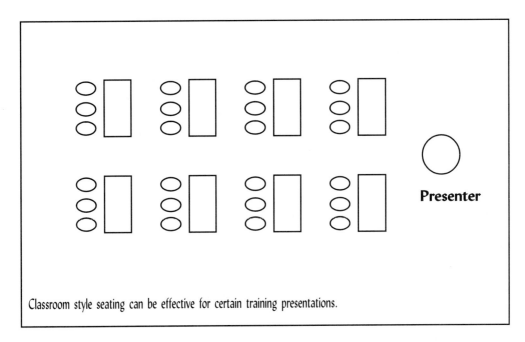

Classroom style seating can be effective for certain training presentations.

Another popular style would be theater style, with rows of chairs. You would probably use this style if the audience does not need to take notes and you want them to focus on you.

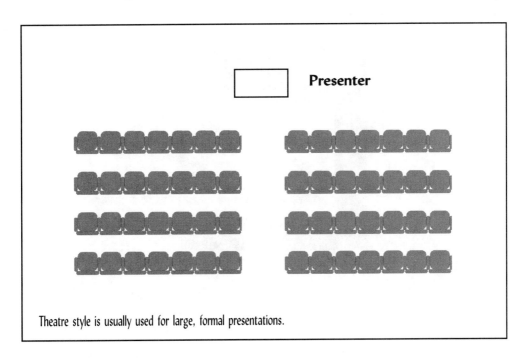

Theatre style is usually used for large, formal presentations.

A setting with round tables would be particularly good if you are going to ask people to have small group discussions as part of your presentation.

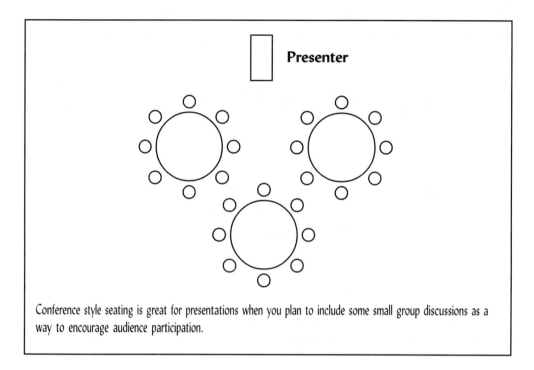

Conference style seating is great for presentations when you plan to include some small group discussions as a way to encourage audience participation.

A "U" setting is particularly good for smaller groups, where you want the audience to be able to see each other and any visual aids that you are using.

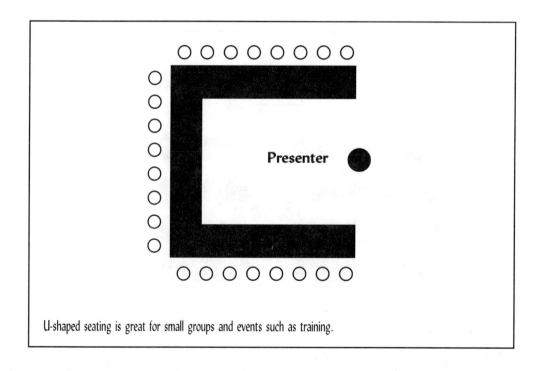

U-shaped seating is great for small groups and events such as training.

Finally, a chevron setting is good when you need the audience to see your visuals easily but audience members need to take notes as well.

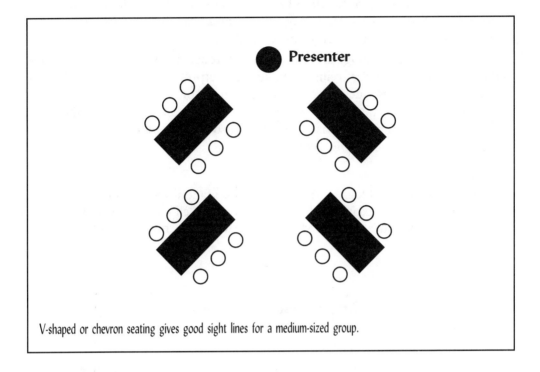

V-shaped or chevron seating gives good sight lines for a medium-sized group.

Another concern is the acoustics of the room.

It is always a good idea to have someone stand in various parts of the room to let you know if he or she can hear you, even if you have a microphone. Mark the correct volume for the microphone as you set up. Use a small piece of tape or a washable magic marker so you can tell if someone has changed the settings without you knowing about it.

The other key concern only comes into play if you decide to use your laptop for the presentation.

Make sure the connection between your computer and the projection equipment is compatible.

There is no universal standard yet, and it can be very difficult for you if your computer cannot "talk" to the projector. **I usually recommend a backup set of overheads and an overhead projector—just in case.**

We will look at visuals and technology in Chapter 15, but here's a reminder: Always be prepared for problems with equipment. Make sure you have spare bulbs for projectors, extra markers or pens if one runs dry. Also, make sure you know how to use the LCD panel.

Managing multiple audiences simultaneously

Increasingly, technology makes it possible to present to a variety of audiences that are located in multiple locations. Often these same audiences can participate in the presentation, ask questions, and hear the answers even though they may be separated by several time zones!

However, the technology around videoconferencing is still in its infancy. The difficulty for the presenter trying to make a Bulletproof Presentation is the lack of some of the basics, such as eye contact. Focus on trying to create a lot of energy in your presentation. Remember that, for the audience, the experience will be similar to watching television. Speak clearly and carefully choose the words you use. Use action verbs and active voice.

Consider this

Great presenters will tell you that a great presentation is 80-percent preparation and 20-percent exciting delivery. Or as Texas Tech's legendary basketball coach Bobby Knight says, "Everybody has the will to win, but precious few have the will to prepare to win!"

———

Activity: Covering all the bases

1. Consider the presentation you will have to make or one that is typical of presentations you make.

2. Refer to the logistics list on pages 45 and 46 for common elements you will need to consider when making that presentation. You may not need any of these items, or you may need items that are not on the list. The main thing is to feel comfortable and confident that you have not overlooked anything in evaluating your situation. Each of these elements provides challenges that must be overcome to have a Bulletproof Presentation. The last column is to help you note who *exactly* will provide the item.

Bulletproof advice

➤ **Analyzing the situation is crucial to a Bulletproof Presentation.**

  ▪ Consider a number of factors, including the size of the group and whether you are considered an Insider or an Outsider within the group.

➤ **Be aware of the agenda.**

  ▪ Elements such as the time of day and the time you have allocated are important for you to know.

➤ **Consider all aspects of the location and facilities.**

  ▪ The mood of your presentation will be set by the facilities and the acoustics and layout of the room.

➤ **Use the checklist to make sure you do not forget anything.**

Presentation checklist		
Check Off	Item	Responsibility
❏	Confirm date and number of people.	
❏	Confirm seating arrangement.	
❏	Ensure that everyone can see screen.	
❏	Get directions to location.	
❏	Confirm set-up time.	
❏	Confirm name of AV person.	
❏	Confirm table for handouts and backup materials.	
❏	Confirm size of room.	
❏	Confirm chair for presenter.	
❏	Confirm lectern with light.	
❏	Confirm table for refreshments.	
❏	Confirm breakout room(s).	
❏	Request water pitcher and glass (where you can reach them).	
❏	Locate temperature control for room.	
❏	Locate light switches or dimmer switch.	
❏	Confirm location of restrooms and phones.	
❏	Provide name tags or tents.	
❏	Provide masking tape.	
❏	Pack business cards (if needed).	
❏	Confirm proper dress for the occasion.	

	Audio-visual requirements	
Check Off	Item	Responsibility
❏	LCD panel.	
❏	Computer.	
❏	Remote mouse.	
❏	Note cards.	
❏	Backup overheads.	
❏	Extra transparencies.	
❏	Overhead projector (with masking tape for squaring image).	
❏	Spare projector bulb.	
❏	Stand for projector.	
❏	Pointer (if needed).	
❏	Flip-chart pads and stands.	
❏	Markers for flipchart.	
❏	VCR monitor and video.	
❏	Extension cord.	
❏	Screen (with extension to prevent keystone effect).	
❏	Podium.	
❏	Workbooks or handouts.	
❏	Models or props.	
❏	Microphone (type?).	
❏	Video camera and tripod.	

CHAPTER 5

HOW PEOPLE
LISTEN

All your planning, talents, and good execution will be in vain if you fail to recognize one simple—and critical—law of nature: how people listen.

Consider this

> A professor who had taught for many years was counseling a young teacher. "You will discover," he said, "that in nearly every class, there will be a youngster eager to argue. Your first impulse will be to silence him or her, but I would advise you to think carefully before doing so. He probably is the only one listening." Sometimes we think that those who do not argue with us agree with us. We have to realize that maybe the real answer is that they are not listening!

In the 1970s the Navy did a study to find out how long people can listen to other people talk. The objective of the study was to determine how to best use the time of instructors and students throughout the Navy's education system. The answer surprised a lot of people. Most people expected that students could sit and listen attentively for about an hour. The answer was not an hour—or even half an hour. The answer was just 18 minutes. The Navy found that whether in a classroom, presentation, or lecture environment, people's ability to focus on what the speaker is saying, and then remember what was said, drops off at 18 minutes. Even in the best of circumstances, the audience members would remember only about 25 percent of what they had heard unless they had taken notes. Unfortunately, very few people are aware of that study or the resulting vital number. If they were, we would save thousands of wasted hours and untold lost productivity in schools and businesses in the United States every day.

However, for any number of different reasons, most of us cannot limit what we must say to 18 minutes. In real life, particularly in business situations, we find that presentations usually go longer than 18 minutes. Frequently we see, for example, management presentations, analyst presentations, and new business presentations run approximately 40 minutes or longer—and it's not uncommon for a presentation to take an entire morning or afternoon or, on rare occasions, a full day.

How can a presenter who seeks to give a Bulletproof Presentation get around this problem?

I see four ways to get around the 18-minute problem.

- ➤ **Go to Q&A.** Address all the essential points in your presentation in 15 minutes, then set aside 30 minutes for Q&A to touch on details and elements that you feel might need further explanation or fleshing out. Questions, by the way, are your chance to redeem yourself if you feel that the presentation itself did not go particularly well. Most of us tend to be more effective in handling questions, anyway, because questions will allow us to be most ourselves and most conversational. We can establish a more personal rapport with the audience and reinforce positions that contribute toward whatever objective we may have—whether it is seeking endorsement, demanding a plan of action, enlisting help, or asking permission. (In Chapter 12, I will give you specific help in answering questions effectively.)

- ➤ **Use another speaker.** Have an associate speak for two minutes or so to highlight, clarify, or amplify a particular area of expertise. Then the clock starts again with you. You may repeat the process before the next 18 minutes are up, but human nature probably would not allow you to use the strategy successfully a third time. You can also use an associate to help during the question period if that would be appropriate. When I speak at various conferences around the country, I will often invite a colleague or client along to provide his or her insights on the topic of the presentation. It takes a little more coordination, but it is highly successful. If you decide to use this technique, you should refer to Chapter 18 (Team Presentations). Many of the issues are similar and that chapter can help you prepare for a presentation with someone else.

- ➤ **Show a videotape.** Bring along a videotape that shows, for example, your company at a glance, a new manufacturing process, a new research facility going up, a news clip pertinent to the issue at hand, or clips of other speakers—and insert the tape into your presentation at the appropriate time. (You can also drive these types of video clips right from your laptop.) The tape can run up to 10 minutes or so and be a nice addition to your presentation. Then you can safely continue to talk for another 18 minutes.

- ➤ **Tell a business story about every 10 minutes.** Borrow a tip from professional speakers and use stories and anecdotes. I don't mean to try to be funny, and I don't mean to make your presentation a story hour. I do mean to do what they do so well—and that is to tell an anecdote every 10 minutes that helps drive home your theme, the point you are trying to make. Whatever anecdote you use—a personal recollection, something you saw on TV or read in the newspapers, something somebody told you—should be aimed squarely at your message, with the specific intention of reinforcing that message. This is why someone such as nationally known professional speaker Patricia Fripp can talk alone on a stage for two hours—because she is talking about a subject that is perceived to be of vital interest to her audience, using well-chosen illustrations to vividly back up the points she is making. All those points, I might add, are not just scattered or used randomly; they are linked to one clear theme. In fact, this technique is so important, I have devoted an entire chapter (Chapter 9) to help you develop stories that you can use.

Recognize the listening style: How do people listen?

Listening-skills experts Dr. Kittie Watson and Dr. Larry Barker did some very good research and discovered four basic patterns in the way people listen. What they learned could help you when you are analyzing the audience and the approach you will need to take. There is no "best" listening style and sometimes people's style will change during a stressful situation. Watson and Barker divide listeners into four categories and describe the positives and negatives of each style:

➤ People-oriented.

➤ Action-oriented.

➤ Content-oriented.

➤ Time-oriented.

Let me describe each type and the strengths and weaknesses of each.

People-oriented listeners: These listeners care for and are concerned about others. They are very concerned about how people will react to any solutions you pose, and negative people reactions will hurt your arguments with this type of listener. They are usually nonjudgmental and are interested in building relationships with others. They will provide you with clear verbal and nonverbal feedback. The negative characteristic for this style of listener is the inability to see the faults in others. That can hurt the presenter who finds him or herself in a competitive situation and must differentiate him or herself from less able presenters. And sometimes these listeners can be overly expressive in their feedback. That can be very disconcerting for the presenter during a question-and-answer session.

Action-oriented listeners: Action-oriented listeners want the presenter to get to the point quickly. They will be quick to tell you about their expectations and will encourage a speaker to be organized and concise. They will also quickly recognize inconsistencies in the message they hear, so beware! If they sense that you are rambling, they can be very impatient. They may ask questions that can seem pretty blunt. They do not necessarily mean to sound that way, but it just comes out. Also, they may appear overly critical, but again, do not read too much into that.

Content-oriented listeners: These listeners value technical information. They will constantly listen to test for clarity and understanding. They will encourage you, as the presenter, to provide support for your ideas. Do not think they are trying to "trick" you; they value complex and challenging information. The negative for this style of listener is the tendency to discount information that does not come from experts. For these listeners, establishing your credentials during the introduction will be vital to get them to listen to you respectfully. They also tend to discount nontechnical information in support of an idea or argument. Unlike the people-oriented listener, who always is concerned about how people will feel about something, you will not impress a content-oriented listener with that type of point.

Time-oriented listeners: Time-oriented listeners are very conscious of time and particularly of saving it. They will usually let you know how much time you have, and you had better stick to it! The downside of these people is their tendency to be impatient and perhaps even interrupt a presenter. They may also glance at their watches or a clock regularly. Do not let these tendencies rattle you as a presenter. They are really not necessarily unhappy with your presentation; this is just part of who they are.

Listening orientations—PACT

Each of the listening orientations (people-, action-, content-, and time-oriented) has positive and negative characteristics associated with it.

People-oriented Listeners

Positive characteristics	Negative characteristics
Are concerned about others.	May get overinvolved with others' feelings.
Are nonjudgmental.	Avoid seeing the faults in others.
Provide clear verbal and nonverbal feedback.	Internalize the emotional state of others.
Notice others' moods quickly.	Are overly expressive when giving feedback.
Are interested in building relationships.	May not be discriminating enough in building relationships.

Action-oriented Listeners

Positive characteristics	Negative characteristics
Get to the point quickly.	Tend to be impatient.
Give clear feedback concerning expectations.	Jump ahead and finish the thoughts of others.
Concentrate on understanding the task at hand.	Get distracted by unorganized speakers.
Help others focus on what is important.	Ask blunt questions.
Encourage others to be organized.	May appear overly critical.
Identify inconsistencies in message.	May minimize relationships and concerns.

Content-oriented Listeners

Positive characteristics	Negative characteristics
Value technical information.	May be overly detail-oriented.
Test for clarity and understanding.	May intimidate others by asking pointed questions.
Encourage others to provide support for their ideas.	Minimize the value of nontechnical information.
Welcome complex and challenging information.	Discount information from non-experts.
Look at all sides of the issue.	Take a long time to make decisions.

Time-oriented Listeners

Positive characteristics	Negative characteristics
Manage and save time.	Tend to be impatient with time.
Set time guidelines for meetings and conversations.	Interrupt others.
Let others know of time requirements.	Let time affect their ability to concentrate.
Discourage "wordy" speakers.	Rush speakers by frequently looking at watches or clocks.
Give cues to others when time is being wasted.	Limit creativity of others by imposing time pressures.

Multiple preferences

In particular situations we may switch from our preferred orientation to use another one. The circumstances that may cause us to change orientations include:

→ Time pressure.

→ Interest or motivation in speaker/topic.

→ Communication setting.

→ Presence of others during communication.

→ How much listening energy an individual has available.

Activity: Considering how my audience listens

1. Think about your presentation, or one that is typical of presentations you give.

2. Think about the people who will be attending in great detail. (Refer to your audience analysis). What type of listeners will you have there?

   ▪ Who will be people-oriented?

   ▪ Who will be action-oriented?

   ▪ Who will be content-oriented?

   ▪ Who will be time-oriented?

3. How will I need to tailor my presentation to meet these listening types?

Bulletproof advice

Remember that listeners can only listen, on average, for about 18 minutes.

➤ **Vary your presentation style through question and answer.**

➤ **Use another speaker to highlight or amplify your message.**

➤ **Show a videotape, or video clip, to add interest.**

➤ **Tell stories that illustrate your points.**

➤ **Recognize the listening styles within your audience.**

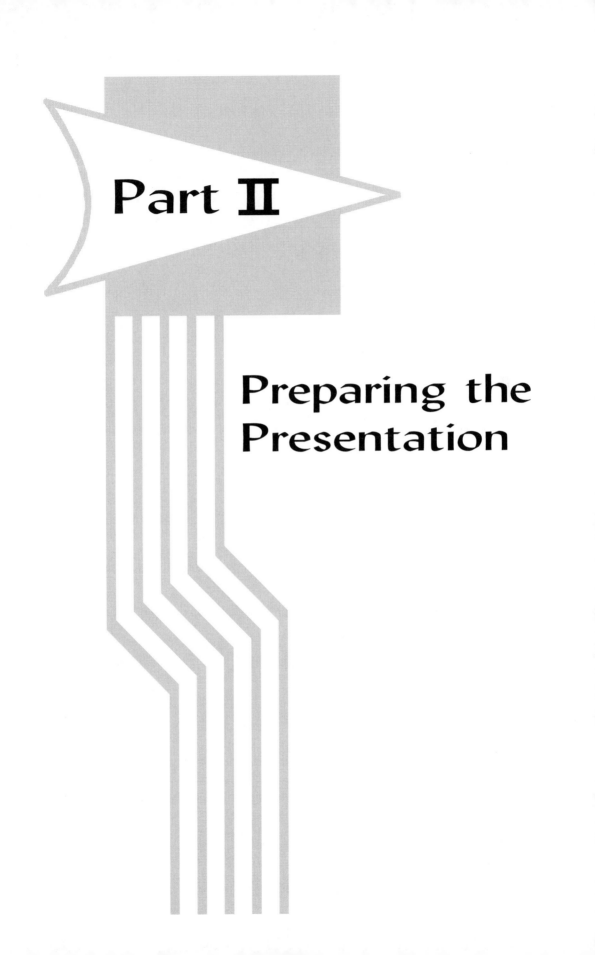

Part II

Preparing the Presentation

CHAPTER 6

ESTABLISHING RAPPORT IN THE INTRODUCTION

"Tell them what you're going to tell them."

A wonderful old minister that I knew as a young man used to tell me that he had three parts to every sermon. He said, "I tell what I'm going to tell them, then I tell them, and then I tell them what I told them." Over the next few chapters, we will see why that's such an effective approach.

Consider this

> In every Bulletproof Presentation I have ever done, I always make sure I make a connection to the personal life of as many people in the audience as possible. I may tell a story that illustrates a point, but it also features one of my daughters (I have three) and connects me to people in the audience who have children. Those connections are the emotional glue that cements the logic of the argument you are presenting. The audience is thinking that you must be good because you make sense and *you are just like them!*

If you remember back to the Rules of Primary and Emotion, you will understand how important rapport in the introduction is to any Bulletproof Presentation. In this chapter we will look at the various elements that must be part of any introduction. Examples will illustrate those points. Those essential parts are:

- ➤ Rapport (how to establish it).
- ➤ The grabber (to "grab" the audience's attention).
- ➤ Purpose (why are we here?; this topic is covered in Chapter 1).
- ➤ Benefits (what will the listener get out of it?).
- ➤ Roadmap (the main points to be covered).

Rapport

Establishing rapport with your audience is very important. You may think that it is not that important, but remember how you listen to speakers.

**Your audience is always looking for validation
that you are qualified to speak on a particular topic.**

That is what I mean when I recommend establishing "rapport." Unless you are a celebrity in your field or a true Insider, it is always important to give the audience a reason to listen to you. Sometimes someone else will introduce you. You can do that person a favor and establish your rapport by writing the introduction for that person. Be very specific about the qualifications you bring to the topic. Even when you present internally, it may be wise to consider establishing your credentials.

Whatever you do, a cardinal sin in presentations is apologizing when you first begin speaking. There is nothing that can take momentum out of the presentation the way apologizing because the room is too warm or the lights are not right and so on does. Just live with the situation and go on!

Consider this

It is really hard to beat a good story, particularly one that your audience can relate to easily. Consider this story:

"This is a true story of a young snowboarder who left the ski trails and got lost in the mountains of Colorado. The young man had three choices in the way he could handle the situation and survive. It just so happens that the way he chose that day could also help you survive in your business."

Who could resist that kind of introduction?

―――

The grabber

Gaining the audience's attention is your first challenge.

The grabber is any effect that will help draw the audience to you at the beginning of your presentation. It can be an interesting story (that relates to your presentation), a startling statistic, or a quote from a famous person.

**Rule of Primary: Listeners will remember ideas or information
they heard first during a speech or presentation.**

When you begin any presentation, you must realize that everyone listening to you is still engaged in whatever they were doing before. Maybe it was a phone call they just finished, a meeting they just left, and a conversation they just concluded. That little "tape recorder" in their head is still rerunning that event.

**Your job with the grabber is to turn that recorder off
and get the person to focus on you exclusively.**

Pay attention to all the good presenters, and you will notice how they get you engaged immediately: They use a good grabber.

Consider this

> When Senator John Glenn, the first astronaut in space, was asked about his thoughts just before taking off into space, he responded, "I looked around me and suddenly realized that everything had been built by the lowest bidder!"

―――――

The challenge of the grabber

Consider this

> "The world is too big for us. Too much going on, too many crimes, too much violence and excitement. Try as you will, you get behind in the race, in spite of yourself. It is an incessant strain to keep pace.... And still you lose ground. Science empties its discoveries on you so fast that you stagger beneath them in hopeless bewilderment. The political world is news seen so rapidly you are out of breath trying to keep pace with who is in and who is out. Everything is high pressure. Human nature can not endure much more!"

―――――

This commentary represents the way many people think today. However, it originally appeared on June 16, 1833, in the *Atlantic Journal*. Wouldn't this story be a good attention-getter if you wanted to begin a presentation on the pace of change and how to cope with it? However, frequently, speakers will start with sentences such as these:

➤ "My topic today is to address you."

➤ "I learned only yesterday that I was to speak."

➤ "I'm not very good at speech making, but...."

Would any of these statements at the beginning of a presentation fill you with hope? Probably not. You would likely think, *Oh no. What kind of torture will this be?*

There are eight major types of grabbers available to you.

1. **An attention-grabbing rhetorical question (a question you don't expect them to answer) or statement:** "What would you do if you earn one million dollars in the stock market?" or "Every one of you could earn one million dollars within the next 10 years."

2. **An appropriate quote from a well-known person:** "J.P. Morgan once said, 'You can tell the cut of a man by the type of investment he makes.'"

3. **A startling or interesting statistic appropriate to your audience:** "In the 45 minutes since this meeting began, American investors have pumped $10 million dollars into mutual funds."

4. **A personal story or anecdote of relevance and interest:** "You all know my company's famous Small Cap Funds—at least I hope you all know them, since we spend an awful lot of money on advertising. Well, let me tell you the real story of how they came to be available."

5. **An appropriate and related reference to a current event:** "I'm sure you've all heard the news from Washington today about the mutual funds that can be placed in an IRA, but withdrawn later without penalty."

6. **Unusual or unexpected biographical information:** "I've been asked to speak to you today because of my position as chief executive officer of Consumers Friend Investments, and I appreciate the honor. But did you know that I'm also a real-estate broker and, before that, a teller in a bank!" (Be careful not to sound too egotistical.)

7. **A challenge to your audience:** "Ladies and gentlemen, we have no one to blame but ourselves for the sorry state of the mutual fund industry! It is my hope, though, that we can come out of this meeting tonight with goals and an understanding that will put us all back on the road to prosperity." (A note of caution here: Be careful not to set an impossible assignment. Your audience may recognize it as such and tune you out, or they may blame you for failure if the challenge is unmet).

8. **The use of common ground, including shared values, coupled with an appeal for a fair hearing:** "You and I have one major goal in common: to do everything possible to ensure the survival of the mutual fund industry. However, the escalating number of mutual funds imperils our survival, and our challenge is to work harder on quality rather than quantity. Please hear me out, because we need to understand the full picture before we make any decision or take any action." This combination of tactics is particularly appropriate for a hostile audience, especially one that values directness and candor. (Although this example gets to the heart of the speaker's case quickly and directly, it is devoid of jokes, illustrations, and other more creative types of grabbers that might appear too manipulative under the circumstances.)

Rhetorical devices frequently used in speeches and prepared in advance can act as a similar grabber.

Repetition

Repeating a word, phrase, or sound can add and elevate the overall energy of a message. Recapping information during your presentation is an effective way to help the audience remember your main points. When planning your presentation, build some repetition into the presentation at the end of each main point and into the conclusion. However, simply repeating the same words you have already delivered previously is *not* appropriate. Use different wording to keep the ideas sounding familiar but fresh.

➤ **Repeating a phrase:**
Now is the time for us to increase our sales.
Now is the time for us to seize a greater market share.
Now is the time for us to achieve true leadership in our industry.

➤ **Repetition is also effective at the end of a phrase:**
Our plan is ready. Our team is ready. Our people are ready.

➤ **Or in succession:**
Reorganization. Reorganization will help us capture our potential.

➤ **Alliteration is the repetition of consonant sounds:**
Three keys to credibility are character, competence, and compassion.

➤ **Assonance is the repetition of vowel sounds:**
Every effort must be exerted to educate our employees about the expected benefits of reorganization. Note that both alliteration and assonance can be especially effective if they do not draw too much attention to themselves.

When to develop the grabber

My final point will be to recommend that you not attempt the grabber until you have completed the rest of the presentation. There are two reasons for that:

1. You might get "writer's block" trying to figure it out.

2. The best grabber will probably not appear until after you have developed the rest of the presentation.

Too often I have worked with people who tried to think of a grabber right away. They want that dazzling start. The problem they find is that it does not jump right out at you very often. And so they spend a tremendous amount of time worrying about the grabber and lose precious time building the rest of the presentation.

**A grabber is important, but wait
until you have all the other pieces of the presentation ready,
then tackle the grabber.**

Benefits

There are distinct differences between benefits and features. Too often people will talk about features, which may or may not appeal to the audience. Think of it this way: Imagine a car salesman is telling you all about the audio equipment on a particular model. He explains it in great detail, because this is a great sound system, much better than the competition offers. The problem? You are buying this car for your spouse, who carpools kids all day and never listens to the radio, tapes, or CDs. In this imaginary situation, how valuable would that audio system be? Probably not very! The car salesman is touting the features of the car. More important to you would be the benefits of the roominess and safety features of the car while your spouse is carting those kids around town.

**Explaining true benefits to the audience will get the
maximum results from a presentation.**

Think about that old adage WIIFM (what's in it for me?). That is really what the audience wants to hear. Think of questions or problems the audience would like to have answers for. For example:

➤ How will you get my work finished faster?

➤ How can this make my job easier?

The answers to these questions will help you frame real benefits and not features of your products or ideas.

Refer back to your audience analysis and flesh out the benefits with the audience in mind. That will help ensure you develop a Bulletproof Presentation!

The roadmap

The roadmap is the way you orient your audience to the topic and outline what you will talk about. It will also help audience members to focus on your presentation and give them a sense of the direction you are going to take.

The basic technique is to give your subject a recognizable beginning, middle, and end. For your presentation to be Bulletproof, it is important that you follow the basic format that you will present in the roadmap.

With the roadmap, you help the audience to understand the main points of your presentation so audience members will understand where you are and how you will arrive at your conclusion.

It is important to give the audience these clear signals at the beginning of the presentation.

Remember the Rule of Frequency? **Listeners will remember ideas or information they have heard more frequently.**

In the roadmap, you are telling them, for the first time, the topics or main points you intend to cover. These are going to be covered in far more detail in the body of the Bulletproof Presentation, so don't give them too much detail. Only give them enough to know where you are going.

Finally, in your roadmap, you may want to let the audience know some of the ground rules you intend to observe during the presentation.

For example, you might want to mention when questions are appropriate (anytime during the presentation or at the end of the body). If you will be presenting for more than an hour, you might consider a break as well. Be sure to let the audience know. If listeners know a break is coming, they may wait for the break before leaving for the restrooms or refreshments.

Consider this

Once you have developed your introduction and grabber, it is best to stay with it. You may want to do some last-minute changes within the presentation, but not in the introduction. The reason is simple: You will be the most nervous when you start. You do not want to be making changes at the last minute, or you could end up confusing yourself and going off track right from the beginning—and that will make you nervous throughout the rest of the presentation.

———

The final step in planning the introduction is to build a smooth transition to the first main idea in the body.

The transition can be simple, but it should signal the audience that you are now moving into the body of the Bulletproof Presentation.

Consider this

If you want to take the air out of your presentation sails right from the beginning, do what I heard a person do recently after he was introduced to the audience. He said, "There are probably a lot of people here today who know more about this subject than I do, but I would like to share my thoughts with you." The first question that came to my mind was, *Who invited this guy to speak?*

―――――――――

There are three cardinal rules about introductions:

1. Don't sell yourself short the way the speaker I just described did. You are the expert or you would not be there, and these types of statements will create serious doubts in the minds of the audience before they hear anything else from you.

2. Write out the introduction for the person who will introduce you so he or she can get it right.

3. Never—and I mean *never*—apologize when you begin a presentation.

Bulletproof advice

➢ **Establish rapport with the audience during your introduction.**

■ The audience will be looking for validation that you are qualified to speak on the topic.

➢ **The grabber will get the attention of the audience and focus audience members on you as the speaker.**

■ Start with an interesting story, fact, or challenge that will engage the audience immediately into your topic. Don't try to develop your grabber until later in the development of your presentation.

➢ **Establish the benefits to the audience members if they listen to you.**

■ Refer back to the audience analysis and make sure the benefits you state are important to this audience.

➢ **Roadmap the topics you will cover in the presentation.**

■ Help the audience understand the main points of your presentation and give the audience confidence that you are not speaking "off the top of your head."

CHAPTER 7

USING HUMOR IN A BUSINESS PRESENTATION

William Davis once said, "The kind of humor I like is the thing that makes me laugh for five seconds and think for ten minutes."

Humor can be effective in your introduction or at any other point throughout your speech. While tickling the audience's funny bone, humor can relieve their tension and yours, demonstrate your friendliness and approachability, make a point, and ultimately enhance your credibility. In short, effective humor can put your audience in a frame of mind conducive to meeting your substance and image goals—to your capturing the persuasive edge.

Consider this

A man flying in a hot air balloon realizes he is lost. He reduces height and spots a man down below. He lowers the balloon further and shouts, "Excuse me, can you tell me where I am?"

The man below says, " Yes. You are in a hot air balloon, hovering 30 feet above this field."

"You must work in Information Technology," says the balloonist.

"I do," replies the man. "How did you know?"

"Well," says the balloonist, "everything you have told me is technically correct, but it's of no use to anyone."

The man below says, "You must work in management."

"I do," replies the balloonist, "but how did you know that?"

"Well," says the man, "you don't know where you are, or where you are going, but you expect me to be able to help. You're in the same position you were in before we met, but now it's my fault!"

It's a good story, but what does it have to do with making presentations? Good question. I once had a boss who thought all good presentations should start with a joke. He tried time after time to get a response from the audience, but all he got were groans. He was a very nice person with a good sense of humor, but his timing and delivery were terrible.

Avoiding the biggest mistake

Although this rule would seem to be common sense, I have seen it routinely violated by many people making business presentations. In fact, the single biggest mistake made by untrained speakers today is the use of irrelevant humor. Fortunately, a few simple precautions can help you from falling into this trap.

The biggest humor sin is to be irrelevant!

People who use irrelevant humor come from all walks of business life. They are managers, executives, salespeople, and engineers. They speak at company meetings, industry conferences, training sessions, and employee banquets. They are really quite well intentioned. They are good people who want to communicate successfully, and they know that successful presentations they have attended in the past have often used humor effectively. But they have a problem. After taking weeks or months to prepare an important presentation, they take 10 seconds to throw in their favorite joke. Inevitably, they use it as an opening and more often than not, it is a dud.

This unfortunately produces two reactions, one in the presenter and the other in the audience.

One group of business presenters swears off humor forever. They decide that they "can't tell a joke" or that they "aren't funny," so they take a vow to always be serious in any presentation and revert to the stiff, overhead-laden school of business communication. Another group has an even worse reaction. They remain undaunted at their failure. They continue to inflict irrelevant humor on additional audiences with the same result. Neither reaction is desirable or necessary. A few preventive measures enable anyone to use humor in a safe and effective manner.

Within audiences, a poorly told joke at the beginning of a presentation that is totally irrelevant to the topic makes the audience groan and begin to discount the presentation right from the beginning as irrelevant.

> **If you decide to use humor in your presentations
> (and I strongly advise that you do!),
> the first step in harnessing the power of humor is to
> use it for a purpose.**

Irrelevant humor is a distraction. Whether you are speaking to one person or to 100 people, humor is more effective if it makes a point.

Here is why: Relevance reduces resistance. There is a basic principle of audience psychology that says that people resist humor if they think someone is deliberately *trying* to be funny. They put a comedy "make me laugh" filter on their listening. This is a problem faced by professional comedians every time they stride up to a microphone and begin their routine. The typical audience attitude is: "You think you're funny? Prove it!" Professional comedians work very hard to overcome this automatic resistance.

By contrast, when humor is used to make a point, the audience reaction is likely to be more generous. We are more open to accepting the humor. We realize that the person is using humor to make a point and not "trying to be funny." That same psychology in audiences will decrease the resistance. Consequently, there is a much greater chance that the audience will be amused by the speaker's humor.

Most important, even if the audience does not think the speaker is funny, the humor still makes a point and still moves the presentation forward. The speaker is not left in the embarrassed limbo called "el bombo" by Johnny Carson.

The presenter simply moves on to the next part of the presentation. As long as the humor makes a point, it will always have a place in the speech, even if it does not get the laugh you anticipated.

Let's consider an example.

A Phillips Petroleum Company executive addressed a group of chemical-industry producers about the problems of government regulation. Specifically, he discussed how environmental restraints had slowed construction of a Phillips chemical plant. He summed up his main point by saying, "I got to feeling a little like Moses crossing the Red Sea with the Egyptians in hot pursuit. When Moses asked God for help, God looked down and said, 'I've got some good news and some bad news. The good news is that I'll part the Red Sea, let your people pass through, and then destroy the Egyptians.' 'That's great,' said Moses. 'What's the bad news?' God said, 'First you have to file an environmental impact statement.'"

If his audience thinks the joke is funny and tries to remember it, then they are remembering his main point. If they do not think it is funny, he has still reinforced his point. The story won't bomb, because the audience will recognize its relevance. It supports and illustrates a major theme of the presentation.

How to make humor relevant

How can you ensure that your humor is relevant? Just follow this simple three-step method:

1. Authorize.

2. Analyze

3. Analogize.

Authorize means that you, as author, should write your serious message first. Do not start with the humor. Add it after you develop what you are going to say. Humor should complement and augment your basic points; it should not be the message.

Analyze means that you carefully review the points presented in your serious message. You cannot make your humor relevant if you have not carefully analyzed the points you are making.

Analogize means that you relate a quip or anecdote to one of your points. Your humor should help introduce, summarize, or highlight one of these points. This process ensures that you won't force irrelevant jokes into your presentation.

Humor linkage is all-important.

The three-step method requires a small investment of time in order to be used effectively. You need time to think about the humor within your presentation. A half-effort will not work. Throwing in your favorite joke without much thought about the point you are making is a prescription for disaster. Think of this process as an insurance policy: It reduces the risk of bombing. The "premium" you pay is preparation.

Let's examine the process in action with a case study. An executive had to give a speech to the shareholders at his waste-management company's annual meeting. During the fiscal year, the company had lost several million dollars by acquiring a small operation and losing a lot of money in the process. The speech had to both acknowledge and explain how this mistake could happen. When the executive asked me for advice, I suggested using the three-step process.

Step 1: He wrote a detailed explanation of how the subsidiary had been acquired, including what went wrong.

Step 2: An analysis of his major points quickly revealed the main point that he wanted to make in his speech: He wanted to admit that the company had made a mistake by purchasing the subsidiary.

Step 3: I suggested that he explain the events leading up to the subsidiary's failure and then analogize it to the following story: It's like the fellow who went to a florist and ordered a floral arrangement for a friend who had opened up a new office. Then he went to the new office, and there was a wreath that said, "Rest in Peace." Well, this fellow was mad. He went back to the florist. He screamed and raved and ranted. Finally the florist said, "All right, I made a mistake. But calm down. It's not that bad. Just think. Somewhere today, someone in the city was buried under a floral arrangement that said, 'Good Luck in Your New Location.' "

The story had the desired effect at the annual meeting. It admitted the mistake while provoking laughter from the shareholders. The story eased the tension and helped the audience accept the executive's explanation.

The power of the analogy method is limited only by your imagination. After all, any quip or anecdote can be analogized to an infinite number of points. It is up to you to make the connections.

A good example comes from the sales force of a company that sells storage space for backup tapes of computer data. They break the ice with prospects by using this anecdote:

One of the most important things to consider with any information system is your backup plan. A consultant asked a group of people how many of them had one. One brave soul from a bank raised his hand and said, "I've got a disaster recovery plan—complete and ready to go into action. It's real simple, just one page." And the consultant asked, "A one-page disaster plan? What would you do if your computer center blew up, or flooded, or caught on fire? How could you recover with just a one-page disaster plan?" He said, "Well, it's really very simple. It's a two-step plan. First, I maintain my resume up-to-date at all times. And second, I store a backup copy off-site."

The story is effective because it illustrates the storage company's key selling point: Be prepared. But note that the story could illustrate other ideas. It would be equally effective for making points about resourcefulness, looking out for number one, career change, and the superiority of simplicity. In fact, the story can be used to illustrate any point to which you can analogize it. Its effectiveness is limited only by your inventiveness.

A side benefit of using the analogy method is that it forces you to examine your serious message carefully. It keeps you focused on your key points. And it helps you discover the parts of your message that don't clearly make a point. In other words, it's a wonderful editing tool that compels you to stay on track.

How to use old jokes

But is staying on track really enough? Does making a joke relevant guarantee its success? What if it's an old joke? What if everyone has already heard it? People often ask me if old jokes should be avoided. They worry that a joke won't be funny if it's too familiar. Nothing could be further from the truth.

Make it fit

First, recognize that part of what your audience will find funny is the way that you have analogized a joke to one of your points. Using an old joke in a new way is a creative act. It can produce surprise and amusement. Second, old, funny jokes can be likened to old hit songs: Most people enjoy hearing them once in a while. Third, what is old to you may be new to someone else. The bottom line is that an old joke will work if it makes a point.

A good example comes from the 1984 presidential campaign. Senator John Glenn of Ohio talked about an old man sitting on a porch in a fenced-in yard watching a dog run around. A visitor came up and asked, "Does your dog bite?" The old man said, "Nope." So the visitor walked in. As soon as he did, the dog ran up and bit a chunk out of his leg. The visitor said, "I thought you said your dog didn't bite." The old man said, "It's not my dog."

Glenn then analogized the story to Ronald Reagan and the federal budget deficit: "He says it's not his dog that's biting us." Detailed accusations followed.

The story about the dog in the yard is an old joke. But after Glenn started using it, he received a lot of favorable media coverage about his "newfound" sense of humor. In addition, his campaign message reached new voters every time the media quoted the story. The old joke worked for Glenn because it made a point.

Why personal anecdotes work better than jokes

What if you cannot tell a joke to save your life? Are you forever condemned to a prison of serious utterances? Will you never experience the joy of hearing laughter at one of your remarks? Is there no reprieve?

Stop worrying. Even if you can't tell a joke, you can tell a humorous personal anecdote relevant to your presentation. Anyone can.

"Funny" is more important than new

I base this claim on the assumption that you have at least one mildly amusing story that you have been telling for years for no particular purpose. You tell it when you meet people. It is an icebreaker. You tell it at parties and social functions. The story may involve something that was embarrassing years ago but seems funny now. It may relate to home, school, or work. It may even be a story about something that happened to someone else. (If you want more information on developing stories, refer to Chapter 9.)

Whatever the form of your personal anecdote, it will possess two important traits. First, it will be real. And second, you will be comfortable telling it. After all, you've already been telling it for years, so no special comic delivery will be required.

The key to success with personal anecdotes is developing points that your story can illustrate. An exercise I conducted for managers at a defense contractor making a presentation during a bid for a NASA contract demonstrates the process. After explaining the value of personal anecdotes, I asked for a volunteer to share a story with the group. In exchange, the group promised to come up with a point that the story could make.

The volunteer turned out to be the company's chief engineer—the person who oversees development of the shuttle systems. He was a soft-spoken, shy individual, and his colleagues seemed surprised that he had volunteered. His delivery was not dramatic or embellished. He possessed no special comedic skills. And he told his story in a matter-of-fact way:

> "When I first joined NASA, I was a young engineer just out of college. My first mission was to assist in the first orbital mission to send a satellite around the earth. My training was very complete and I was sent to a listening station in the middle of a jungle in Madagascar. The jungle was hot, steamy and miserable. Then the fateful day came. There I was, in the middle of the jungle, halfway around the world when suddenly the radio came to life. Then I was talking to John Glenn as he circled the earth hundreds of miles above me! That was the most exciting day of my life. All of the sudden, I began to cry, not out of sadness, but just because I was so overcome by emotion. And I am as excited about the work I do today, as I was the day in Madagascar."

During the engineer's recitation of his story, his coworkers listened intently to every word. Their full attention was focused on this tale about an important moment in their colleague's life and the life of the nation. And they began to congratulate him as he ended the story. Why? Because the story is real. And it comes across as real. You just can't make up stuff like that.

In order to keep our end of the bargain, I asked the group what points the story could be used to illustrate. Immediately the company's marketing manager jumped up and came up with the overriding theme right then and there. (Refer back to Chapter 2 for additional information about the overriding theme.)

When the applause died down, the project manager noted that he could use the story. One of his major tasks as a project manager was to establish the experience and credentials of the team without appearing to be giving resumes during the presentation. The chief engineer can now accomplish this task by telling them the story about his first NASA mission. By doing so, he will achieve something even more important than making a point about work habits: He will begin to establish rapport with the potential customers within the government's space program.

The story of the first mission is the type of information that starts the bonding process. New employees will feel honored that the chief engineer has chosen to share something so personal. In addition, the story has a humanizing effect because he admitted that he had cried, something not easily admitted to.

Most important, the chief programmer can *relate* his personal anecdote. He cannot tell a joke, but it does not matter. He can tell the story about his experience. He's been telling it for years. Now he can tell it to make a point.

The personal anecdote is one of the most powerful tools in your humor arsenal. It never fails to gain attention, and it can be used by anyone. Take advantage of it. Try to recall key events in your life—your first date, your first job, your first driving lesson. All of them offer potentially amusing stories. Mine your memory for anecdotes. They are a precious resource that each of us possesses in great abundance.

So now you know the secret. Using humor successfully is not very difficult. It's no different than using any other type of communication. It will work if it makes a point. Whether you're talking to one person or one hundred, you will better serve your audience if your jokes serve a purpose. And if you can't tell a joke, use a personal anecdote. Just remember to analogize it to your message. As long as you make it relevant, you'll be on your way to using humor for business success.

Comedians and speakers who are good at using humor in presentations are good at assessing risk. They regularly give the following advice about when to use humor:

1. If you are not, by nature, a good joke-teller, chances are that you will have difficulty telling one well during a speech (just as my old boss—remember my example from earlier in the chapter?). Nothing kills a joke the way an uncomfortable delivery does. It's better to use a humorous story or anecdote—particularly if the object of the humor is you! People resonate to stories more than jokes, and stories also give them an opportunity to get to know you better, too!

2. If you have a good sense of humor but are not a terrific joke-teller, putting in a quick one-liner may be better suited for your presentation.

3. Remember that your humor must be relevant to the situation or the occasion. If it is not relevant to the audience, setting, or occasion, it should be relevant to the content of your message.

4. I strongly suggest against humor that may be overtly or even subtly sexist, ethnic, racist, risqué, or overly critical of a person or group. Although you may want your presentation to be memorable, such jokes may make your words *too* memorable and then you may want more than your presentation to be Bulletproof! If you have any doubt about whether your humorous story or one-liner is funny, try it out on your friends or another reliable critic.

Consider this

Ronald Reagan was 69 years old when he ran for president in 1980. Despite continual criticism, he won the election and never passed up a chance to use humor when referring to his age. Reagan used to delight audiences with comments about his age. On one occasion, he said, "And I want to say that I don't mind at all any of the jokes or remarks about my age, because Thomas Jefferson made a comment about the presidency and age. He said that one should not worry about one's exact chronological age in reference to his ability to perform one's tasks. And ever since he told me that, I stopped worrying!"

**If you have any doubt about whether
your humorous story or one-liner is funny,
try it out on your friends or another reliable critic.**

Make sure your "critics" understand the point you are trying to make and the context in which the story is to be used. If you have any doubt after you try it out, forget the humor—and resist the temptation to put it back into the presentation later.

Humor is not only a good icebreaker for your introduction, but an occasional sprinkling within the body of your speech can add sparkle and interest to even the driest subject.

Don't forget the Rule of Emotion: Funny stories and anecdotes touch our emotions and create memorable presentations.

**The Rule of Emotion:
Listeners will remember the ideas and information
that touched their hearts.**

But the keys in using humor are to make it appropriate for the audience and to *never* embarrass anyone. We all know the risks of the proverbial lead balloon and the skunk at a garden party.

Activity: Personal anecdote checklist

Personal anecdotes are easy to deliver but sometimes difficult to recall. The following checklist will help jog your memory to help build a catalog of humorous stories.

- ❏ Your most embarrassing experience.

- ❏ Your first date.

- ❏ Your first day on the job.

- ❏ The funniest thing that ever happened to a friend.

- ❏ The biggest mistake you ever made.

- ❏ A strange dream.

- ❏ The most bizarre thing you've ever seen or heard.

- ❏ Your wildest vacation story.

- ❏ Your hobbies.

- ❏ The funniest thing that ever happened at a business meeting.

- ❏ Stories about eating out (strange restaurants, waiters, food, poor service).

- ❏ Learning to drive.

- ❏ High school stories (prom, teachers, classes).

- ❏ College stories (dorm, professors, exams).

- ❏ Something that seems funny now but didn't when it happened.

- ❏ Your first job interview.

- ❏ The strangest gift you've ever received.

Activity: Using humor in your presentation

1. Think of your presentation, or one that is typical of presentations you give.

2. Ask yourself if there are some humorous stories or anecdotes that you can include in the presentation to lighten the tone?

3. Now ask yourself if the humor is relevant to the point you are trying to make, or if you just have it inserted for a laugh.

4. Try out the humorous story or anecdote on some close friends or family members to see how well it connects.

5. Pay attention to what these friends or family members had to say about your timing and delivery.

Bulletproof advice

➤ **Use humor if possible.**

- Remember the Rule of Emotion: Humor touches people's emotions.

➤ **Make your humor have a purpose.**

- Use relevant humor that links to a point you want to make.

➤ **Providing humorous personal anecdotes is better than jokes.**

- Never embarrass anyone (except maybe yourself).

- Try your humor out first on family or friends.

CHAPTER 8

BUILDING THE BODY AND CHOOSING A STRATEGY

"Tell them."

In developing the body of the Bulletproof Presentation, you will need to first think of the main points that will support the purpose and overriding theme of the presentation. In this chapter, we will work on delivering the message through a clear strategy.

Consider this

Benjamin Disraeli, British prime minister in the 1880s, once said, "There are lies, damn lies, and statistics." Many presentations are just chock full of numbers and statistics. As a presenter, your job is to take your audience behind the numbers or statistics and tell the audience what they mean—to you and to the audience. The key to using numbers and statistics in a Bulletproof Presentation is to help the audience see the important ones and keep summarizing. They will welcome your insights and dub you a brilliant analyst rather than a boring person who crunches numbers.

Consider this

Content is what makes any presentation Bulletproof. When the content fails to convince the audience, delivery will suffer. Delivery alone, no matter how good it is, cannot carry the presentation alone. It is akin to a beautiful house built on a foundation of sand: It will not stand for long! To make a Bulletproof Presentation, you must focus on the content.

Delivering the message well begins with a clear strategy!

We have all heard the "slick" speaker who is all show and no substance. However, we have all heard a speaker who has a lot of knowledge but is hard to understand. The good speaker is the one we have heard who presents the information logically and who cares about the topic and about our ability as the audience to hear and understand.

Those are the presentations we remember. Those speakers had substance and delivered it well.

Before you begin the process of choosing a strategy, sit down and write out all the main points that you can think of to include in the presentation. For many of these points, you will probably be able to later group them into common areas. But first, get those ideas out. Don't worry if you can't use them at this point, and don't start editing or debating! The main purpose of the exercise is to elicit as many ideas as possible. As you begin the process in this chapter, you will undoubtedly come up with additional ideas, stories, or anecdotes.

Many presentations are too long and too general. All too frequently, they are loaded with unnecessary words and ideas. Remember the old adage "Keep It Simple, Stupid."

Here are some guidelines for considering some of these ideas:

➤ Simplicity.

➤ Timeliness.

➤ Association.

➤ Perspective.

Simplicity. Keep the examples and information as simple as possible given the audience. You do not want to talk down to them, but you need to remember that in listening, people cannot "go back over" something they missed the way they can when they read. So keeping the information as simple and practical as possible will help ensure that you do not "lose" people along the way to your conclusion.

Timeliness. Keep your examples and information as timely as possible. If you give examples that recall the Vietnam War, that may be quite appropriate for 40- and 50-year-olds, but very difficult for people in their 20s and 30s to relate to.

Association. Choose familiar images to support your ideas. For example, I live in Houston. At a technical presentation on air pollution, the speaker described one part per million as "like a small glass of water inside the Astrodome." This really helped the audience understand his point. Also look outside your standard area of expertise for analogies that illustrate points vividly and in a concrete fashion.

Perspective. Keep in mind the perspective of the audience. Refer back to your audience analysis, but only after you have jotted down all of your ideas.

Once you have completed these steps, you are ready to consider a strategy. **One of the greatest weaknesses of presenters is their lack of a clear strategy.**

So often, presenters will choose a topical approach and have no persuasive style that brings home the main points. I will illustrate the different strategies that you can use to give a far greater impact to the information you present.

Look at the following numbers. Try to figure out the logic for why these numbers are in this order:

8   5   4   9   7   6   3   2   0

It is very logical. If I gave you a hint and asked you to pick the number that seems to be missing, you would pick "1". If I told you that the number "1" goes between the 9 and the 7, would it help? Probably not.

If you are like most people, you have turned this into a math problem, looking for mathematical relationships between the numbers. It is much simpler. They are in alphabetical order.

What's the point? What may seem very logical to you will cause others in your audience to work very hard trying to connect with you. Believe me when I tell you that most audiences will not work that hard. They will tune you out very quickly. Use one of the more common strategies for developing your ideas.

There are a variety of strategies that you can choose from in organizing your presentation. There is no "right" or "wrong" strategy. All of them will fit many situations, but the key element is to have a strategy!

Consider this

> Remember: You have to be clear in your message, or the audience will have trouble understanding what you mean. Take, for example, that confusing yet creative communicator, Casey Stengel, former manager of the New York Yankees. Addressing his baseball team one day he said, "Now all you fellows line up alphabetically by height." What was the message? Who knows? Don't let yourself be caught in "Stengelese." Carefully craft the message and use the pointers in this book to build a Bulletproof Presentation.

In a team presentation, there could be a strategy for the overall team presentation and then another for each individual presentation. *They can be different!* However, during a presentation, you will not have enough time to mix strategies within an individual presentation unless that presentation is more than one hour long.

A basic rule of thumb is to give the general idea first and then back it up with facts. The problem with using the reverse approach (giving the facts first and then following with your conclusion) is that the audience may understand the facts and reach an entirely different conclusion before you get there. Now you have the doubly difficult task of trying to steer them in a different direction along with convincing them of your ideas.

You are the presentation!

How you deliver your ideas and support them will really determine whether your audience will know, think, or do what you ask of it. If you structure the presentation logically and then deliver it effectively, you will have a Bulletproof Presentation!

Traps to avoid

When you talk about verbal communications, you're also talking about productivity and time management. In the many corporations where I have been a consultant, too often people spend time preparing presentations that are too long, overwrought, poorly designed, poorly structured, and ineptly delivered. The result is not a good use of the audience's time—because typically most people leaving the room can't pass a quiz on what they've just heard.

Worse, I have seen people spend a month preparing for a presentation when two or three days would have been sufficient.

Whether you tie up 200 or 20 people in a room for several hours and the audience members feel as though they have wasted their time and have nothing to show for it, then you really have wasted everybody's precious time—presenter and audience alike—whether you agree or not! The same can be said for smaller but equally vital business presentations.

A few years ago a vice president of a Fortune 500 company spent a solid month preparing for his first big presentation to the chairman. For 10 days he focused his concentration and productivity time into building something he wasn't quite sure how to build.

When the big day finally came, it was the second day of a long, two-day marathon of presentations. The time was 4:50 on Friday afternoon. The vice president was so consumed with the moment and the fast-approaching culmination of all his recent efforts that he failed to correctly gauge the mood in the room. He did not notice, for example, that some of the senior officers were stirring restlessly and impatiently glancing at their watches. Even after a forgettable start to his 40-minute plus presentation and the chairman's curt interruption to request that he speed things up and get to the point—because some people had to catch planes—the vice president marched doggedly onward. Apparently fired by fear of failure, and too rigorously prepared to be flexible, he seemed not to have heard the chairman's admonition.

Meanwhile, waves of thinly disguised impatience swept the room. Soon it became apparent even to the hapless vice president that things were threatening to slip out of control. After 10 minutes, when the vice president had apparently still not gotten to the point, the chairman rang down the curtain. He put an end to the meeting, an end to the presentation, and, as it turned out, an end to the vice president's career in the company.

What he did wrong

The lesson here was a need for flexibility and perhaps even an entirely new approach in a world where change is a daily fact of life and every second counts. Several elements conspired to make things go badly for the vice president.

First, his presentation was designed improperly. He never would have had the problems he did had he simply reversed the order—in other words, he should have started with the conclusion. That, after all, is what his audience was waiting to hear—and never did.

Second, he had planned to speak too long: 40 minutes. A maximum of 18 minutes, plus 22 minutes of questions and answers, would have served him better.

Third, he used too many visual aids. Not only that, but he used them incorrectly and picked the wrong ones.

Fourth, he allowed the presentation itself to dominate everything—even himself. He forgot about the big picture, the message, the main points, and instead focused only on the mechanics of trying to tell too much detail—an exercise I liken to trying to force an elephant into a golf bag. The presentation overwhelmed him and subsequently overwhelmed his audience.

Fifth, he had no theme, no "take-away" that his audience could remember a week later.

Sixth, for all his preparation, his basic lack of faith in his own presentation showed, and he came across as uncomfortable and nervous.

So despite all his best efforts, the vice president failed. Instead of seizing an opportunity, he walked into a series of common traps and wound up a victim of his own undoing. Just a few simple guidelines, covered in this book, might well have saved the day.

Consider this

When I watch one of my favorite shows, The Practice, one of the questions that often is asked by the judge is this: "Counselor, where are you going with this line of questioning?" Often, I think audiences wonder that same thing about presenters who have not structured their presentations with a clear strategy in mind. They cannot follow the speaker and have no idea where these points are heading. In a Bulletproof Presentation, the audience never needs to ask that question because it knows exactly how the points tie together because the strategy is clear.

Here are some of the most common strategies to assist in developing the logic:

- ➤ Chronological.

- ➤ Topical.

- ➤ Problem/solution.

- ➤ Most critical to least critical.

- ➤ Big picture/small picture.

- ➤ Procedural.

- ➤ Compare/contrast.

- ➤ Motivated sequence.

- ➤ Spatial.

Chronological

This strategy is basically a time sequence. It is very helpful in walking the listeners through a series of events in the order they occurred. It can also assist listeners in connecting events where you may wish to show a cause-and-effect relationship between the events. Finally, this strategy is helpful in situations where the audience needs to look at the past, present, and future.

Topical

Here the strategy is simply to present a variety of topics. This is a very popular approach in technical areas, but it is not very persuasive in its orientation. The major problem with the strategy is connecting the topics. Remember the logic earlier in the beginning of the chapter? Often the relationship between the topics is not clear to the listeners, so if you use this strategy, be very careful to establish the connections among topics. This means the transition between topics (the segue) is critical to success. My suggestion would be to test progression of points on someone who is not familiar with the topics to see if he or she can follow the presentation logic. If he or she has difficulty, then I would recommend choosing a different strategy.

Problem/solution

The information given during a presentation using this strategy cycles back and forth, first stating a problem and then the presenter's answer for solving that problem. This pattern is most often used in persuasive presentations, but it's also used in some technical presentations. If your audience analysis suggests that the audience will have a variety of questions about your topic, this is a good approach. It will allow you to anticipate the questions and provide the answers. It is almost guaranteed to be Bulletproof if you have answered all the questions. This approach is very similar to the technique often used in pamphlets and brochures. A variation of this strategy is the question/answer, in which you pose the questions and then answer them for the listener. Again, the trick is to do a good audience analysis in the planning stage.

Most critical to least critical

This strategy is very useful where a series of variables have had an impact on the outcome of the decision or proposed solution. Start with the most critical elements and move to those that are less critical or more common. For example, if you were considering a number of vendors for a project, some of the qualities would be very critical in presenting the vendor you chose for the project. You would want to highlight those critical factors first and then move progressively to those qualities that all the vendors possessed. However, the audience analysis plays an important role in this strategy, too. Be sure that the listeners also see the qualities that you have identified as equally important. If your priorities do not match theirs, they will almost surely question your logic and your judgment. If that happens, the presentation will not be Bulletproof!

Big picture/small picture

This strategy is very persuasive for presentations to upper management. This approach helps the listeners to see how you are applying the data and information, along with the recommended solution, into the larger goals of the department, division, or company. Here, the goal is to tie your ideas or solutions to the overall goals of the company, department, or client. You explain how your ideas will help the listeners achieve these goals. Again, for those people whose compensation is tied to performance against goals and targets, this is a very persuasive approach!

Procedural

This approach lays out the procedure in a step-by-step fashion. This strategy is obvious in its development. However, there is one significant danger to address. If you have ever heard a presentation where the speaker begins by telling you he or she will now cover the 15 steps in the process, you know what I am talking about. People will begin to tune out almost immediately and wonder why you did not put the information in written form. The best way around that is to break the multiple steps into two, three, or four groups or categories.

Compare/contrast

You can use this strategy very effectively with a persuasive presentation. The basic approach is to compare (show how things are similar), and contrast (show how things are different). For example, you might use this strategy to demonstrate how you are different from the competition.

The strength of this strategy is that it allows you to stress the differentiation that would be important to the audience. Although the strategy is called compare/contrast, you are not limited to that order. There are some situations where it might be advantageous to explain the contrasting points first, but that would normally be the exception.

Motivated sequence

In this approach, you establish with the audience that you understand its needs, then you explain how you can satisfy those needs, and, finally, give the audience a call to action. This strategy is often used in sales situations and can be persuasive if used correctly. However, if you have not established rapport and credibility in advance, this approach will "turn off" the audience because it will seem too much like a sales approach.

You need to:

➥ Get their attention.

➥ Generate interest in your approach.

➥ Present the data to support your approach.

➥ Call them to action.

Spatial

With the spatial strategy, you are trying to get the audience members to literally see something "in their mind's eye." For example, if I wanted to describe what I saw on my last trip abroad, I might use the spatial strategy to allow the audience to travel with me in their minds and "see" what I saw.

> **No matter which strategy is chosen,
> the presenter will constantly keep the purpose in mind,
> as well as reinforce the Overriding Theme.**

Consider this

An old story tells us of two men who were walking along the streets of London, when the music of some wonderful chimes in a nearby cathedral floated through the air. One of the men remarked to the other, "Isn't that wonderful music?"

"I didn't hear what you said," replied the other.

"Aren't those chimes beautiful?" replied the first man. But again, the other man failed to catch the words, and the first speaker said for the third time, "Isn't that lovely music?"

"It's no use," came the answer. "Those pesky bells are making so much noise, I can't hear what you are saying!"

The presenter needs to think about the type of listener the key decision-maker is and orient the strategy to best fit his or her style of listening and the way he or she thinks.

People can only process so much information at one time. Think of the last time you were at a social event where you met several new people. How many names did you remember? Not more than four or five is my guess. That is because of the way our memory works. Once we hit a certain level, we go into "overload," and that causes us to shut down further information. The same principal applies to presentations. Try to choose three to five main points for the body.

For example, if I had a presentation to discuss a new procedure that had 12 steps, I would certainly use the procedural strategy. However, I would try to break those 12 steps into three or four groupings that will allow people to sort and remember them better. If I simply present 12 steps as individual items, I would not be successful. The structure of this book is an example: 19 chapters grouped into five main parts.

First or last

When you have total freedom to choose, you might question where in your presentation you should place your strongest major points: first or last? Some will argue for placing your strongest points first. When you believe that the greatest effect in creating change in the attitude of the audience will be most affected by putting your major points first, do it! Others will argue that the greatest impact on the audience will occur when the strongest major point is placed last in the presentation.

The real answer will probably lie in your audience analysis. Although there is no conclusive research regarding which position has the greatest benefit in a persuasive presentation, the following general guidelines may be helpful.

Even if you cannot decide whether your strongest argument would be more effective first or last, either is better than "burying" it in the middle of your presentation.

Consider beginning and ending a series of arguments with your two strongest arguments; this allows you to take the fullest advantage of being able to start strongly and finish strongly. When you and your audience differ greatly on an argument, consider dealing with it early in your presentation—probably even first. Otherwise the listeners might become preoccupied with their position on one issue while you are presenting others, and they are not listening to you.

If you are making a persuasive presentation, many presenters prefer to build their case to a climax at the end. This may be stronger than presenting your strongest argument first. If a major point is weak and leaving it out would not be considered conspicuous or unethical, leave it out.

Involving the audience

You can often change the entire mood of an audience by getting it involved. You can do that by asking questions—and then waiting until someone gives you an answer. For example, you can ask a question and ask for a show of hands. Often the audience will assume you are asking a rhetorical question and are not really looking for them to answer. By waiting, or encouraging the audience to answer, you remove that assumption and the audience will be more likely to answer future questions.

You can also involve the audience by initiating a roundtable discussion or doing a short, simple activity after you have spoken to get people involved. Perhaps you can ask them to share impressions or questions with the people sitting beside them and then pose them to you for the group to hear.

I have had great success with these techniques and am convinced they are a key reason why I am always rated very highly as a speaker. It is a simple technique that you can use with a little planning.

Using examples

In using examples, you need to appeal to the two sides of the audience's psyche: the logical and the emotional. In appealing to the logical, you will need to support your points with facts and data.

Any presentation that does not have the proper data to support it is doomed in most cases. But most people do not think about the emotional side. You must use examples that touch people's emotions: whether happiness, sadness, worries, or whatever.

Remember the Rule of Emotion? Stories are a great way to move to that emotional side. If you think about the great presenters you have watched, I bet you remember their stories more than any data or facts they used. Try to think of personal experiences you have had that relate to your topic. You can relate the stories of others, but they often are not quite as good, and they may have heard someone else tell that same story. It is not as effective as if you have an original.

Bulletproof advice

➤ **Delivering a message well begins with a clear strategy.**

- Keep the presentation logical and connected to the audience so listeners can follow your ideas easily.

➤ **In most cases, you will want to use one of the common strategies.**

- Except in unusual circumstances, you will probably want to use one of the nine common strategies outlined in the chapter to develop your ideas.

➤ **Try to choose three to five main points for the body of the presentation.**

- People can only process so much information at one time; this should help you to keep them focused.

➤ **Use examples that appeal to people's emotional as well as logical sides. Using examples and stories that touch people's emotions is a great way to do that.**

CHAPTER 9

DEVELOPING
STORIES FOR
YOUR PRESENTATION

The more we learn about the human mind, the more we understand how important stories are to the way we learn. This chapter will focus on how to develop stories that you can use in your Bulletproof Presentations, even business or technical presentations.

Computer scientists working in the area of artificial intelligence confirm the notion that we are natural-born storytellers. Various experts point out that stories are a terrific way to reach a listener or group of listeners. In several companies my firm has worked in, stories are an integral, albeit informal, way of passing along information on the history and culture of the company. The point is that for most of the history of the human race, people have used stories to organize and remember important experiences.

Humans have always used stories to
organize and remember important experiences or events.

Several experts will point out that not every experience makes a good story, but, if it does, the experience will be easier to remember. Throughout a variety of cultures, stories helped our ancestors understand the world around them through an oral history. This oral history was established by a series of stories that were told and retold to successive generations. **People's ability to understand and use these stories in new and unique ways is a hallmark of most civilizations and cultures today as well**.

However, we do not have to go to that level if we think of our own experiences. The last time you attended a wedding or funeral, my guess is that you heard several people telling stories about the members of the family. They are also part of our personal history.

Much of psychotherapy is also based on the premise that each of us creates our own life story from the time we are born. Such theories and Transactional Analysis, using life scripts and Alfred Adler's theory that the order of birth affects our life, both build on the premise of these stories that we create internally. It is a natural, inevitable process in our maturation. It's also one in which these therapies contend that we can consciously and creatively examine and effectively rewrite in order to "change" our past and restore our psychological health. First, however, we need to reclaim that core part of ourselves where our individual stories reside. To that end, there is a relatively new approach that has developed over the past few years called *narrative therapy.* This approach assists people to rewrite their stories and revise or replace their negative stories with new ones that are more positive and practical. The concept behind the therapy is that by rewriting our personal narratives, we can change the negative images that have been recorded into our minds and become healthier and happier people.

For example, if a man is suffering from memories of having been pushed around all his life, he might be led by a therapist to rewrite his concept of his past around the times when he, in any way, felt strong, confident, or in command. According to this theory, he could accomplish this "mental shift" by consciously developing new, more positive stories of these occasions in his life that will compete with, and eventually replace, the negative stories he had repeated internally to himself and others over the years. By using this approach, he would be tapping into the same, internal storytelling mechanism that developed the original negative events that lead to the negative stories from the past. He would be essentially reconstructing his personal identity, making a new, more positive person out of old, damaged materials. Or so narrative therapists claim.

The core of the human mind, according to Michael White, an Australian counselor and early advocate of narrative therapy in the 1980s, is a storyteller. The human mind cannot take in the full range of sensory, mental, and emotional experience that it encounters without some sort of artificial frame of reference, so it consolidates these experiences into stories. These stories are certain to change on their own, to some degree, as time goes by, not only in details and structure but also in tone, significance, and relative rank of importance within the story person's mind.

In telling stories during presentations, our personal stories can change the most. If you have told stories about a childhood incident many times over the years, you have probably changed it somewhat to improve the telling and to get the point across.

In telling personal stories during a presentation, you must ask yourself the same question about "the truth": Is it about factual accuracy or helping the audience to see the point.

You will need to decide the issue on a story-by-story basis and come to your own personal decision. You can do this by listening with the inner voice that we all have—that inner part of ourselves that answers the ethical questions we confront using our personal values.

Many have heard the writer Anna Quinlen tell a personal story about the time she ran out into the street and got hit by an automobile when she was five years old. In a *New York Times* column on October 7, 1988, she recounted the ending she usually gives to her story: "My mother, who was pregnant, runs to the scene and promptly passes out. After all is said and done, I have nothing more to show for it than a black-and-blue mark on my backside that is shaped like the continent of Africa." When the author commented later on the "facts" contained in the story, she is really not sure if her mother was pregnant or not. She is fairly certain that her mother did not really faint. And she is almost positive that the "bruise shaped like Africa" is a something she made up to give the story color. "I could swear that I looked at my back view in the mirror on my closet door and that I had a bruise that was shaped like Africa," she has said.

Would it be wrong to use the story if every detail was not exactly accurate? I don't think so. I often tell a story about my youngest daughter and the surprise I received one day about an assumption that I had never thought about. The story goes like this:

My daughter was at a Brownie outing at a neighborhood pool near my home. I had dropped her off just after lunch on Saturday and went home to do my usual lawn work. I arrived back at the pool at the designated time later that afternoon to see my daughter sitting against a tree all by herself. She is a very social person, and for her to be alone was quite unusual. When I asked her why she was sitting alone, she said, "Well, Daddy, I just wasn't feeling well." My immediate response was to ask her why she had not called me to pick her up. After all, I was just doing lawn work and could easily have come to get her.

She said she had tried to call, but she could not get the telephone to work. That made me very curious and I asked her what was wrong. She said, "The phone had this round thing on the front and I kept pushing the numbers in the little holes, but it would not work." My daughter had never used a rotary dial telephone before! If you had asked me prior to that day, I would never have believed that would be a problem. It goes to show you the assumptions we make!

In telling that story to illustrate a point, I have worked on it to help it resonate with the audience, build rapport with them, and make a point.

Is that exactly the way it happened? I am not even sure today, but it did happen and it helps me connect with my audience so I am not concerned with absolute accuracy and you should not be either!

The other reason for using stories to illustrate points is to connect with the audience on an emotional level. Much of the information we use in presentations is factual in nature. It connects very well with the logical side of people's brain. However, it usually does very little to connect to the emotional side. Stories connect on this level. Hearing about my daughter not only illustrates a point I want to make during the presentation, but it gives audience members additional information about me as a person. They find out that I have a family with at least one daughter (actually, I have three). They also learn something about me as a father and share a laugh at the situation because they can relate it to similar situations they have encountered themselves. That is the emotional connection.

Generating family stories and using them to illustrate points is a great way to connect with the audience on an emotional level. This is how exceptional presenters build rapport with the audience. To try to add stories to your presentations, recall family stories that you have told before and see if any are applicable. They can be stories from work, too. (We will cover that in the next chapter.) You might get better results—sharper images and, therefore, more applicable stories—by focusing on a more specific topic: for example, "my daughter," "my habits," "things my mother said," or "my father's favorite possessions."

After you have come up with topics to explore based on your own personal memory review, consider any other questions that are appropriate to the subject in general or that you'd like to ask the particular people you plan to talk to about the stories. I have found that the following questions posed to various family members often work well to bring stories to light:

➤ **What was your childhood like?** Your home, neighborhood, school, parents, siblings, pets, chores, meals? Your favorite things to do? The ways you celebrated good times, coped with bad ones, conducted daily or weekly business?

➤ **What stories or legends did you hear about as a child related to your family background?** Ancestors, migrations, name origins? Heroes, villains, victims, oddballs? Triumphs, catastrophes, courtships, marriages, feuds, alliances?

➤ **What goals or dreams did you have as a young person?** What people, events, and things influenced you the most? What major learning experiences did you have?

➤ **How did you first meet various people?** Your spouse or mate, your mother-in-law, an aunt or uncle that was a real "character."

➤ **What difficult/successful/unusual experiences stand out?** In your job history? In your friendships? In your marriage? In raising a family?

➤ **What memories do you especially associate with significant people, places, or events?** For example, your father's or grandfather's funeral? Boy Scout camp? Vietnam War protests? Me (the potential storyteller) as a child?

Here are some guidelines for interviewing family members—and other people—as you try to develop stories based on your personal life. These should make it easier and more productive.

1. If possible, try to meet with other family members alone—that is, on a one-to-one basis, not with the other people present. Keep in mind that interviewing two people separately about the same event can be very informative, especially with regard to the relativity of "truth."

2. Choose a time, place, and situation that is comfortable for both you and your interviewee and free from disturbances or distractions. Stay focused on the interview. Don't divide your attention by simultaneously eating a meal, playing cards, or taking a walk.

3. Start out the interview on common, familiar ground, so that both of you can relax into the spirit of things. Bring an old photograph, object, or document that you believe the other person might know something about, or ask the other person to recount a story that you remember him or her telling before. You're almost certain to hear something new now, when you're paying closer attention.

4. As much as possible, keep the interview flowing in a conversational manner, even though the other person will be doing most of the talking. To encourage lengthy discussion, ask open-ended questions that can't simply be answered with yes or no. For example, ask, "What was Uncle Darrell like as a kid?" instead of "Was Uncle Darrell mean?" The second question will more than likely only get you a yes or no answer. The first question can give the other person a lot more latitude and will probably get you more information.

There are two important considerations that can become components to making a successful presentation. When successful presenters talk to audiences, they appeal to both the logical part of the audience and the emotional side. Any presentation that only focuses on one or the other may be seen as "okay" by the audience, but it will be left less than satisfied. The trick is to mix your facts (which appeal to the logical side) and your stories (which appeal to the emotional side) in an interesting way. By moving between the two, you will really capture the audience.

Whatever way you decide to link the points, data, and stories is not as important as the fact that you have them.

Here are ways that you can lay out the stories and facts to make key points during a presentation. Remember: You should not use the same layout every time or the repetition will get boring.

▷	Sample layout	
Topic 1	**Topic 2**	**Topic 3**
1. Point	1. Story	1. Data
2. Story	2. Point	2. Point
3. Data	3. Data	3. Story
4. Point	4. Point	4. Point

Depending on the presentation, any of these formats would work. Mixing them slightly can add sparkle to your presentation.

Clearly define the ending of one section of your presentation and the beginning of the next in the structure of your presentation.

Even with a clear strategy and the roadmap you developed earlier, linking the various points together and moving among them easily will go a long way toward making your presentation Bulletproof!

Finally, when you must decide what and how much information to include in the body of the presentation, you might consider dividing the information into three distinct categories:

1. Information the audience must know.

2. Information the audience should know.

3. Information that it would be nice for the audience to know.

This listing can help you to pare down the information into the key points, either during the planning stage of your presentation or if you are asked to reduce your time at the last minute. The latter happens more often than you can imagine. Having made the decisions about the importance of the points in advance will help you decide what can be edited out and what needs to remain within the presentation.

Activity: The family beat

Gathering the personal recollections of individual family members can not only give you good story material, but it can also bring you and your interviewees closer together.

First, identify at least one person in your family who you feel reasonably comfortable about contacting for this purpose. Ideally, the two of you should be able to meet face to face for an hour to engage in the type of discussion described in this chapter. If it's impossible, impractical, or undesirable to meet with an actual relative, then identify someone who knows (or knew) your family or who has long been a part of your chosen "family" of intimate friends.

Once you've identified this person, ask yourself the following questions:

1. What people, places, or events in my own past might this person know more about? (State at least two.)

2. For each major person, place, or event that I have identified, what specific, open-ended questions could I pose to this person? (State at least three questions for each item.)

3. Apart from his or her connection to, or insights about, the people, places, and events in his or her past, what things most interest me about this person's life? (State at least two items.)

4. For each subject of interest that I've identified, what open-ended questions could I pose to this person? (State at least three questions for each item.)

5. How, specifically, should I approach this person and describe the meeting's purpose?

6. What are three different options I could propose to this person for meeting with me? (Include date, time, place in each option.)

Bulletproof advice

➤ **Use stories to help your audience remember your key points.**

- Don't get too concerned with the absolute accuracy of the story.

➤ **Search your own experience to develop your stories.**

- Use family members or friends to gather information.

➤ **Use stories to build connections with the audience.**

CHAPTER 10

STORYBOARDING YOUR PRESENTATION

In this chapter, we want to look at how to lay out the stories within your presentation for the best effect using the technique that comic book creators and animation and cartoon illustrators have used for years: storyboarding.

Whether or not a picture's worth a thousand words, a comic book can tell a pretty good tale, as any story-loving kid well knows. Once we have identified and, to some extent, planned the key scenes in a story, we may want to structure it in a more thorough and systematic way by creating a comic book-style storyboard.

The word *storyboard,* coined by filmmakers in the early days of the film industry, commonly refers to a large board holding sketches that depict step-by-step plot progressions in the early stages of developing a movie. As with its Hollywood counterpart, a storyboard for plotting your stories and overall presentation is a series of images that represent not just the key ideas in a presentation but each and every significant shift of fact, perspective, or subject from the beginning of a presentation to its end.

**We can evolve a storyboard solely in our
imagination or we can write it out,
using an outline format with short phrases for each shift.**

If we really want to be thorough and give ourselves some valuable, right-brain exercise, we can even make note cards for each idea and the transition steps in between. Symbolic images—for example, an apple or a dollar sign to represent a point in a story where we go to a financial statement—are generally easy to remember and, therefore, can function as excellent memory aids. More realistic sketches can help us, as we are drawing them, to "see" all the more deeply into that moment of the presentation.

After we create a storyboard that satisfies us, we can then store it in our memory bank, so that it's there to help us practice and present during the many rehearsals prior to the actual presentation. In a sense, the storyboard serves as a compromise between keeping in mind the key ideas in our presentation (which is simpler to do, but may not offer enough guidance for longer presentations or more formal occasions) and, at the other end of the spectrum, memorizing a complete script (which offers more support, but is much more work and may ultimately make our delivery sound stilted or staged).

At this point in the discussion of the crafting stories process, I would like to offer a more complete, fairly long sample personal tale as a basis for further discussion and illustration. Because this is a book and not a workshop, I will give you an example of one of my stories and you can see how it develops.

Harmon Killebrew

I am a great fan of baseball. The roar of the crowd, the smell of hot dogs and popcorn, and the excitement of seeing some of the greatest athletes on earth is my special treat. I love standing during the seventh-inning stretch and singing *Take Me Out to the Ball Game* along with thousands of other baseball fans.

One of my favorite players as a kid was Harmon Killebrew of the Minnesota Twins. He was a big, brawny player who swatted towering home runs on a regular basis. His career and personal character certainly earned him a spot in baseball's hall of fame. However, he did not get elected into the hall of fame immediately. In fact, he was 60 years old before he finally made it, several years after he had retired from the game as a player and coach.

I think it was with a great deal of relief that he finally was elected into the hall of fame, and during the ceremonies he was as excited as any kid. During one of the breaks in the festivities, a writer from *Sports Illustrated* magazine interviewed Killebrew. The usual questions came up about his career and his excitement at being elected to baseball's elite status. However, the writer decided to veer off into another set of questions to get Killebrew's opinion of the current game. "Mr. Killebrew," he said, "how many home runs do you think you could hit playing today?"

Killebrew rubbed his chin for a moment, in deep thought, and then said, "Oh, I guess maybe 20 or 25." This from a player who had hit well more than 500 home runs in his career? The writer was stunned that the number was so low.

"Wow," said the writer. "You regularly hit 35 to 45 home runs every season. Is the lower number because of more night games now? Or different pitching styles?"

"Hell, no!" responded Killebrew. "It's because I am 60 years old!"

The story is humorous and builds on all the key elements of a good story. The audience members have to imagine they are there with all the different elements. Here are some of the key elements of building a good story:

Appeal to all five senses

Incorporate in your story details that stimulate all five senses in your listeners' minds: sight, sound, smell, touch, and taste. You can appeal to a different sense in each of several different images, but it's even more effective to invest a single image with several different sensations.

In my Harmon Killebrew example, I appeal to the senses of sight and sound in particular when I refer the excitement of the baseball game, the food, and the singing of *Take Me Out to the Ball Game.*

You may have to expand or change your original story line so that it *can* invoke all five senses. In a story about your first boss, for example, you may have to include, somehow, his or her favorite food in order to have an image that appeals to the senses of smell and taste. This addition may seem rather mechanical when you first make it, but it helps to guarantee that the portrait of your boss has a well-rounded life of its own when you share it and that it can come to a similarly full life in your audience's imagination.

Now that I have encouraged you to use sensory images in your stories, I urge you to be careful in how you use them. Including too many descriptive details can weigh down your narrative, making it sound more like a written story. When you tell a story, it needs to be livelier and more action-oriented to hold the attention of its listener than a written story. This means being selective about details, choosing only ones that are especially clear and help you to make your point.

Include ear-catching words and phrases

Every now and then, drop into your story expressions that are appropriately (or, for a humorous effect, inappropriately) colorful, humorous, sophisticated, graphic, or poetic. These special uses of language not only bolster and reward your listeners' attention, but they also help you remember the parts of the story and where they occur. For example, when I tell the Harmon Killebrew example, I make it a point always to use the expressions that remind baseball fans of the emotions they feel at a game. However, the story has enough information and impact that even listeners who are not baseball fans can get the point—and the humor that the situation calls for.

Interesting metaphors or comparisons can also add more flavor to a story. Suppose you want to say that the sauce you once ate at a business dinner was incredibly spicy. Think of yourself as a stand-up comic and imagine voices shouting from your audience, "How spicy *was* it?" In this case, you might say, "It was so spicy that my eyes watered so much that people came over to offer condolences."

Add interesting facts or allusions

Often, a story is doubly valuable to a listener if it includes interesting pieces of relevant historical or educational information. For instance, in describing the trait of independence you want in your employees, you might include a tale involving your cat's special meaning in your life. In addition, you could refer to the fact that in ancient Egypt cats were worshiped as gods, and given special treatment and care.

You could also make allusions to other works of art (paintings, musical compositions, novels, movies, poems, folktales) that are similar in theme to your story or that help to capture the quality of something you mention in the story. In some respects, alluding to another tale can become a miniaturized version of the story-within-a-story format discussed later on.

Colorado-based storyteller Jan Cooper tells a story about dating the prettiest girl in high school in which he uses an extended *Sleeping Beauty* analogy. Alluding to the hundred-year paralysis that the whole kingdom endures between the time Sleeping Beauty falls into a coma and the time the prince kisses her, Cooper speaks of the house where the girl lived as being frozen in a spell, surrounded by thorny hedges, empty streets, and silent, neighboring houses with their curtains pulled shut. He says he worried about what might happen when he finally worked up the nerve to kiss the girl on her living room sofa. He feared that at the first smack of their lips, her never-used fireplace would burst into flames, her drab walls would spew forth wedding decorations, her elderly parents would dash from their rockers to get the preacher, her lazy hound dogs would start dancing around them, and her neighbors would rally in front of the house, cheering, waving gift-wrapped toasters, and blocking his escape.

By using the story, Cooper gives his personal story an ironic twist for two main reasons. First, the audience relates to the familiar story from childhood and connects a great adventure that gets all the more caught up in familiarity. Second, Cooper is able to talk about himself from a third-person perspective, adding to the story's humor and avoiding the pitfalls of being too sentimental, self-important, intimate, or boring.

In addition, ironic connection to a well-known story accomplishes what another kind of allusion does: images from the broader audience that helps make Cooper's own story deeper, more resonant, and more universal.

Build in repetitions to build interest

Repeat important or interesting words, phrases, facts, or sentence structure. You want the structures during the course of your story to lend it a pleasing sense of structure and familiarity. Repetition can also add to the story's humor. But perhaps best of all, it can help both you and your listener remember things. Children especially like repetition in stories for all these reasons, but all audiences will enjoy it as long as you do not overdo it.

In the Harmon Killebrew example, I repeat the full name "Killebrew" a lot, partly so people will be more likely to remember it.

Plan appropriate pacing and inflection

The best possible equipment for telling personal stories is your own natural voice and vocal style. At this stage in story development, when you have just finished putting your story together, it helps to note the parts of it that you think, or feel, should be told especially slowly or swiftly, loudly or softly, seriously or comically, insistently or tentatively.

Review your story carefully. There are two ways you may use pauses for dramatic effect. One way is to pause for a few seconds to let what you've just said linger in the listeners' minds. In other cases, pauses can build suspense, reflect the passage of time, change the mood, provide a transition from one subject to another, and give the audience a chance to recognize something or offer you *and* your audience a brief opportunity to rest.

Pauses can be some of the most effective moments in a tale. They can also be some of the most difficult to deliver. As a presenter taking a pause, we tend to get very nervous as the silence passes. In radio, this is called "dead air," and most radio stations work very hard to eliminate it from their programming. For this reason alone, it is good to plan certain significant pauses in advance. Another reason to include at least a couple pauses in your story is to give yourself some time to remember, just in case you need it. In addition, if you have already paused once or twice in a natural place (without appearing preplanned) as you are telling a story, it is easier to insert yet another *unplanned* but still natural-seeming pause when you need to buy time to recall something you've forgotten. (As you'll see later in the delivery section, this is also a great spot to take a drink of water!)

If you make a mistake, handle it as best you can without breaking the presentation's momentum. Pretend you have other people listening and therefore need to provide a fairly smooth delivery, even if it means sacrificing or changing certain story details on the spot. For example, one time I was making a presentation to a group of company executives to illustrate the steps they would need to take to drive change through the company. I was using a theater metaphor for change developed by Winford E. "Dutch" Holland in his book *Change Is the Rule.* To illustrate the ideas, I was using a publicly known story of another company from the newspapers. However, the morning of the presentation, the company I was addressing announced the purchase of another company's assets that would have a tremendous change on the company's character and business. Instead of using the public example as I had planned, I switched gears and used the new company assets to illustrate the points I wanted to make. In doing that, I knew the points of the story very well, and they were very excited because I was able to tie the major points of my presentation, and the story, to something that was clearly on their minds that morning. Needless to say, the presentation was definitely Bulletproof.

If you want, you can think about one or more of the other enlivening techniques during additional practice sessions.

Anytime you tell your story, to yourself or to others, it is best to tell the whole story—rather than just part of it—and then to wait for a while (at least a couple of hours, preferably a day or more) before telling it again. In this way, you preserve the natural, overall flow of the story and allow yourself some time after each telling to reflect on what you've heard. Also, this type of rehearsal will help you if you need to adapt your story "on the fly," as I illustrated earlier.

Our lives consist of worlds within worlds within worlds: private domains and public sectors; family circles, business rounds, and social spheres; fantasy realms and brutal realities; present, past, and future scenarios. Through personal stories, we can journey among all these realities in a host of new ways that benefit ourselves and our audiences as we deliver a Bulletproof Presentation.

There are some distinctions between big stories (about major, self-defining life events) and little ones (about smaller-scale dramas). Often presenters find themselves more comfortable with one category rather than another. There is nothing wrong with that. However, if we develop the habit of telling *only* one type, fearing or discounting the other one entirely, we can severely limit our true potential. In this case, growing as presenters means learning to love communicating *both* kinds of stories.

An even more common and possibly more critical occurrence is the tendency to tell personal stories in only a few contexts. We may tell them:

➤ To our family members and friends, but never to our coworkers.

➤ In our homes and offices, but never in our community.

➤ To get laughs and make points, but never to inspire the audience.

➤ When we are with people we know, but never among strangers.

It is crucial for you as a presenter to learn to love bringing your tales into every major context of your life. Only then can the stories evolve into an integral aspect of who we are and how well we present our ideas. Only then can we connect with our audiences on both the logical and emotional levels. And only then can the stories perform their full magic in our own lives and those of our audiences.

In this and the next two sections in this chapter, we will explore two major life contexts for storytelling:

1. Storytelling at **work**: to our coworkers, staff members, bosses, trainees, clients, and business associates.

2. Storytelling in the **community:** to individuals and groups in our neighborhoods, towns, cities, countryside, ecological niches, and spiritual congregations.

As you read these sections, you may think of other contexts for storytelling or different ways to describe the ones I discuss here.

Equipping ourselves to tell personal stories in each of these two contexts may require us to develop and deliver distinct varieties of stories:

➤ Some about domestic or family matters.

➤ Others relating to the workplace.

➤ Another batch involving local, regional, or spiritual issues.

It is far more likely, however, that the same tale will work in one or both contexts, with only slight modifications in the way it is introduced and/or delivered. This is especially true of personal experience stories, which are highly flexible in their structure, length, wording, emphasis, and tone.

Here's an example of how a personal story can be adapted to fit both of the contexts.

When you work to help people make a change, you must learn to be flexible and even start over again if necessary. I learned that tip from Michelangelo. Yes, *the* Michelangelo! On a trip to Italy, my wife and I visited the Galleria dell' Accademia museum on a glorious fall day that was a perfect setting for visiting beautiful works of art. The Galleria dell'Accademia has a wonderful display area for one of Michelangelo's most famous statues: the statue of David that you have probably seen pictures of. The statue is huge and is displayed in a large hall that allows visitors to view it from a 360-degree perspective. It is magnificent!

Also contained in this museum are interesting collections of incomplete works of Michelangelo that artists of that time period called "slaves." They were given that name because the artist believed that the beautiful art inside them could not be released and was therefore held captive within the stone.

One in particular drew my attention and I decided I had to talk with my museum guide about it. This incomplete work looked very much like Michelangelo's famous work titled the *Pieta* that is housed in the Vatican in Rome. This statue is the one where Mary is holding the dead Jesus in her lap. How many of you know the statue I am talking about? Show of hands?

There was a slave there at the museum, an incomplete sculpture, that looked very much like that very famous statue that we had seen just a couple of days earlier. I asked the guide, "What happened here?" "Why did Michelangelo quit working on this statue?" The guide said, "Well, of course we don't know exactly what happened, but probably one of two things happened. Number one, Michelangelo discovered there was a flaw in the marble. That could create a problem in that it might very well break because of that flaw. Or number two, and this is more likely, the statue was not turning out the way he wanted it to, so he made a decision to start over."

Of course, he did start over again and created the masterpiece that I had seen a couple of days earlier in the Vatican. That particular piece became world-famous and is admired by millions of people every year.

I could understand the idea, and I admit that I do not know a lot about sculpture, but as I looked at this slave, I was amazed at the detail in it. Again, it was so detailed that I could tell it was an incomplete rendition of the *Pieta*. So I asked the guide, "How long do you think he worked on that slave before he quit and decided to start over?" The guide said again that he could not be 100-percent sure, but knowing how fast sculptors generally work, knowing generally how fast Michelangelo worked, and based on their best estimates, most experts believe that he probably worked on that piece for somewhere between two and three years before he quit and started over.

Can you imagine? Michelangelo worked on that slave for more than two years and then threw it away to start over. Talk about patience! And he always kept the results he wanted in mind. Michelangelo felt strongly enough about how he wanted to complete that statue, and he made a decision. He must have said something along the lines of, "It is not coming out the way I wanted, so even though I have spent more than two years on this project, I am not going to try to 'fix it up' and go on. I am going to start over again and do it right."

We have our plans, too, and sometimes they do not turn out the way we thought. We have to be flexible enough to recognize that when we are not getting what we expected, that it's okay to start over again.

When I want to gear this story toward a particular context, I introduce and tell it from a slightly different, expressly appropriate perspective—adding, subtracting, minimizing, or maximizing details accordingly. I never actually change the core of the narrative or stray from the truth of what happened. I simply choose my emphasis, tone, language, and interpretation to fit the audience and the situation.

Here are some of the adaptations I make for each context:

Community storytelling: I spend more time talking about my home environment, daily rituals, and my family as we saw these incredible, albeit, incomplete statues. The point of view centers more around kinds of frustrations we find in our personal lives every day and the need to overcome them.

Storytelling at work: Because I am a public speaker and consultant by profession, I more pointedly use words and images that evoke the themes of long-range plans that do not work out, communication between the craftsmen who had to abandon their work, and inspiration that these same craftsmen could, and would, start over to ensure the quality of their work. In the larger field of business in general, the tale can be told as a parable of supply and demand, customer service, quality in the work environment, and/or management challenges and responsibilities.

To give the story a more spiritual cast, I dwell on how moved I was by the sacrifice that Michelangelo and his craftsmen made, and their intelligence, bravery, and trust, as well as by the fact that I felt connected so strongly to that group of people despite the incredible number of years that had passed since they lived. I create a dramatic contrast between the frustration of making a decision to start over with the joy at creating a beautiful masterpiece that still inspires millions of people hundreds of years later. The story talks about motivation on a number of different levels.

Each of these storytelling contexts (work and community) offers its own unique learning experiences and enrichment opportunities, which is why we have so much to gain from applying ourselves to both of them.

Storytelling at work

Long ago, before the printing press, when communication among people almost always went directly from mouth to ear, telling personal stories was a major means of conducting day-to-day business. After all, when human beings themselves are the medium, even work-related messages tend to be narrative in style and experiential in content.

Today, a wide variety of machines—e-mail, cameras, fax machines, photocopiers, computers, satellites, and so on—have done much to make overall business communication far more technical in style and data-driven in content than it used to be. That doesn't mean, however, that stories no longer have a function in the workplace. I believe they continue to play a more vital role in work-related operations than we acknowledge, and they could serve us even better if we would pay more attention them.

Certain jobs intrinsically call for *some* kind of oral storytelling, such as teaching, journalism, selling, counseling, preaching, and tending bar. The same goes for certain activities that are common to many different types of jobs, such as giving speeches, making presentations, participating in workshops, networking, and entertaining clients. There is no reason why job-appropriate *personal* tales should not be included in the mix of stories that are told. In the working world in particular, personal tales can relate the presenter to the work, the listener can connect to the presenter, and the listener to the work in many unique, fresh, and constructive ways.

If you are self-employed, are engaged in a small, entrepreneurial venture, or perform some sort of specialized service for a living—whether it is brain surgery, computer repair, or television repair—personal tales may be your best vehicle for rendering the demands, experiences, and motivations of your unconventional work life more comprehensible to others. If you are employed in the corporate world, where individual identities sometimes tend to get lost, personal stories may represent not only a life-saving means of humanizing your work relationships but also a vital tool for communicating your unique wisdom, needs, and goals to others.

Superficially, the corporate environment may seem the least likely place for telling personal stories. In fact, the activity already thrives there under other labels. Some of the more common labels are mentoring or training as examples. Others seem somewhat negative: schmoozing, gossiping, or trading "war stories." I have often said, to the knowing nods of my audiences, that the "rumor mill" seems to spread information faster than e-mail.

Regardless of the label or how it is regarded, the simple act of sharing personal tales in an otherwise impersonal environment always helps individual storytellers and their listeners invest more of themselves in each other. This ultimately means that they can apply themselves to their jobs more wholeheartedly, which benefits them *and* their company.

David Boje, associate professor of management at Loyola Marymount University in Los Angeles and editor of the *Journal of Organizational Change Management,* advises, "Think of an organization as a big conversation. People are conversing all day long. An organization is an ongoing storytelling event." Given this situation, it pays for corporate employees to put extra effort into crafting personal stories that are interesting and more germane to their jobs when they are making presentations, and therefore more effective in improving the quality of their day-to-day work and explaining it to others.

David Armstrong, vice president of Armstrong International and author of *Managing by Storying Around: A New Method of Leadership,* knows from firsthand experience that storytelling can do wonders within a corporation to forge partnerships and teams, to pass along ideas and information, and to enhance workplace reporting, interviewing, evaluating, and recruiting processes. He has virtually institutionalized storytelling in his company, taking it upon himself to be one of the key tellers, listeners, and spreaders. "I average only about one meeting a week," he told Larry Pike, a writer for *Storytelling* magazine. "Ninety percent of the time I'm walking around, talking to people." Corporate America would recognize that as "managing by walking around."

Armstrong also firmly believes in the value of developing good stories in advance, rather than leaving matters to chance. Comparing story communication to marketing, he states, "Too many people think, 'I don't have much time; I'm just going to blurt it out real quick.' Well, if you want to sell somebody an idea, you've got to present it properly. If you want to sell a story, you got to present it properly, too."

Here are suggestions for getting down to business with your personal storytelling:

1. In a workplace atmosphere, it is best to tell tales that are relatively short, realistic, and plainspoken. It is also essential that they clearly illustrate a specific point.

2. Because work is so achievement-oriented and workers are so often overstressed, give special consideration to developing and telling personal stories that can somehow empower your listeners: ones that offer them new information, trigger fresh ways of thinking, encourage them to realize their goals, validate what they are doing, or simply put them in a better frame of mind. Think of Michelangelo's craftsmen.

Be alert for problematic workplace situations, issues, projects, or relationships that might benefit from the novelty of personal stories. Quite often, the activity in itself—apart from the actual content of the stories—can lead to more innovative points of view. John Ward, a corporate consultant in what he diplomatically calls "creative communication" (rather than "storytelling"), believes that stories develop a businessperson's peripheral vision. He describes this visionary asset as the ability to see beyond the dots, referring to the famous puzzle involving a nine-dot square (three rows of three dots), where you are asked to connect all nine dots using no more than four lines, with no backtracking or lifting the pencil off the paper.

Ward's theory is that stories set in motion a different way of thinking that can result in workplace breakthroughs: "Stories can potentially support thinking beyond the dots by arousing emotions and awakening the imagination." He believes that storytelling is particularly effective in helping to resolve those problems in a corporation that somehow relate to communication. He therefore offers this suggestion: "As a storyteller, think about or discover where an organization might be vulnerable in the area of communication, then find a story to suit the situation— or search out one from inside the organization that gratifies the communication need."

Consider proposing a creative-thinking or team-building program or retreat for your work group that includes sharing personal tales. Possible topics for story telling might be: success, failure, leadership, problem-solving, work versus home, your toughest assignment, your best working relationship, lessons learned, ethics and values, quality, and service.

Activity: Working with personal stories

Here are some questions that will start you thinking about how storytelling might benefit you, the people who work with you, and your business:

1. Thinking about your work history—not just your present job, but all the jobs you've held in your life—ask yourself these questions:

   - What experiences did I enjoy the most? Why?

   - What experiences were the most difficult to handle? Why?

   - What important lessons did I learn? How?

2. Thinking about individuals or groups that are involved in your present work situation, ask yourself:

   - What kinds of personal stories would I like to tell this person or group?

   - What kinds of personal stories would I like this person or group to tell me?

Activity: Developing your story

In this activity, you'll tell yourself the "final" version of the personal tale you have been developing during this chapter, thinking of exactly where you will use it in the presentation.

As you tell your story, you will also be listening to it. Chiefly, you should simply enjoy feeling the story come to life using your voice and hearing it come to life in your ears. In addition, you can be listening for ways to enhance it, either as you go along—provided you can do so without interrupting its natural flow—or later, as you reflect on your telling.

Follow these guidelines:

1. Reread each of the story-enlivening techniques already discussed:

   - Appeal to all five senses.

   - Include ear-catching words and phrases.

   - Add interesting facts or allusions.

   - Build in repetitions to build interest.

   - Plan appropriate pacing and inflection.

2. Choose *one* of these techniques as you focus on how you tell your story.

3. In your usual talking-out-loud practice area, or some other quiet spot where you can be alone and undistracted, assume a comfortable standing (or sitting) position and tell yourself your story as naturally as possible from beginning to end, without stopping, repeating yourself, or jumping ahead.

Activity: Shifting perspective

Examining how you might alter the introduction, content, or delivery of a personal tale to fit different contexts helps you to recognize and take advantage of more opportunities to tell it.

Think about the story you developed earlier, or any other personal tale you want, and ask yourself these questions:

1   What aspects of the story (or its background) might especially interest family members or close friends?

2. What aspects might especially interest people with whom I work?

3. What aspects might interest different people or groups who live in my community or who attend the same religious institution I do?

4. How could I introduce the story, modify it, or adjust the way I tell it to better appeal to each of these three audiences.

Bulletproof advice

➤ **Use a storyboard to help you "see" the flow of your presentation.**

➤ **Appeal to all five senses in your story.**

➤ **Include words and phrases that will bolster the audience's attention.**

➤ **Build in repetition; remember the Rule of Frequency.**

CHAPTER 11

MOTIVATING
DURING THE
CONCLUSION

"Tell them what you've told them."

Remember the great minister I mentioned earlier and his approach? He said, "I tell them what I'm going to tell them, then I tell them, and then I tell them what I told them."

Consider this

Socrates said, "I can not teach you anything. I can only make you think."

———

This is your last chance to make an impact on the audience. You must close strongly if you are to have the results you are looking for. These are the steps to follow:

Closing steps

**First and most importantly,
notify the audience that you are finishing.**

Remember our attention curve earlier? You want to get that attention curve back on the upswing. You can use any words or phrases (in conclusion, in summary, for my final point, and so on) that you feel comfortable with. It is simply a device to capture audience members' attention if they have wandered off mentally. **Restate the main ideas of your presentation, or the overriding theme, whichever is most appropriate.**

Again, with the attention curve in mind, some of the key individuals may have mentally "checked out" at portions of your main content, and you want to remind them of what you covered during the presentation. They will often be grateful for the opportunity to review any points they may have missed during your presentation.

At this point, you may want to ask for any questions from the audience.

In Chapter 12 (on stage fright), I will outline suggestions for handling questions and formulating your answers so you answer clearly and concisely. Summarize the benefits you hoped they would achieve from hearing your presentation.

If possible, link your final statements to the grabber you used at the beginning. It will remind your listeners of that story or quote that got their attention in the first place. Finally, **say "thank you" as a way to tell the audience that you are finished.**

This notifies the audience you are finished speaking and cues listeners to begin your well-deserved applause.

Time crunch

When pressed for time, presenters will often push as much as possible into the body and neglect the conclusion. **Evidence suggests that cutting back on the conclusion is a flawed strategy.**

The conclusion is the time to make that lasting impression and really motivate the listeners. **If you are pressed for time, carefully examine portions of the body of your presentation.**

There are probably details and data that you could put on handouts that will allow you the time you need for an effective conclusion.

Why restate everything?

The Rule of Recency:
Listeners will remember the last ideas or information they hear.

The main reason for restating all your main points, benefits, and overriding theme is that most people are poor listeners. And do not forget our four Rules for Presentations, especially the Rule of Frequency.

They will have "checked out" on you at times during the presentation. Finally, believe it or not, the audience may have already forgotten many of these key elements. To make a Bulletproof Presentation, the presenter wants to remind listeners of the benefits they have gained in listening to this presentation. **During the conclusion, *never* bring in new information!**

However, it is usually appropriate to ask for questions.

Finally, a strong, dynamic finish will round out the presentation. A Bulletproof Presentation will leave the audience wishing for more.

Evaluating the presentation

When it is appropriate, you may want to use an evaluation form to help you with feedback from the audience. I would recommend a simple, one-page form that asks for information on a 1-to-5 scale from poor to excellent. Ask the audience to rate your:

→ Content.

→ Organization.

→ Visual aids.

→ Delivery.

Include space for any other comments the listeners want to give you. I always ask for five words that would describe the presentation because those words often give me better feedback than the rating. However, only use this type of form if it is appropriate for the situation.

Bulletproof advice

➤ **Handle any last-minute questions or write down any information you need to supply people after the presentation.**

➤ **Either restate the main ideas of your presentation or the overriding theme, whichever is appropriate.**

- Get the attention of the audience back by notifying them you are finishing and, using the Rule of Frequency, state your main ideas one more time.

➤ **Restate the benefits of listening to you.**

- Don't forget to remind them of the benefits you believe they will receive because they have listened to you. Believe me: They will have forgotten them!

➤ **Don't forget the Rule of Recency!**

- Remember that, in a time crunch, you do not want to short change the conclusion; it is too important!

➤ **Finally, do not bring any new information into the conclusion.**

- Information during the question period is fine, but do not add *new* information once you have gone into the conclusion.

Part III

Presenting

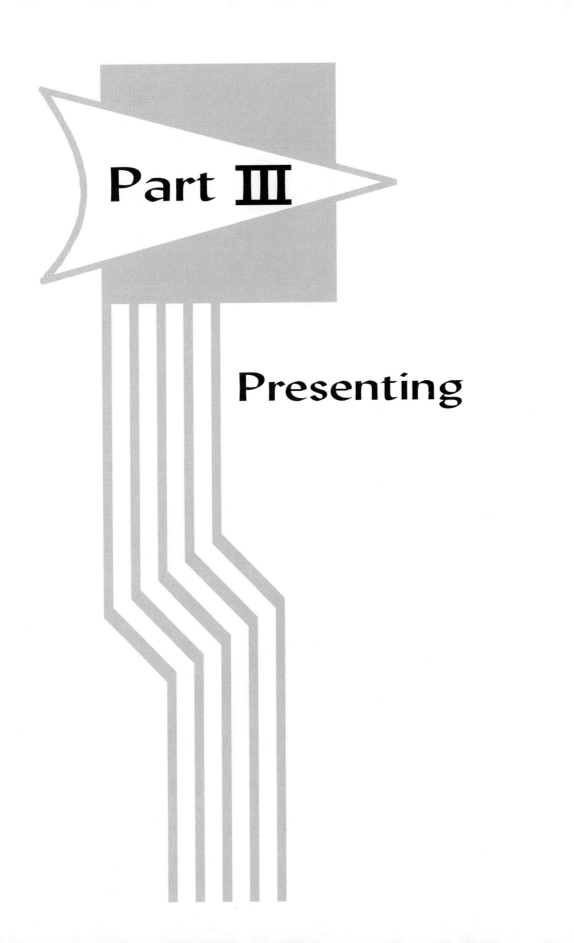

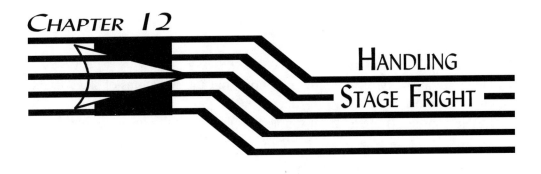

CHAPTER 12

HANDLING STAGE FRIGHT

Speaking in public is the number-one fear of Americans according to research started by the Brushkin Report in the 1970s, and supported by additional research since. How to overcome this fear of speaking is the focus of this chapter.

Consider this

Winston Churchill is said to have controlled his nervousness before a speech by imagining his audience naked. That helped him to realize that he did not need to be intimidated by the audience. Personally I think imagining people naked would be a little distracting in itself! I think good preparation and practice would be far more helpful in overcoming nervousness.

President Franklin Delano Roosevelt delivered a great line in his first inaugural speech that describes the best approach to stage fright better than any other passage I have every read (even though he used it in a different context): "Let me assert my firm belief that the only thing we have to fear is fear itself—nameless, unreasonable, unjustified terror, which paralyzes needed efforts to convert retreat into advance."

There are examples galore in the entertainment industry of people who had great difficulty with stage fright, even in the business they were in. Here are just a few examples:

→ Johnny Carson had audience members sit far away from the stage on *The Tonight Show* because they would be out of the lights and then he would not see them. He had grown up in radio and still had terrific stage fright even after years of being on television in front of live audiences.

→ James Garner would not attend television's Emmy awards for fear he would win one and be forced to give an acceptance speech.

- ➤ The late Sir Alec Guinness actually developed psychosomatic symptoms of sharp pains in his back and legs due to the stress of stage fright.

- ➤ Bob Hoskins, a popular British actor, is so used to throwing up prior to the curtain rising on opening night that he actually gets worried if it does not happen!

What exactly is stage fright?

There are a variety of different definitions, but the symptoms of stage fright are quite common:

1. Nervousness, ranging from simple jumpiness to full blown anxiety attacks.

2. The inability to concentrate.

3. Failure of the memory.

4. A gnawing conviction that something is definitely wrong.

5. A pounding heart.

6. Dryness and constriction in the throat.

7. Increased perspiration.

8. Clammy palms and trembling hands.

9. Gastrointestinal discomfort, including vomiting or diarrhea.

Preventative measures

If you can be alone for a few minutes prior to delivering your presentation, do some yawning and stretching to help relax you physically. Here are some other techniques to help overcome the symptoms of stage fright:

- ➤ Take a series of slow, deep breaths. Breathe in and hold, count to four, and exhale slowly. Repeat two more times.

- ➤ First arch your back, stretch your arms, and clench your fists. Then ease up and shake your hands and arms loosely.

- ➤ Move your head in a slow, circular motion. Do the same with your jaw.

- ➤ Take a few minutes to rise up and down on the balls of your feet, tensing and relaxing the muscles.

- ➤ Gently clear your throat and take a sip of water. Then try humming a few bars of one of your favorite songs. You can also recite the Pledge of Allegiance or Mary Had a Little Lamb.

- ➤ If you feel you may actually throw up, there are some good over-the-counter medicines you can take to help out. Also, you may want to see if you can force the issue before you speak. That sounds pretty drastic, but President George H. Bush would have been far less embarrassed in Japan if he had done that prior to the state dinner he attended.

Two on-stage precautions

Here are two simple precautions you can take to spare yourself onstage embarrassment from some of the symptoms of stage fright:

1. Always have a large glass of water within easy reach when you're speaking. If your mouth suddenly goes dry, take a sip. It's perfectly normal behavior and no one will mind.

2. Carry a large, absorbent cloth handkerchief in a side pocket. If your forehead or upper lip is suddenly flooded by perspiration, similar to the fate Richard Nixon suffered during his first presidential debate, wipe it away slowly and deliberately. The more thorough the wipe, the less often you'll have to repeat it.

The need for perfection

Consider this

Keep this thought in mind as you progress through the development of a Bulletproof Presentation:

- Before you give your presentation, you are focusing on getting yourself ready. You are getting together the information you need, developing the strategy you will use, and preparing the visual aids that will help you present with "sparkle."

- While you are giving the Bulletproof Presentation, you are focusing on your audience. You think of how they are receiving the information, the questions they might have about your topic, and the concerns they may have about your ideas.

Before your presentation, take care of yourself; during the presentation, take care of your audience.

———

Whenever we give a presentation, we always want to do as good a job as we can.

**If we strive for perfection, we are probably
doomed because there is a
one-in-a-million chance that we will get it perfectly!**

Even veteran professional speakers I know admit to times when they missed a story or forgot a fact. And if we are focusing so hard on perfection, we are also focusing on ourselves instead of the audience—where our attention should be! So do not strive for perfection. Rather:

➤ Focus on the message.

➤ Know your material.

➤ Prepare well.

If you do these things, you'll have the Bulletproof Presentation you really want!

Fear of embarrassment

Another major fear behind speech anxiety is the fear of embarrassment.

Consider this

The Greek poet Hermessianex lived about 400 B.C. Although we don't know much about him, he left us with a four-word phrase that still has meaning today: "as within, so without." The attitude you possess within determines external attractions.

Consider also the story of two young women working in a community hospital. They decided to quit their jobs. They were tired of dealing with ungrateful patients, backbiting between employees, and an apathetic administration. Just before quitting, though, these two women decided to try an experiment. They resolved, just for the fun of it, to bend over backwards for everyone they encountered on their last day of work. No matter how someone looked at them, talked to them, of treated them, they overwhelmed people with encouragement, courtesy, and appreciation. Before long, an amazing thing took place. Patients did not seem so miserable, staff smiled at them, and the administration seemed surprisingly interested in their work.

The two women experienced a basic law of nature: The very situations that caused frustrations were reflections of their own attitudes.

In trying to determine the specific fears that concern speakers the most, I have narrowed them down to four categories. They are:

1.   Forgetting or drawing a blank.

2.   Having your fear obvious to the audience (through excessive perspiration, stiff delivery, or quaking voice).

3.   Being unable to answer a question posed by a key decision-maker.

4.   Making a mistake in fact during the presentation.

> **The major value of using the process outlined in this book is that it will help you to control your fear.**

That is not to say that you will not be nervous. You will probably always be nervous. That is a normal human response to speaking in public. Try to value your nervousness as a sign that you are ready to perform very well.

This chapter will help you capture that nervous energy and put it to positive use during your presentation.

If you use the information in this chapter, it will help you capture that nervous energy and put it to positive use during your presentation. Anyone who claims he or she is not nervous is probably lying (or unconscious). However, that does not mean that you cannot be confident. You can be confident because you know you are well prepared. That is very different. Obviously, the key is preparation.

A theme established in this chapter (and carried throughout Part III) is the importance of practicing.

Practice, more than any other strategy, will help most people become more relaxed and confident in their speaking ability.

Consider this

I am often asked how many times to practice before making a presentation. You never want to practice the excitement out of your presentation. The correct number of practice times will vary, but you must know what you are saying and where you are going during your presentation.

Many inexperienced speakers will avoid practice for the same reason they are afraid of making mistakes. However, just saying the presentation in your head is *not* practicing! When I talk about practicing, I mean standing in front of a podium (or a makeshift podium) and delivering the presentation as closely to the way you expect it to go "for real."

―――

Consider this

Practice your presentation in front of a full-length mirror if you can. The mirror will give you great "feedback" on how you look without a word and will never laugh at you.

I also highly recommend that you videotape yourself during your practice sessions. I know that is difficult, because it allows us to see those nasty little habits we have that we don't like. I feel intimidated by the prospect when I do it, too, and I am a very experienced presenter. However, wouldn't you rather see those flaws in the privacy of your own home? Wouldn't you rather work to correct them in private rather than ignore them and let everyone see them? You will correct many of them during your practice sessions, and that will help you feel more confident when you finally present. Finally, stop taping yourself a few days before the presentation, even though you should continue to practice. The main reason for my suggestion is that I do not want you to become too self-conscious as you get close to the actual presentation.

―――

I have also learned through experience that people are much harder on themselves than the audience is.

The other major factor that causes fear in people is the feeling that somehow they will be made to look stupid or silly during a presentation. Worksheets that you can use to eliminate that fear of the unknown are provided in the Appendix.

The other key to practice is to become familiar with your material and the situation you will face during the presentation. Think back to your first day at a new job. Didn't you feel a little nervous and scared? Most people would say yes. However, within a few days, you became more comfortable and the anxiety of the new situation wore off.

The same is true in presentations.

To make a Bulletproof Presentation, you need to practice enough so that when you finally give the presentation, you almost have a sense of déjà vu, as though you have been there before.

And in a very real sense, you have. However, that means practicing as closely as possible to the actual presentation.

Remember the chapter on analyzing your situation earlier in the book? That is important for your practicing, too. When you practice, you want to replicate the situation as closely as possible. That may mean practicing in an auditorium, a large room, or a conference room that most closely resembles the room you will present in. Set up the tables and chairs in a similar pattern to the room, and know where the podium and computer (if you are using one) will be placed. This will reduce your anxiety tremendously and you will feel far more comfortable and confident than you will if you see the room for the first time when you arrive to present.

Try to reframe to control your stage fright. Reframing is a way to change the way you look at a situation and redefine what you are feeling. Imagine an athlete before a big game. Many athletes will tell you they get "butterflies," those same butterflies you get before a presentation. However, the difference is that they will tell you that they are excited and need that rush of adrenaline to perform well. They have just reframed their feelings from a negative (nervousness) to a positive (excitement). You can do that same thing! The way successful athletes reframe the situation is to imagine successfully shooting the ball, hitting the shot, or knocking down all the pins. They try to imagine these things in great detail, including hearing the crowd roar its approval.

Another important consideration in reframing is to take the focus off of you and put it on the audience—where it really belongs! When you are thinking, *Can they hear me?, Did that make sense to them?,* and *How can I explain what I mean so they get it?*, you are putting the focus in the right place, and you will find yourself more comfortable in the presentation.

Another technique successful athletes use is called visualization.

Close you eyes and imagine a whole room of people who are excited to hear what you have to say. Imagine yourself as looking cool and confident. See the audience members smiling and nodding as they agree with your key points. Feel yourself truly enjoying the experience of giving a Bulletproof Presentation! Finally, hear the audience applaud as you take your seat, with a big smile on your face. That is visualization in a positive way! Do that before every presentation you make.

Think positively

Remember to think positively.

Repeat positive and encouraging thoughts over and over again to yourself as you prepare for your Bulletproof Presentation.

It will boost your confidence and calm last-minute fears. Remember that your topic is interesting to your audience, and the listeners feel you have something valuable to say; otherwise, they would not have invited you to talk with them.

In addition to the Worksheets in the Appendix, here are a few suggestions that will help with fear and prepare you to give a Bulletproof Presentation:

➤ Complete checklists.

➤ Strong focus.

➤ Good notes.

Dealing with "dry mouth"

Generally, giving a presentation—any presentation—will cause your mouth to become dry. If you have watched experienced speakers, you will notice they always have a glass of water available. The water allows them to moisten their mouth when they begin to experience that dryness.

Water is really the best choice. Often, inexperienced speakers will use coffee. The major problem with using coffee to moisten your mouth is the caffeine. **Caffeine actually contributes to the dryness in your mouth,** so using coffee is actually aggravating the problem you are trying to solve! The same is true of soft drinks. It contains caffeine and can cause the same problem as coffee. An additional problem with soft drinks is the carbonation, which can cause gas pockets to build up in your stomach. If they are released at an inopportune time, you could be embarrassed. Finally, caffeine can get you really "jumpy" if you drink it before a presentation. Combined with the nervous energy you already have, you may have trouble reining in your energy and focusing on the presentation. This is a long explanation to say stay away from caffeine in any form prior to your presentation.

Fruit juices can work, but again there can be a significant disadvantage—namely, the sugar within many fruit juices can cause your mouth to get sticky and hurt your enunciation.

My best advice is to use water!

Besides, it gives you another advantage. If you happen to lose your place in the presentation, you can stop to take a sip of water. Audiences have seen speakers do that for years and think nothing of it. While you are getting that sip of water, you can search your notes for your place and the audience will never know.

Watch the food you eat

Be careful of hot, spicy food that will be hard to digest. You have to deal with what you eat, so make sure you can comfortably eat a certain food and then rise to make your presentation. Only you know the answer to those questions.

Control your breathing

Focus on your breathing to help you control your nervousness. Concentrate on the rhythm of inhaling and exhaling and work to slow it down. If you can do that, you will be able to take control of your breathing and, with it, your nervousness. Also, breathing is the key to using the volume of your voice effectively. If you are too nervous, you will probably start breathing too shallowly, and that will adversely affect your voice. As you practice, pay special attention to your breathing.

**You will need to breathe correctly to create
a complete sound when you present.
As you practice, pay special attention to your breathing.**

What about pauses?

A pause is to a speech what an exclamation point is to a composition. It draws attention and builds energy and anticipation, much the same as holding your breath. The pressure is released only when you resume speaking. To grasp the power of this, notice your own reactions when a speaker, or even someone on the radio or TV, simply stops communicating for three to five seconds.

Insert pauses into your talks during the practice sessions in the final polishing stage. Position them sparingly, carefully, and at key points for emphasis and attention. Timing is important, and you can regulate the length of a pause by your breathing. A slight pause is about half a breath long. A regular pause is approximately a full breath, and a long pause is two breaths. If you have the courage and want to have a major point scream off the walls, try a three- or four-breath pause.

Be prepared for the pressure buildup, and do not be overwhelmed by it. After you get the feel of this, go the next step and try a spontaneous pause to bring people to attention when you sense they are not listening closely enough. It works! Pauses are basic equipment for the verbal artist; learn to use them skillfully and with power.

Questions and impromptu presentations

Consider this

When answering questions, it is usually best to be as brief as possible. Journalists are constantly pushed to be brief.

A certain beginning journalist picked up what he believed was a "hot story" that would make front-page news. He hurriedly e-mailed his editor with the news. He wrote, "Column story on scandal. Shall I send?"

The answer came back promptly: "Send 600 words."

The enthusiastic young journalist was depressed and wrote back, "Can't be less than 1,200 words."

The editor's reply came back immediately: "The biblical story of creation of the world told in 600. Try it!"

One of the more difficult tasks during a presentation can be questions. Sometimes they can be very easy, but sometimes you can be surprised by a question. This section will give you some tips on how to structure your answer for the best impression.

It is important to handle questions well.

In fact, good presentations have been negated by a speaker's inability to field questions well. First of all, be sure to prepare for questions that might occur just as you are preparing your presentation. As part of your audience analysis, you may decide that certain questions are likely to come up. Have another file or additional handouts in case those questions do arise. Ask friends and colleagues who are giving you feedback on your presentation to point out any gaps or natural questions that they have thought of while they listened. Have answers for those questions, or consider putting that information in the body of the presentation.

First, try to assess whether the answer to the question is required to be factual or purely a matter of personal opinion.

If it is simply a matter of opinion, you are on much firmer ground, because you can admit not knowing the facts but still give a reasonable answer based upon your own past experience to personal opinion. If it is purely factual, then see the following tips.

Don't be too hasty in answering questions.

If you are not sure about the question, you might ask the person to clarify what he or she is seeking. Don't be too hasty in answering questions. Make sure you have heard the question correctly.

If more than one person seeks to ask a question, be sure to acknowledge people and keep control of the presentation. Only handle one question at a time. Also, don't get drawn into a lengthy discussion of a minor point of your presentation. Suggest to the questioner that you take their question "off-line" and move on—in other words, speak to that person after the presentation in a one-on-one setting.

Never try to fool the audience
with an answer if you are not sure.

If you cannot answer a question for any number of reasons, there are standard replies you can use. Ask the audience if anyone knows the answer to the question being posed. Sometimes an audience member will have the answer and you can either amplify it or simply move on.

Here are some other standard responses:

➤ "I don't know the answer, but I can find out for you. If you will leave me your e-mail address, I will get back to you."

➤ "I hadn't considered that one. I need to think about it and get back to the question later."

➤ "I'm not sure I know the answer to that. Maybe we could talk about it after the session is finished."

➤ "There are really no right or wrong answers to that question. However, my experience has been...."

Typical questions

There are certain typical questions that seem to come up over and again during presentations. Learn to recognize them so you can deal with them successfully. Here are a few:

1. **The Summary Question:** "You seem to be saying.... Am I right?" This person is trying to get a recap or clarification of what he or she has heard already.

2. **The Direct Question:** "What can you tell me about your company's office in Africa?" This person simply wants some direct information.

3. **The Me Question:** "When I tried what you suggested, it didn't work. How can you explain that?" This person is challenging your point by using his or her personal experience when it failed. Use some of your own personal experience to reinforce the point you were trying to make.

4. **The Logic Question:** "How can you say A at the same time you insist on B?" This person is trying to use logic to defeat the presenter. Again, personal experience backed by data or evidence is the best counter.

5. **The Well-Connected Question:** "When I talked to my friend Bill Gates, he said something different." This questioner is trying to demonstrate power or influence. Again, refer to your experience and data and try to take the discussion off-line.

> **The best way to anticipate questions from the
> audience is to take the time
> to make sure you do your audience analysis thoroughly.**

This will allow you to better understand the opinions, feelings, and biases of those who are likely to disagree with you. However, treat these questioners politely or they can ruin an otherwise outstanding presentation. If, on the basis of your homework, you anticipate disagreement, or if the nature of your subject is somewhat controversial and likely to arouse strong feelings, you should address the disagreement before it addresses you. The best way to ward off trouble is to "head it off at the pass." The way you can do that is to acknowledge during the introduction of your presentation that there are some other points of view on this subject.

If you are the one to bring up these other viewpoints, then you can explain them in your words and within the context of the approach you are going to present.

That will often burst the balloon of hostile troublemakers. You have stated their case for them and, in doing so, taken much of the sting out of their comments. The audience will appreciate your fairness and evenhandedness in recognizing other points of view. The bottom line effect of this is to lend credibility and strength to your presentation.

Here's some further information on other types of troublemakers and techniques of neutralizing, defusing, and minimizing their effect.

Troublemakers

You need to realize that out of every 100 people, there is at least one nut. You need to recognize that you are simply not going to convert a hostile attitude about your company, your product, your service, or a new idea in a one-hour presentation.

What you can hope to do is to neutralize the participation and the effect of the hostile troublemaker. Furthermore, even among fair-minded people, not everyone will want to follow your prescription or suggestions. It is important to have a realistic attitude about your audience and your expectations. If you anticipate the troublemaker during your audience analysis, you are less likely to become rattled when someone in the audience says, "It'll never work."

The hostile troublemaker

Consider this

I was doing a presentation to a group that seemed to be going great for the first five minutes and then a man raised his hand and told me that he thought most of what I had to say so far was horse excrement. I figured I had three options in responding to that kind of statement:

1. I could lose my temper and tell him what I thought of his heritage or some other equally pithy response. I know it would have felt great, but I knew the audience was gauging my actions and I might lose them all if I followed this option.

2. I could ask him why he felt that way and begin a discussion that might persuade him that I did have something to say worth listening to, but I worried that I could get pulled into a quagmire and never get out.

3. I could say that he had an interesting observation, and if he would be available, I would be happy to discuss his observations after the presentation with him one-on-one.

I can't tell you which option you should pick, it probably depends somewhat on the situation you are in. However, the third option worked well for me, and it may help you to handle that kind of situation if you ever find yourself in it. I would not recommend option one, because the potential damage to this approach will almost certainly be to you personally and professionally.

This person is the worst of all. He or she is the one who will come out with statements such as, "That'll never happen"; "It'll never work"; and "I don't agree." His or her remarks may even take the form of a personal attack on you.

**Another strategy for handling the hostile troublemaker
is to persuade the rest of the audience to your way of thinking
before the troublemaker can do any damage.**

The way to do this is to set ground rules during the introduction to your presentation with a remark such as, "For the next 30 minutes, I am going to present a new idea. I would like to ask that all of you keep an open mind and hold your comments or questions until I finish. Is that all right?" That is a reasonable request, and the group will agree that it is all right. However, it may be difficult to make that type of request if you will take more than 30 minutes, so keep that in mind. Then, if the troublemaker tries to interrupt, you can simply refer to the agreement of the group that everyone will hold comments until you finish the presentation of the new concept. If you have followed the Bulletproof Presentation method, you will have persuaded the audience to your view. If the trouble-maker makes a statement such as, "It'll never work," you will have the audience on your side and the troublemaker will be viewed as not having an open mind. Rather than you responding to the troublemaker's comment, it's more effective if you let another member of the audience answer. Now his or her disagreement is not with you, but with the rest of the audience. That's like a whack on the side of the head. The message to the troublemaker is, "shut up"!

Another way to defuse the troublemaker is to use the weight-of-evidence technique.

Using this technique has been very successful. Because you know what you are going to present, you will also know the more common objections. That being the case, you can prepare yourself in advance with facts, figures, references, quotes, and so forth for the common objections. The strategy is to drown the trouble-maker with the weight of the evidence you have prepared or collected. He or she is usually disadvantaged, because he or she is not as prepared as you are for an intelligent discussion. Your comment might sound similar to this: "You may be right, but let me review some additional facts and evidence that supports my position." You can now, once again, turn to the audience for support.

Hostile questions sometimes have hostile words that you can identify within the question, such as *rip-off, sneaky,* and *hedging.* You can defuse these words by asking for clarification.

Do not repeat hostile words when you rephrase the questions.

In fact, a truly hostile question that is loaded with emotion should not be repeated. Approach it instead as follows:

➤ "I can't answer your entire question."

➤ "If what you mean by the question is that, then my answer is this."

➤ "If what you would like to know is that, then my answer is that."

Clearly state your position, but do not let the troublemaker bait you into a debate or an emotional argument. Again, it is far better to ask for a response from someone in the audience whom you know agrees with your opinion.

Another way to handle troublemakers is to let them destroy themselves. You do this by answering a hostile question with a question. Say, "If you feel that way about the situation, then what do you think should be done to correct it?" The answers to these kinds of questions tend to be recognized by the audience as more emotional than well-thought-out, logical answers. The longer he or she talks, the more the troublemaker hurts himself or herself. It starts to become apparent that he or she has an ax to grind. However, this approach may invite the hostile questioner to take over the presentation and you may not get it back!

A word of caution: Negative comments or questions are not always hostile.

Some people just like to argue or play the devil's advocate. You say it's hot, they say it's cold. Their comments or questions tend to be nitpicking, directing attention away from your central point. The strategy here is to get their agreement on the larger issues. You can then respond with, "Although we have a few differences on the details, we seem to be in agreement on the concept."

The worst thing you can do is lose your temper. Avoid eye contact with the troublemaker. The more visual contact you have with the troublemaker, the more irritated you will become and the more emboldened he or she will become. If all else fails, just say, "It looks as if we have different views on this subject. Why don't we discuss it in more detail after the meeting?" The strange thing is that troublemakers rarely want to discuss the subject after the meeting. They seem to be more interested in a verbal interchange in front of an audience. If that is so, that tells us something about the troublemaker.

The know-it-all troublemaker

This sort of person has a weapon he or she uses to intimidate people. Some types of weapons are:

➤ Years of service with the company.

➤ An advanced degree.

➤ Experience.

➤ Title or responsibility.

➤ Professional status.

This person's remarks are prefaced with statements such as:

➤ "I have a Ph.D. in Economics and."

➤ "I have worked on this project more than anyone in the room and."

➤ "In my 20 years of experience."

➤ "As a senior systems analyst my opinion is."

The basic assumption here is that he or she knows more than you do, and therefore he or she is right and you are wrong.

The key to handling the know-it-all is to stick to the facts.

Don't speculate. Stick to your own experiences and the documented evidence you gathered for your presentation. People can legitimately disagree with your theory or proposition. But they cannot question your experience or documented facts.

Consider this

When former senator Paul Simon from Illinois disagreed with someone, he had a great approach that can avoid many of the problems that start a battle ,particularly during a question-and-answer period.

"Let me see if I can help you with this," he would start. "There are two ways to consider the matter. The way you just mentioned—and a way that starts from a slightly different base."

He would continue on speaking pleasantly, outlining his opinion on the issue. Senator Simon always made sure that the issue did not become personal. He stressed that he just looked at things with a different perspective. The point is to never say another person is wrong. It is disrespectful and will usually start a nasty little battle.

———

Another way to handle the know-it-all troublemaker is to use quotes of other experts whose credentials are even more impressive than those of the troublemaker.

Let me tell you another approach that I have used successfully in the past. If you know in advance (or can find out in advance) about any potential know-it-alls in the audience, arrange a meeting with them in advance. Acknowledge their credentials. Tell them what you are going to present and ask for their support. You will be amazed more often than not to find that they will support or possibly even endorse your program. What started out as a problem person becomes an ally and supporter.

Human beings are interesting in that we are very comfortable with things in threes. When you are formulating your answer, you want to take advantage of that natural predisposition that all people have for threes. Here are two suggestions to help you organize your thoughts. Use the one that makes the most sense for you and the situation.

REP

This is a three-step process for an answer to a question. REP stands for:

1. Rationale.

2. Evidence or example.

3. Point.

When answering a question, first explain your **rationale** for answering the question in this way. It gives the listener an understanding of your reason or reasons. Also, if you have misunderstood the question, it gives the questioner an opportunity to correct you before you begin a long response that misses the mark.

Then, follow up with an **example or evidence** that supports your viewpoint. Try to think of something in your experience that supports the reason you gave earlier.

Finally, make your **point,** a concluding statement that sums up the answer to the question you were asked.

The person asking the question may want some further elaboration, but you have set the tone and given a clear, cogent answer. That will impress the audience with your ability to think "on your feet" and allow your technical expertise to come through.

Sometimes, the answer you need to give will require much more detail and almost becomes a mini-presentation.

Think "3"

Sometimes, someone in the audience will ask you a very insightful, probing question that needs a lot more discussion than you had planned during your presentation. If it is not of general interest to the audience, then try to speak with the questioner after the presentation is complete.

However, if you feel that the entire audience would benefit from hearing the answer to the question (and you are sure of any facts you will need to reference) then you may choose to go into a totally unrehearsed presentation.

Use our basic model for a presentation.
There are three parts: introduction, body, and conclusion.

Remember to include all three of those elements in an answer. Within the body, try to think of three things you can say. That will help you organize your thoughts and help the listeners to understand better.

This is also the way to handle "impromptu" presentations.

Impromptu presentations can happen at any time—for example, your boss lets you know 10 minutes before a staff meeting that you will need to make a presentation on a project you are working on!

Use the Worksheets

Finally, using the Worksheets found in the Appendix will give you the confidence that you can be successful in making this presentation.

You will probably not lose the nervousness entirely, but you really shouldn't. Any time a presenter says he or she is not nervous, I get nervous! You need that nervousness to make a brisk, energetic presentation. If you are too laid back, you may be lackluster and bland.

You can feel confident, in spite of the nervousness, that you have a solid presentation, and that it will be Bulletproof!

Bulletproof advice
➤ **The major cause of stage fright is the fear of embarrassment.**

■ If you try to strive for perfection, you will be frustrated because that will only happen one in a million times. Focus on your message, know your material, and prepare well, and you will be Bulletproof!

➤ **Practice, more than any other strategy, will help you be relaxed and confident in your presentation.**

  ▪ Practice your presentation several times, and videotape yourself if at all possible.

➤ **Prepare for dry mouth and control your breathing for the best results.**

  ▪ Lay off the caffeine and use water. Practice controlling your breathing for containing nervousness and using your voice effectively.

➤ **Handle the questions with confidence using the techniques discussed in this chapter.**

  ▪ Most questions can be anticipated during your audience analysis, so you can be prepared. If not, use the REP method to answer them.

CHAPTER 13

WHAT IF I HAVE TO READ THE PRESENTATION?

Prepared text does not make sense for everyone. For most people, speaking from notes or AN outline or even extemporaneously is more effective and certainly more believable. Sometimes, though, prepared text is the clear choice.

For example, use prepared text when:

➤ The legal beagles insist you say every word on the page.

➤ There is a consistent party line that everyone in your organization has to adhere to.

➤ You have a precise time slot to fill.

➤ You have no preparation time, your speech was prepared for you by someone else, or you find yourself having to give someone else's speech.

➤ Your speech has an accompanying slide show requiring rehearsal and precise cues.

➤ You feel more confident and comfortable reading from a text than trying to speak extemporaneously or from notes or an outline.

However, if you read, it will be very important to pick your words carefully.

Consider this

Words are powerful. Choose them carefully. Not only organize your thoughts before you speak, but determine which words best communicate the message you want to send. One thought in choosing those words: Attempt to speak in the other person's (that is, your audience's) language rather than your own. Consider Lee Iacocca's comments about the leader as communicator: "It is important to talk to people in their own language. If you do it well, they will say, 'God, he said exactly what I was thinking.' And when they begin to respect you, they will follow you to the death."

Reading from a script while trying to appear *not* to be reading is a neat trick. But that is exactly what we have to do if we expect people to take us seriously and be willing to listen to what we have to say.

———

Few people—either in public or private life—know how to handle a prepared text properly. Unless they are using TelePrompTers, even U.S. presidents look as if they're reading a text verbatim.

No one can master the art of prepared text delivery from a book—because until now no book has been able to explain correctly how it should be done. But a few simple tips, plus some practice in front of a mirror, can still make a measurable difference in how you come across.

Don't read until you can see their eyes

The key to great prepared-text delivery is really quite simple. Most people, when they speak from a script, begin almost every sentence with their face and eyes pointed down at the page. Then they raise their eyes in the middle of the sentence, before looking right back down to catch the words at the end of the sentence. If you have seen a speaker repeat this action three or four hundred times during the presentation, you probably thought it was a pretty dull presentation. Here's how you can change that awkward reading style with one that will look far more natural to the audience.

First, practice reading the presentation by looking at the words on the page without speaking. Then, raise your eyes and begin speaking to the audience. When you finish with that thought, move your eyes back to the page (again without speaking) to find the next thought. Remember that the key to success here is *thoughts,* not necessarily complete sentences. In a long sentence, you may lower your eyes a couple of times, but keep in mind that eye contact is critical. The central idea is to be speaking, as much as possible, only when you have eye contact with the audience. Most of the time you are looking at the written presentation, you are silent. That may seem difficult, but with practice, it will become easier. It will also have a dramatic effect on the audience. In order to use this technique effectively, you will need to prepare your manuscript differently. Following are some ideas that have proven helpful to me in the past.

Preparing the text

The up-down-up drill sounds easy, but for people not used to it, it can feel awkward. To make the procedure as easy as possible, prepare your scripted speeches so that:

➤ **Each sentence is a separate paragraph.** This makes it a lot easier to use the technique just discussed (that of not looking down). If the original text has several sentences in a paragraph, you can indicate which separated sentences belong to the original paragraph by not indenting those sentences. They would still be separate, just not indented on the speech copy. The only indented sentence would be the lead sentence of the original paragraph.

- ➤ **Make sure the letters are big enough to be read easily from three to four feet away.** Laser printers can quickly produce enlarged conventional typeface, which should be about a half inch high.

- ➤ **Double-space each sentence and triple-space each paragraph.**

- ➤ **The last sentence on the page should end on the page.** The sentence should never continue on to the top of the next page so it will be easier to track with your eye.

- ➤ **Put page numbers on the top and the bottom of each page.** This will make it much simpler to pull your notes together if you happen to drop them on the way to the podium.

You will now have more pages, but you can easily move each page with almost no distraction by sliding the page while looking at the audience as you speak the words from the last sentence on that page.

Some further points are:

- ➤ If you insist on keeping your hands folded behind your back, you may wind up looking a little too much like a bad imitation of the British royal family.

- ➤ Arms folded across your chest is a nonverbal signal that you feel vulnerable. You look as though you're protecting yourself and would probably rather be some place else.

- ➤ Hands raised up to your sternum (heart) with fingers touching is almost priestly.

Feet

If you have to stand at a lectern (and if you've got a prepared text, you most certainly do), then you've also got to position yourself in one place and stay there. Paradoxically, I tell people that rather than stand planted with feet apart, they ought to place their feet fairly close together—6 inches or so.

The reason for this is simple. Most people doing a prepared text get anxious or bored and start shifting their weight back and forth from one foot to another. This is enormously distracting and sends the signal that you're not really committed to, or even involved in, what you're saying. By contrast, if you put your feet close together and try to shift your weight, you will probably tip over. Plus, you'll get another inch or two in altitude, and sometimes every little bit helps.

But now that you are stuck in one spot, you'll feel trapped unless you have some way to move around a little. The answer is to stay in the exact same place, but to *turn slightly, by small moves of your feet,* to face different parts of the audience (some of the best political and evangelical speakers do this well, including former president Bill Clinton and Texas governor Rick Perry).

Now let's quickly walk through what happens when you're called up to speak. Listen carefully to the introduction. The person doing the introducing might say something very personal, poignant, or even witty. Sometimes these seemingly offhand remarks just beg for a response—and if you don't respond, you could appear to be not plugged in to what is happening around you. With luck, you will be able to respond with a line that not only spins off the introduction but also makes a business point relative to what you've come to talk about.

But don't push your luck. If you have a prepared text and can't figure out a way to weave in a one-liner without hurting your strong start, forget it. Just go ahead and begin the way you had planned.

If you are carrying your speech with you (that is, if it is not already waiting at the lectern), conceal it as much as possible by wrapping it around your thigh away from the audience. As you walk to the lectern, carry the speech close to your leg.

You should have already practiced and probably memorized at least the opening line or two, perhaps the first couple of sentences, so there is no need to look down once you get to the lectern.

At the lectern, while still trying to keep your manuscript hidden, ease the speech onto the lectern. Look at your audience as you do this. If you are right-handed, place the body of the speech on the left side, with the top page on the right. Reverse that procedure if you are left-handed. The reason is that with the speech spread you won't have to move the page for at least the first minute or so.

Now position yourself back far enough so you can still touch the lectern, but at the same time have a good angle for your eye to hit the page. If the lectern is adjustable and someone else spoke before you, adjust the lectern so the rear portion is just below your sternum.

Once you begin speaking, slide the pages over as needed; *never turn them.* Sliding will minimize the perception that you have a prepared text and help give the impression you are speaking from notes or an outline. This, in turn, will reinforce the perception that you are not reading—which can only mean that you know what you are talking about.

After five or 10 minutes you might begin to get a little antsy, but *resist the temptation to let it show by rocking or swaying.* Stay vigilant and alert to what you're saying. Borrow from the actor. Actors *hear their words in their head* before those words come out of their mouths. So use your pauses as you glance down at each new sentence to *listen to the words* in that moment of silence before you actually say them. Do this hundreds of times, and the effect will be that these words are, in fact, your own—even if someone else wrote them for you or if you are giving someone else's speech.

Pause longer after rhetorical questions and key points. Those pauses may seem agonizingly lengthy (remember that the adrenaline has probably been working overtime), but to the audience you will only look natural, thoughtful, conversational, and comfortable with your subject.

When you finish, don't bolt. Stay long enough to keep your eye contact with the audience. If there is applause, simply say "thank you," pause for another moment, and then leave the podium.

Remember never to show the audience your entire prepared text if you can avoid it. Slip the speech discretely off the lectern and leave it on the shelf underneath, or slide it back to whichever leg is out of sight of the audience as you walk back to your seat.

Prepared text basics

➤ Eyes up-down-up, not down-up-down.

➤ Don't shoot until you see the whites of their eyes.

➤ Pause before speaking and after speaking.

➤ Longer pauses after "credibility" lines and questions.

➤ Let your hands help you do the talking.

➤ Keep your feet fairly close together so you don't sway.

➤ Turn your body to face different parts of the audience.

➤ Position yourself away from the lectern for better angle of eye attack on the page.

➤ Slide pages, don't flip them.

I should add this important note of caution: Learning to give a prepared text speech as if you were just speaking extemporaneously requires lots of practice. As a rule, I spend only two or three sessions on this skill with corporate people. But with politicians, the work sessions can number five or six, because their jobs depend on being able to use one prepared text after another and to *never* appear to be reading.

The rule for prepared text is simple:
If you practice at home in front of a minor and
can't see your eyes, you're doing something wrong.

The most common arena for prepared text is the big presentation, the big (or important) audience, and the big slide show that goes with it. In fact, most prepared-text speeches involve visual aids of one kind or another, which we'll cover in Part IV.

Bulletproof advice
➤ **Prepare the text carefully for your situation.**

 ▪ Make sure the text is large enough to read easily.

 ▪ Make sure the format will assist you in reading it effectively.

➤ **Concentrate on body language.**

 ▪ Remember to gesture.

 ▪ Remember to turn and face different portions of the audience, even though you are forced to stay at the podium.

CHAPTER 14

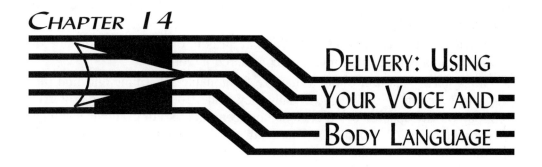

DELIVERY: USING YOUR VOICE AND BODY LANGUAGE

Once you have all the content prepared, you are now ready to put the "sparkle" into the presentation. You do that by using your voice and body language effectively. Remember: You are what the audience will remember even more than the information you presented. How you deliver the ideas and support them with details in a logical manner to influence the thoughts, ideas, or actions of the audience is the key to a Bulletproof Presentation. Don't worry about being perfect—just pay attention to the audience and follow the presentation you have so carefully crafted!

Common grammatical errors to avoid

In developing and delivering a Bulletproof Presentation, there are several common errors to avoid. However, they can easily be overcome if you strive for:

- ➤ Clarity.

- ➤ Accuracy.

- ➤ Gender-inclusive language.

Let's look at each of these elements and see how they can improve your presentation.

Clarity

In order to maintain clarity within your presentation, you should eliminate jargon, buzz words, and clichés; use clear references that your audience can understand; and use parallel structures.

Jargon. The first enemy of clarity is the use of jargon. Every occupation, company, or group has jargon—that is, specialized terms that the general listener would probably not understand. Many of these words come easily to mind, but they convey little real information. For example, using jargon, you might say, "The computer downloaded all the information to the server, but I had to terminate the program before the job was complete." To eliminate jargon, you might say, "The computer sent all the data to be saved, but I had to stop before I could complete the job."

Review your presentation and eliminate jargon, or at least make sure you have defined any terms that might be considered jargon.

Buzz words. These are terms that are fashionable for a time and find their way into everyone's vocabulary. Usually they come from a particular profession or group but are adapted by others to a more general use. For example, you might be tempted to say, "Bob, you and Dan really need to take that topic off-line." To say the same thing without using buzz words, you might say, "Bob, you and Dan really need to address that question after the presentation."

Eliminate buzz words and replace them with better words. They become dated quickly and can easily be misinterpreted by the audience.

Clichés. Although you might use these trite, worn-out expressions during the course of a normal conversation, they are not appropriate for a Bulletproof Presentation. You might be tempted to say, "I think Denise is as honest as the day is long, but in this case, I don't think that project will hold up in the wash." Resist the temptation and instead say, "I think Denise is sensible and honest, but her reasons for supporting this project will not withstand close examination."

Use words that are specific and concrete when you speak. The more abstract the words or phrases are, the harder it will be for people to understand what you are saying. The more concrete you make your vocabulary, the less likely the audience will misunderstand your meaning. When I suggest making your words concrete, think of the five senses. Concrete words refer to things that can be seen, heard, touched, smelled, or tasted. Review your presentation and replace as many abstract words as possible with concrete words.

Eliminating jargon, buzz words, and clichés will help you maintain clarity in your presentation.

References. When you use words to modify or to refer other words, make sure the audience can follow your line of thought. If the references are used carelessly, the audience may draw the wrong conclusion. For example, if you said "We served sandwiches for lunch, which no one felt like eating," the audience is not clear whether it was the lunch or the sandwiches that people did not want to eat.

If you find your references confusing, try one of the following:

➤ Break a long sentence into two or more shorter sentences.

➤ Rearrange the word order.

➤ Fill in the missing reference.

Parallel structures. All phrases and clauses in a series or within a sentence should be parallel. That means they must have the same structure. For example, you would not want to say "We sold our products to the French, the Germans,

Spanish, Italians, and Swiss." Instead, you want to say either "We sold our products to the French, the Germans, the Spanish, the Italians, and the Swiss" or "We sold our products to the French, Germans, Spanish, Italians, and Swiss." Notice how the construction is parallel in either example.

Don't mix the structure in verb forms either. For example, you should not say, "I have completed the research, typed the pages, and printed the report." You have mixed the "have" form of the verb with the simple past tense. Instead, keep the structure parallel by dropping the "have," and then it works!

Accuracy

Another common error is to have someone in the audience discover that you have not been accurate in a fact used in your presentation. Aside from the embarrassment, this situation hurts your credibility and may call into question other facts or statistics you may have used. So what can you do? Here are some suggestions:

1. Double-check all facts, figures, dates, specifications, or any other details. Your motto should be: When in doubt, check it out. Don't rely on your memory for important information.

2. Be sure that all names, titles, and abbreviations are spelled correctly. You don't want to discover that you have a slide with the client's name misspelled during the presentation. Also, find out whether abbreviations you are using are spelled with periods, in all capital letters, or with certain symbols, such as an ampersand.

3. Verify the accuracy of direct quotations. Make sure you are correct in what people said, and report those words accurately. At times, you may even want to cite the source of the quotation or have the source in your backup materials in case a question arises.

Gender-Inclusive Language

Over the past 10-plus years, the public has become much more aware of the inherent sex-bias in the English language. As a result, audiences will expect a presenter to consider that when speaking to them. In addition, using antiquated language can actually confuse the audience. For example, the use of the word "man" has sometimes referred only to men, other times to the human race, and occasionally to both men and women. The transition to gender-inclusive language can be made gracefully and naturally if given some thought.

Here are some tips for using gender-inclusive language:

➤ Try to use female and male pronouns only when referring to specific people. For example, you could easily say, "Carolyn always takes good care of her clients." However, you would not want to say to a group of managers, "A manager must always take good care of his employees." A better way to phrase this might be, "A manager must always take good care of his or her employees," where you aren't using the male or female pronoun exclusively.

➤ Make the nouns and pronouns plural. For example, instead of saying, "The smart executive knows where his money is being spent," say, "Smart executives know where their money is being spent."

➤ Use the first person *we,* second person *you,* or third person *we, us, them,* and so on, where appropriate. For example, instead of saying, "Man's desire for reward drives him to seek the maximum return on his investment," you might say, "Our desire for reward drives us to seek the maximum return on our investment."

➤ Reword sentences to eliminate the pronouns and replace them with a gender-free article, such as *a, an,* or *the.* For example, instead of saying, "The mailman makes his rounds in delivering the mail," say, "The postal carrier delivers the mail."

➤ Use gender-inclusive titles for as many occupations as possible. For example, use *firefighter* rather than *fireman.* There are hundreds of occupations and positions that have been appropriately renamed. You can reference the Department of Labor's *Dictionary of Occupational Titles* to look up an occupation for the appropriate title.

These are all small fixes that allow you to command the respect of your audience as an articulate presenter with a message that everyone should regard with esteem.

Most of the highly regarded speakers that I know work very hard to avoid committing any of these common language mistakes in their presentations.

Consider this

You want to know the best place to watch body language in action? The weekday afternoon "trash" TV shows! You can see all kinds of body language that tells you exactly what that person is thinking or feeling. Try muting the volume and guess the attitudes or feelings of the people as they talk or even just sit there. People may think they can fool you with words, but body language rarely lies. Videotape yourself and then watch it to see what your body language is saying to the audience.

Beginning the presentation

**As you approach the podium to begin your presentation,
do not just launch into it.**

Take a moment and scan the audience with your eyes. Smile! Check your equipment and make sure you have your glass of water. Do not begin until you are confident that everything is ready for you. Remember: You are in charge! You want to demonstrate that "take charge" attitude right from the beginning. Finally, when you are ready, pick out one person in the middle of the audience and begin speaking to him or her. You will want to change your eye contact as you go, but we will look at that later.

**In delivering your presentation, remember that
you are trying to achieve a technique
called "heightened conversation."**

What that means is simply that you want the audience members to hear you almost as if you are speaking to them in a personal conversation. That means several things about the way you must structure your presentation. It is almost as if your audience were a single person. If you think of it this way, it will create an atmosphere that is far more intimate and warm. A presenter who focuses on creating that one-to-one style of atmosphere gives audience members the feeling that they are participating in the presentation.

Consider this

When you have been asked to present to a group of people, no matter how large or small, you are the expert whose opinion people want to hear. People who do not know as much as you do are not asked to give presentations. Therefore, you are an expert in the room and probably know as much as or more than anyone else in the room.

That gives you the license to present a strong point of view. In fact, people expect that from you. It does not mean you can be arrogant or condescending, but you are entitled to your expert opinion and you should present it forcefully.

———

Presenters who do this well make every member of the audience feel that the content is directed right at him or her.

And that will hold their attention. If you are not sure if you sound natural, try tape recording yourself, and then listen with a critical ear. Then change those parts of the presentation that don't have the effect you are seeking. Another clue as to whether you are using your natural pattern is difficulty in certain places while you practice. If you need to stop and carefully work on a particular portion of the presentation, it may be that you are not using your natural pattern.

First of all, your sentence structure needs to be more like normal conversation, all the while making certain each sentence is grammatically correct.

I suggest you use the active voice in presentations (versus the passive voice). For example, using the active voice, you would say, "the software program I used." (Using the passive voice, you would say, "the software program used by me.") Also, generally put the most important points at the beginning of a sentence rather than after a subordinate phrase or clause. For example, say, "Lower costs and increased sales—that's what we need!" as opposed to "We need to lower costs and increase sales." **Grammatically, both are correct, but the syntax is very different and will produce a different response in the audience.**

Using these techniques will sound more natural to you, too! That will help you be more confident and relaxed. You won't be as concerned about "tripping" over the words or sentences because they are in an unfamiliar pattern.

Using a microphone

You must have the right volume for people to hear you. I once tried to listen to a presentation where the speaker spoke so quietly that I eventually gave up. As a looked around the room, I noticed that several others had not paid attention as long as I had. As you can imagine, the presentation was not Bulletproof, because no one really knew what the speaker had said. One way to overcome volume problems, particularly in larger rooms, is to use a microphone.

Microphones come in four different types:

1.   Stationary.

2.   Lavaliere.

3.   Cordless.

4.   Handheld.

Stationary mikes are the typical mike you would see on a podium. The advantage of these types of mikes is your ability to keep your hands free to handle notes and visual aids. The obvious disadvantage is your inability to move from that spot.

Lavaliere mikes are the type that allows you to clip the microphone onto your clothing. The advantage of a lavaliere mike is your ability to not only keep your hands clear for notes and other material, but this type of mike also will allow you to move around. However, it will usually have a long cord attached to it that makes moving about sometimes cumbersome. You are always trailing a cord that can get caught on chair legs and other items. However, it's still better than the stationary mike, in my opinion.

Cordless mikes are the greatest! As is a lavaliere mike, a cordless mike is clipped to your clothing while leaving your hands free. The beauty of this type of mike is the missing cord. It has a small receiver that you can clip to your belt (obviously it requires that you have a belt or other similar accessory) and allows you freedom to roam the room. If you do not have a belt, you must find another item of clothing to clip the receiver to. Sometimes you can slip the clip into the waistband of your pants or skirt. Otherwise, you will end up carrying it around and lose some of the "hands-free" advantages.

Lavaliere microphone

Handheld mikes have the advantage of allowing you to move around the room, but the disadvantage is that you can have fewer gestures, and coordinating your notes will be more difficult.

Again, this points to the advice I gave you in Chapter 4 (Analyzing the Situation). As part of the analysis of your presentation situation, always be aware of the type of microphone that will be available to you so you will know how to prepare.

Using your voice effectively
has a lot to do with how you breathe.

Earlier, I talked about breathing to control nervousness. Here I want to cover the effect proper breathing has on your delivery. Sound is produced when air passes over the vocal cords and makes them vibrate. Breathing correctly will improve the flow of oxygen in your body and improve the blood flow to your brain. That, in turn, will help you think more clearly and order your thoughts as you have rehearsed them. Taking in more oxygen also improves the flow of air over your vocal cords, allowing you to speak clearly and reduce the nervousness that you will naturally feel. Try to learn to breathe from your diaphragm when you speak. The diaphragm is just below your lungs and separates your chest from the abdomen. Breathing from your diaphragm will give more support to your breathing and strengthen the pitch of your voice.

Consider this

The voice is an important part of any Bulletproof Presentation. I am not talking about the words, but the tone and quality of the voice. If you think of people such as Oprah Winfrey or Sean Connery, it is the voice you recognize and remember, not his or her words. Use the suggestions for breathing and the voice given to create a quality sound with your voice.

———

Some other elements of using your voice effectively are:

➤ Fillers.

➤ Pitch.

➤ Rate.

➤ Emphasis.

➤ Enunciation.

Fillers

It's those annoying *ums, ahs,* and *you knows* that we tend to use in presentations that can provide real distractions for your listeners. Fillers occur because our minds can think at a rate of speed about double our ability to talk.

**Usually, fillers come during those times when
we are transitioning between ideas during the presentation.**

There are two sure-fire ways to handle fillers.

The best way to overcome fillers is first to become aware of them. You will need to realize how big of a problem fillers are for you personally. You can do that by recording your presentation and then listening to it afterwards. Another approach would be to have someone listening to you, even one of your children, and have him or her signal you each time you use one. If you will practice this way, it will definitely help the problem because you will be able to transition from one thought to another more smoothly. Practice will do that for you! I often suggest that people use audio recorders or, even better, video recorders as they practice their presentations. You will be your own harshest critic, and your use of fillers will become obvious very quickly.

Pitch

Pitch refers to how high or how low your voice is while you are speaking. When you are making a presentation, you will want to use the lower end of your normal speaking voice. **When you are presenting, nervousness will tend to push you toward the higher end of your normal speaking voice.**

Research indicates that a lower pitch denotes authority and confidence in the mind of the listener. So consciously, at least in the beginning, focus on keeping your voice at the lower end of your normal scale.

Rate

This is the speed at which we talk. You want to speak in a way that will allow your audience to understand you without distraction. Many people who are nervous during their presentation will talk very quickly and never pause. However, presenters must pause, because the audience really likes you to pause. When you stop talking briefly, listeners get a chance to think about what you have said and relax for that moment. Also, certain parts of the country speak at different rates of speed, so try to be aware of that as you practice your presentation and pace the speed of your presentation.

Try to vary the rate of speech depending on where you are. However, remember to provide variety in the rhythm of your speech. Otherwise, you become monotonous.

Emphasis

Emphasis can make a big difference in how the audience interprets what you have said. Read these three sentences aloud and emphasize the word underlined.

"I did not say **she** stole the skirt." (*Who?*)

"I did not say she **stole** the skirt." (*She did what?*)

"I did not say she stole the **skirt**." (*She had what?*)

The way we emphasize certain words will have an impact on the meaning for the listener. When you are communicating with your audience, where is your emphasis?

For key points during your presentation, pay attention to the words you emphasize and evaluate the meaning as a result.

Enunciation

This is the way we form our words, and it is different than pronunciation. Think of enunciation as shaping your words. Complete each sound in the word and be especially aware of dropping the ending off the end of words. The most common effect is for people to drop the "g" in words ending with "-ing"; they end up by saying "somethin" instead of "something." Be very careful to enunciate clearly for your audience. I believe that this is a crucial skill in delivering a Bulletproof Presentation.

Even if you pronounce the word differently than some
of the audience members, they should be able to understand
you if you have enunciated carefully.

Vowels are very important in giving a presentation. Many words (for example, *bat, bite,* and *boat*) are only understandable if the listeners can hear the vowels clearly. Take the time to pronounce vowel sounds carefully and fully. Spend your practice time shaping the sounds so that your listeners hear all of the sounds.

That does not mean to slow down! You need to be clear and concise, but if you slow down too much, you may lose the normal pace and excitement in your presentation. Remember my suggestion earlier about the best form of presentation being heightened conversation? Think of speaking as if you were involved in a one-to-one conversation with another person. That should help you with the right pace for speaking.

Consider this

Remember that you have to be clear in your message; otherwise the audience will have trouble understanding what you mean. Take, for example, that confusing, yet creative communicator, Yogi Berra, the great New York Yankees catcher known for his great sayings. He once remarked, "Public speaking is one of the best things I hate." That was the message? Who knows? Carefully craft the message and use the pointers in this book to build a Bulletproof Presentation.

The main point must be clearly understood by your audience.

———

Rest your voice

If at all possible, try to rest your voice the day before a big presentation. Limiting the amount of speaking you do the day before a presentation will help make your voice stronger during your presentation.

Writing out your presentation

Many speakers I know will spend a great deal of time writing out their entire presentation word for word. For professional speakers who make a living giving presentations and speeches, I believe that is crucial to their success. After they finish writing the presentation and editing it several times, they will then memorize it. However, the biggest difference between you and them is that in all likelihood you will only give this presentation once, whereas they will give a presentation dozens or even hundreds of times.

Most businesspeople who write out their presentations end up reading them to the audience.

Presentations that are read are not Bulletproof, because they are generally boring and stiff. They are not spontaneous and do not seem to have natural rhythm, because what looks good on paper sounds quite different to the ear. The only exception that I can think of that makes sense is for a team presentation.

If you feel that circumstances may mean your portion of a team presentation may ultimately need to be given by another team member, then I would definitely support writing it out. That way your team member will have your words and ideas even if he or she must edit them to suit his or her speaking style.

Extemporaneous speaking

When most people think of extemporaneous speaking, they think of impromptu or off-the-cuff speaking. **Instead, this speaking style involves the selection and organization of your ideas in advance and relying on a written or mental key-word outline.**

You prepare the basic outline of thoughts, ideas, and supporting facts, but not necessarily each and every word that will be spoken. This is a very popular form of presenting in many situations, although busy executives often prefer a text for outside speaking engagements.

Extemporaneous speaking has both advantages and disadvantages for you as the speaker.

Advantages:

➤ Your language and delivery are much more natural, allowing for maximum connection with the audience.

➤ It encourages eye contact, especially when the speaker uses a good set of notes, because you are not reading a script.

➤ The speaker has greater freedom to leave the podium, use a variety of gestures, and move closer to the audience, thereby establishing a sense of connection with them.

➤ Because you are connected to the audience, you can respond to the audience by adjusting both major message content (for example, restatement, repetition, elaboration, definition, and the providing of additional support) and major delivery adjustments (for example, slowing down or picking up the pace, speaking more loudly or softly, or speaking more or less forcefully).

Disadvantages:

➤ When you speak extemporaneously, you will often sacrifice the precise language of a document or memorized presentation. However, such precision often sounds stilted and, therefore, unnatural. A carefully prepared extemporaneous presentation can usually be sufficiently precise without compromising the naturalness so essential to making a true connection with your audience.

➤ Extemporaneous speaking increases the risk of making a mistake. However, careful preparation and practice using the process outlined in this book can prevent this.

➤ It is sometimes difficult to control the timing of an extemporaneous speech. Sometimes you may "get on a roll" while speaking and lose track of time.

Position yourself slightly *away* from the lectern when speaking extemporaneously. You don't have to be a rocket scientist to figure out that the angle of viewing for your eye is far better the further back you go. This position lets you keep your chin and face up while your eyes go down to the page and do all the work. Remember: You want your eyes to track down to the page *only* in the *middle* of sentences. Short sentences are simple; you just take them in their entirety.

Just standing back a few inches automatically increases your eye contact. You should be 12 to 18 inches away from the lectern, far enough to let you express yourself with your hands if you wish to, yet close enough to still touch the lectern (many people like the comfort of feeling "grounded" to something solid).

Some lecterns are adjustable. If you know in advance you are going to use a prepared text, you should make it a point to request an adjustable lectern. This is particularly important for tall people. Adjust the lectern so that the top of the front is just below your sternum (and just below where your heart is).

You have probably guessed that I prefer the extemporaneous approach!

I place a great deal of value on genuine interaction with the audience and on natural delivery. However, please realize that if you decide to memorize a presentation or read from a manuscript, there are certain circumstances where these are most appropriate. For example, I have coached presenters in sales situations where it was not certain who might deliver the final presentation to the client due to scheduling problems. In those cases, a written script is probably good. That way, anyone can make the presentation and hit all of the important points. In some circumstances you may be best served by a combination approach—that is, making some parts of the presentation extemporaneous, memorizing other parts, and reading a manuscript where accuracy of information is critical.

In some circumstances you may be best served by a combination approach.

For instance, you may choose to memorize the introduction and conclusion of your speech; use a manuscript for sensitive material (to avoid being misquoted or making a factual error) or for reading a quotation, illustration, definition, or technical explanation; and rely on the extemporaneous mode for the overall flow of your remarks.

Here are some suggestions for improving the effectiveness of an extemporaneous speech while minimizing its possible disadvantages:

- ➤ Create a detailed (but not too detailed) outline so that you will keep the proper flow and order.

- ➤ Focus on the goals of your presentation so that you will be less likely to spend too much time on a single idea or be taken too far afield.

- ➤ To control the timing of your speech, allocate a certain amount of time for each major idea, and while you are practicing your presentation, place notations in the margin of your outline to keep track of time as you speak. To do that, you will need to have a watch or small clock within easy sight, and make a commitment to abide by the timing you have practiced.

What to do with your hands

Short of creating a distraction, try to let your hands help you express yourself, for two reasons:

1. Freeing up your hands to "talk" with you helps vent the anxieties that you may feel about speaking in the first place. People experience anxiety or stage fright in different ways. If it's allowed to build without release, anxiety can reveal our fear by making us look nervous or wooden. Nervousness often manifests itself as rocking or swaying. Using your hands helps hide fear by physically releasing tension.

    Of course, your hands should not run away with you. They should always help, never distract. So keep your moves disciplined: short chops to make points, fingertips touching, palms up, palms down, a fist in the palm, all done with some discretion and restraint. Or you could keep your hands busy by holding a pen and occasionally switching the pen from one hand to the other.

2. Gestures will help you look more relaxed and natural. Try to think of gestures that you would use in a conversation with someone while making a point or statement. Practice using at least one gesture for each short sentence, and two or more for longer ones. Continue practicing with the gestures until some feel comfortable. Keep using them, and forget the others.

Notes versus no notes

Use notes! A speaker's total freedom from notes can pay some dividends in the image department. It can project him or her as brighter and more articulate than speakers who rely on them. However, the chances of making mistakes, or going completely blank, outweigh any of those potential image dividends.

The major issue regarding notes should not be whether you use them, but rather how you use them.

I generally recommend using 3x5 index cards because they are easy to handle. However, a trick I learned for using these cards has been very helpful for presenters I have trained. Write on the cards in a vertical fashion rather than the normal horizontal fashion. However, put the notes on the back (blank) side of the card. The cards will fit more easily in your hand and will be much easier to handle that way. Also, once you have your notes in the final fashion, you

---

```
                                      5
Part Two

Three sales mediums              (blue)
   Benefits-
      Fastest response
      Significant results

(Turn to flip chart)              (red)

Methods                          (blue)
   •Direct Sales by existing organizations
      Represenatives of other organizations
      will sell the product for us      (blue)

   •Telemarketing
      Rob will address our plan        (red)
      Market director to the consumer (blue)

   •Direct Sales by B2 Inc.           (blue)
      Principals of B2 will sell direct to
      corporations or non-profit groups
```

Sample Note Card

will want to number them. The reason? If you ever accidentally drop them, you can easily put them back into order and move on. That can be exceptionally helpful if you happen to drop them just before you begin speaking!

Regard using notes during your presentation as an insurance policy against forgetting your ideas and the order of presenting them. Don't make your notes too detailed! If you do, there is a danger that you will start to read them. They should contain just enough information to allow your memory to pick up the words and ideas at that point in the presentation. Also, writing out key quotations or detailed statistics is very helpful, as you do not want to misquote someone or some data. That can be very embarrassing.

You can also color-code your notes in case you need to cut items.

Earlier I noted the possibility that you may not receive as much time as you were originally promised. If you color-code your notes (for example, blue for "definitely keep" and green for "could be removed"), you will be much more comfortable if that situation occurs.

If you are determined not to use notes because you feel they may lower your audience's estimation of you, consider two important questions:

1. Are the notes the problem, or is it the way in which you use them?

2. If you were to avoid using notes, how likely is it that you might forget something crucial to your goals, be sidetracked, feel nervous, devote too much time to an idea, lose smoothness, and so on?

If any of these pitfalls concerns you, you need good notes, not necessarily more notes.

Podium vs. no podium

I am often asked by presenters, "Should I use a podium?" A podium presents a physical—and a psychological—barrier between you (the speaker) and your audience. This is especially true if it is far removed from the first row of the audience members. That barrier is most noticeable if you are a speaker who is unable to appear spontaneous and natural behind a piece of furniture. Why? Because it increases the feeling that you are self-consciousness and nervous about your presentation. *Rest* your hands gently on the lectern; don't grip it and show the "white-knuckle" effect. That will really cue the audience that you are nervous! And it can spell disaster for gestures and eye contact in many cases. If you decide to use a podium for your notes, be sure to move away from it occasionally. Move away from the podium but don't provide any distraction by having the podium block the line-of-sight for any of your audience.

Nonverbal skills

Nonverbal skills are very important to a Bulletproof Presentation. Most people are very visual and make judgments about people very quickly based on what they see. You are your most important visual aid. Learning the following techniques and incorporating them into the delivery of your presentation are critical to successful speaking. Certainly what you are saying matters to your listeners, but how you look and what you do when you are speaking can enhance what you say, or detract from it. Let's look at some ways to improve your chances of success.

Eye contact

This is the most important nonverbal skill. Remember the old saying that "the eyes are the window to the soul"? That is especially true in making presentations. Eye contact is a powerful tool for establishing rapport with your audience.

Consider this

Eye contact is so important that Sam Walton, the founder of Wal-Mart used to say, "You look 'em right in the eye and say, 'How can I help you today?' " Never underestimate the power of eye contact. When he died, Sam Walton was the richest man in America.

**Using eye contact during the presentation
gives the appearance of confidence and competence
(even if you are terribly nervous!).**

Don't sell your audience short by not looking at them. A general rule of thumb is to make eye contact with an individual for about five seconds before moving on to the next person. You must stop and look at the individual or your eyes give the appearance of the garden sprinkler, just sweeping back and forth. If the room is very large, pick about four or five different spots and move among those spots.

Try to find some friendly faces in the audience and move to them regularly.

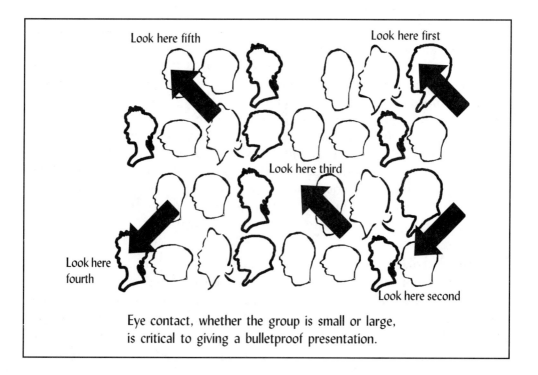

Eye contact, whether the group is small or large,
is critical to giving a bulletproof presentation.

The audience members will think you are looking right at them! Concentrating on your eye contact, your breathing, and your message will help you control your nervousness while exhibiting confidence to your audience.

Speaking into the podium or reading from your notes will break your audience's concentration. If you need to refer to your notes, by all means do so! However, while you are seeking that information, stop talking. Once you have the next thought, raise your eyes and then begin speaking again.

If you maintain eye contact for too long, it may appear that you're staring at someone. Work to soften your focus and begin to move your eyes more frequently.

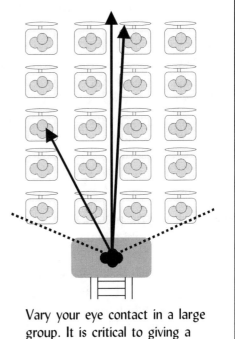

Vary your eye contact in a large group. It is critical to giving a bulletproof presentation.

Stance

Your stance is also an important component. When you first arrive at the podium, assume "the speaker's stance." This means:

- **Stand tall with good posture.**

- **Place your feet about shoulder-width apart.**

- **Square your shoulders to the audience.**

- **Keep your hands at your side or rest them slightly on the podium.**

The only exception to these components in the speaker's stance applies to women. Sometimes women prefer to stand with their feet together. That is quite acceptable as long as you do not begin to sway. Inexperienced speakers have the habit of rocking by shifting their weight from one foot to the other.

Be careful not to rock back and forth during the presentation.

Rocking is usually caused by having either your feet too close together or having one foot in front of the other. If you begin to do this regularly, your listeners might begin to get a mental picture of Elvis, which can distract them from your message! However, if you stand with your feet too far apart you may begin to look like the proverbial "gunslinger."

From the speaker's stance, other body movements can be used to accentuate verbal points you are making during the presentation.

For example, leaning forward slightly will appear positive and friendly to your audience. It appears to the audience members as if you are encouraging them to get involved with your topic. Leaning backward will have the opposite effect.

Standing on one foot with the other crossed not only makes for an unstable stance, but it also makes you appear less authoritative. To the audience, an unbalanced stance can be translated into an unorganized mind.

As part of working on a good speaker's stance, another important consideration is *where* you stand! **Always make sure you are not blocking the view of your audience as you reference any visual aids.**

Many experts recommend the speaker be to the right of the projection screen, as seen from the audience's point of view. The rationale has to do with that natural left-to-right movement that people use. They will look first at the visual aid on the screen and then the speaker. It aids them in focusing on the right thing at the right time.

Mobility during the presentation

If at all possible, make every attempt to move around during your presentation. Don't get "stuck" behind a podium, because you look insecure. Of course, if you cannot move because of the size of the group or the room setting, that is okay, but movement is preferred if at all possible. If you take my suggestion and move around, maintain eye contact and make your movements smooth and steady. Be careful that you do not begin to pace, as that will make you appear nervous and "like a caged tiger."

Never stand with your back to the audience!

If you must write on a white board or flipchart, stop talking while you write and don't begin to speak again until you are facing the audience. The same principle is true when referring to a projector screen behind you. Stop speaking as you point to the screen and then begin again when you face the audience. If you need to gesture to the board or screen and talk, stand to the right or left and point with the hand closest to the screen allowing your chest to face the audience.

Gestures

Gestures are very important during any presentation. Watch people talking naturally in conversation and you will see a good deal of gesturing.

Somehow, when we begin to give a presentation, we suddenly forget how to use our hands for gestures. As you begin to speak you will need to incorporate gestures into the presentation. When using gestures, make all the gestures larger, and more theatrical, than you might feel is normal.

Many good organizations, such as Toastmasters, are very strict about speakers who put their hands in their pockets during a presentation. The main reason for this concern is the lack of gestures that occur when you have your hands in your pockets. However, many people do move their hands to their pockets as a "rest position." Rest positions are what we do with our hands when we are not gesturing. Entertainers such as Jay Leno and David Letterman put their hands into their pockets regularly and, as a direct result, I believe have lowered some of the restrictions in this area.

You will be okay putting one hand in your pocket, but I would discourage both hands, because you'll have no gestures at all!

However, if you have a habit of putting your hands into your pockets, it would be a good idea to remove your keys and loose pocket change. Why? Because many people I have coached (as well as yours truly) have a bad habit of playing with the change or keys. It gives a *Jingle Bells*–type problem during the presentation, and the audience is very distracted by the noise.

Consider this

Take off your watch during your presentation. You may remember the 1992 presidential debates, when President Bush looked at his watch during his debate with Bill Clinton and Ross Perot. Few remember what he said that day, but many commented on the glance at the watch, because it sent a signal that he did not want to be there and that he was anxious to finish. That is not the message you want your audience to get.

When using gestures, make all the gestures larger, and more theatrical, than you might feel is normal.

The reason for that is tied to the way people listen. If the gestures are too small, or not seen by the audience, the audience gets tired of listening more quickly. For example, if you are making a point that requires a gesture of three fingers, the gesture will need to come all the way from your arm, not just your hand. Again, the reason is more theatrical. People are generally visual during presentations, and they must be able to see your gestures for them to be effective. At first, exaggerating your gestures may seem odd or awkward, but as you practice, it should become more natural and normal. Don't be afraid of big gestures or long pauses in your presentation; they will seem normal and natural in the eyes of the audience. They can be used very effectively. In any case, do not reduce or ignore gestures, as they are critical to a Bulletproof Presentation!

Research has shown that listeners mentally "check out" about every five to seven minutes. However, because most people are so visual, their attention will last longer if the gestures are congruent with the words.

As you practice, use a video recorder or mirror to notice how the gestures tie into the points you are trying to make. Videotaping can be invaluable in improving your gestures. Turn the sound completely off and watch your gestures. Without thinking about the content of the presentation at certain points, ask yourself, *What are my gestures saying to the audience? Is that what I want them to see?* Improve those gestures that do not convey the right message.

Other rest positions

There are some other common "rest positions" used by inexperienced presenters. Some of the more common are:

The Prayer Position: In this position, the presenter stands with his or her hands clasped in front, as in prayer. There is nothing wrong with this position for short periods, but the operative word is *short*. Don't stand for an extended time in this position or you could send a message to your audience that you are nervous and "praying" for the presentation to be over.

| **The Fig Leaf:** | Here the presenter has his or her hands clasped in front of his or her pelvic region. This type of rest position sends a message to the audience that you are anxious and lack confidence. Clearly, this is not the type of message you want to send in a Bulletproof Presentation. |
| **The Fighter:** | When a speaker is constantly clenching his or her fists during the presentation, the listeners will either conclude you are ready to fight them if they disagree or that you are very nervous and therefore not confident. |

Facial expressions

Facial expressions tremendously impact any presentation. Have you ever been in a situation where you were talking with someone and you felt you were not hearing the whole story? Many of us have had that experience. Researchers tell us that many times the reason for that is has to do with the subtle differences we note unconsciously between the words we hear and the expression we see on the other person's face. (This is probably how your mother could always tell when you were lying!)

Appearance

I don't want this section to turn into a "Dress for Success" session; however, the way you dress will have an immediate impact on your audience. Remember how important your mother told you first impressions were? Well, they certainly are when making a Bulletproof Presentation.

First impressions are very strong and hard to change. People will pick up impressions of you from your dress, your walk to the front of the room, and even the way you stand before you begin. All of these elements help the audience begin to make an impression before you even say one word!

Always dress at least as conservatively as your audience.

If you are not sure, err on the conservative side. Remember that a business suit is designed to make the person who is wearing it look like everyone else. If the business environment is "business casual," then it might be more appropriate to dress that way. The reason you want to be concerned is to make sure people to focus on your ideas, not how you are dressed.

Whatever clothing you wear, you want the clothing to be a minor contribution to your presentation!

Be sure to check on the dress requirements (or expectations) where you are speaking particularly if you are going out of town. The audience may be "business casual" but consider it inappropriate for you to dress the same way.

Ask someone who knows how you should be dressed for this presentation. And remember that it can be different in different places. For example, in Houston it would usually be fine for an engineer to remove his or her jacket and make the presentation in just shirt and tie or business blouse. You would be considered too casual in Dallas if you did the same thing. Make it a point to know the local norms.

If you are not sure, dress one level up from where you understand the audience to be. Where everyone would be in business suits, men will probably want to wear the traditional dark blue or gray suit with an equally traditional tie. For women, a dark-colored jacket that matches the skirt, with a blouse buttoned to the collar or with a high or crew neck, would be appropriate.

If everyone is more casual, then men might choose an outfit with khaki pants and a blazer. Women might wear a more informal ensemble, such as a jacket and skirt that are meant to be worn together even though they do not "match."

For color, generally pick bright colors as accents and choose darker colors, such as navy blue, gray, and black, as the dominant color. However, remember that some colors are hard for anyone to wear in a business setting. Examples might be turquoise or magenta. As you select your clothing, remember how the lighting might affect the colors. Sometimes beige can become an ugly gray, and red can turn orange in certain light.

Also beware of large or shiny pieces of jewelry, which can be quite distracting. Shiny baubles or accessories can distract from your presentation if you are not careful. That includes everything from large earrings to large belt buckles.

For women, manage your cosmetics carefully. You want to wear the right makeup to make you look healthy and natural.

Try to get a good night's sleep the night before your presentation. Make sure you do a check before you begin your presentation in the nearby restroom. Make sure your hair is brushed, your shirt or blouse is correctly tucked in, and all buttons and zippers are in their proper position. Finally, if you think perspiration will be a problem, wear a jacket to hide any telltale marks.

Also remember, you will be moving, talking, and a little nervous. You will feel warmer than you would if you were just sitting and listening to the presentation. Therefore, dress "lighter" or in layers that will allow you to adjust for that additional warmth factor.

Make sure your shoes are shined and your appearance is sharp. If you do not take care of your appearance, you will come across as unprepared and the audience may well assume you are not really the expert you are touted to be. Essentially, a speaker that appears unkempt becomes a distraction to the audience, and that will detract from your important message.

Distractions

Whenever a distraction occurs, deal with it immediately. One time I was delivering a presentation to a group in a hotel in Baton Rouge, Louisiana, when maintenance started to repair the roof directly overhead. It was so loud it was incredible—and a big distraction. I simply told the audience that if the noise became too distracting, to let me know and I would stop and we would see if we could do something about it. If you can, use some humor to break the distraction and get the audience to focus on you again. For example, if a cell phone rings while you are speaking, stop and say, "Could you get that?" to someone who appears to be in the area where the ring came from. The basic premise it to let your audience know you will not be distracted and they should not be either.

Bulletproof advice

➤ **Using your voice and body effectively will put sparkle into your presentation.**

- Remember that in a Bulletproof Presentation, you are trying to achieve a sense of heightened conversation with the audience.

➤ **Understand the microphone you will be using.**

- Knowing the type of microphone and how to operate it will give you more confidence and allow you to give the style of presentation you want.

➤ **Be aware of fillers and eliminate them during your practice sessions.**

- Fillers are the most distracting characteristic of a poor presentation, but they are the easiest to fix because we know they will come as you transition from one thought to another.

➤ **Prepare and use your notes wisely.**

- Use 3x5 cards and write only the key words that help you remember what you wanted to say. If your notes are too detailed, you may be tempted to read them and lose the heightened conversation you are seeking.

➤ **Eye contact is critical to a successful presentation.**

- Using eye contact during the presentation gives the appearance of confidence and competence.

➤ **Keep your audience clearly in mind when you decide what visuals to use.**

- Structure your visuals using standard rules and practice with them several times before the presentation.

➤ **Don't read the visuals you produce.**

- Nothing is more distracting than a speaker who reads everything to the audience. Use the visuals to reinforce key ideas, and then move on.

➤ **Remember that there are a variety of visuals available, from low complexity to high complexity, that can enhance your presentation.**

- Choose the visuals that are appropriate for the audience and that you are comfortable using. Practice with them and don't be afraid to get rid of some that are not helping you.

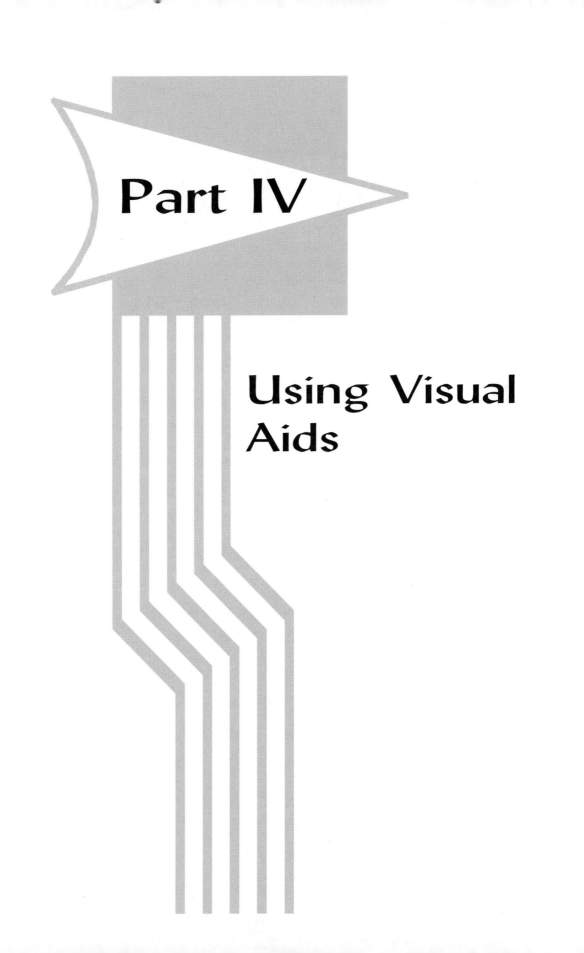

Part IV

Using Visual Aids

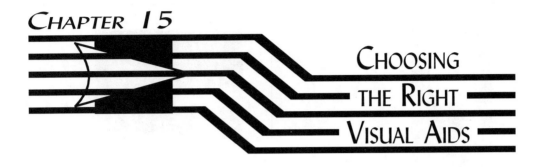

CHAPTER 15

CHOOSING
THE RIGHT
VISUAL AIDS

This chapter will cover when and how to use visual aids. Visual aids need to add dramatic flair and heighten the retention of the audience. We'll explore some of the myths and misguided uses of visual aids. We've all suffered through presentations that used literally dozens of overheads for a 15- or 20-minute presentation.

Consider this

Here are some things to remember about audiovisual equipment (much of which I had to learn the hard way):

- Whatever AV equipment you decide to take with you to the presentation, remember that you will need to carry it or hire someone else to carry it.

- Don't rely on the so-called AV expert at the location where you are giving the presentation to know how to fix a problem with the equipment. You should know how to use and fix any problems with the equipment or you could be in trouble if something fails.

- Don't use AV equipment unless you can use it comfortably. You don't want to be fooling around trying to figure out something and looking shaky to the audience. They may think you are shaky with the subject matter, too!

The types of visual aids available are shown on page 154.

A selection process in today's world is not easy because so many choices are available. Decision-making becomes a major task in today's society.

Consider this

Make sure the visual image you want to convey sends the right message. A man attending a seminar on interpersonal relationships became convinced of the need for him to begin showing appreciation to people. With his family seemed like an appropriate place to start. So on his way home, he picked up a dozen

Low Complexity	High Complexity
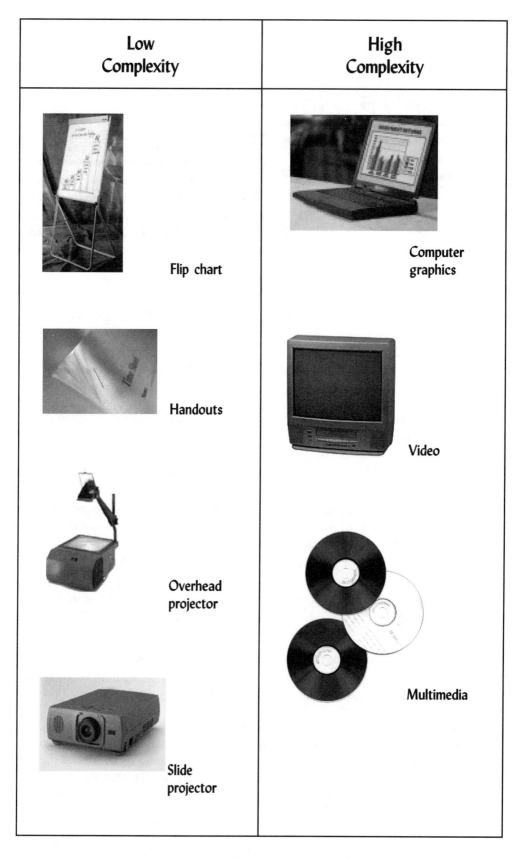	

Flip chart

Computer graphics

Handouts

Video

Overhead projector

Multimedia

Slide projector

long-stemmed roses and a delicious box of chocolates. This was going to be a real surprise, and he was excited to begin showing his wife how much he appreciated her.

Arriving home, he walked up to the front door, rang the doorbell, and waited for his wife to answer. Immediately upon seeing him, she began to cry.

"What's the matter, honey?" asked the confused husband.

"Oh, it's been a terrible day," she responded. "First, Tommy tried to flush his diaper down the toilet, then the dishwasher quit working, Sally came home from school with her legs all scratched up and now, and now you come home drunk!"

———

Yesterday's world consisted of far fewer options. For example, you could select vanilla, chocolate, or strawberry ice cream. Today's world offers the option of Baskin-Robbins' 31 Flavors or more, with additional choices of regular, lowfat, or nonfat ice cream. Or you could choose frozen yogurt with the same decision of regular, lowfat, or nonfat.

Decision-making can be frustrating with so many choices available, but it can also be exciting because of the many unique possibilities not available in the past.

Although presentation purposes are essentially the same as in the past, presentation media has been enhanced by computer technology. The production and delivery processes are more sophisticated, yet easier for the presenter.

The choices of presentation media are categorized as handouts, models, posters and flipcharts, notetakers/copyboards, overhead transparencies, 35mm slides, and computer-based media. Frequently, the choice should not simply be which one to select, but which *ones* to select. Combining media types makes a presentation both more forceful and more interesting.

Selecting and making presentation media is only part of the task. Knowing when and how to use the media appropriately also requires careful thought and study. The focus of the presentation should be on the presenter—not the media. Media is a support or an aid (there's a reason they're called visual *aids*) to a presentation. Without the right use, the intended impact of a presentation can fall short of its mark.

Handouts

The presentation medium used most frequently is a handout: the printed materials used during a presentation. A handout can be used by itself or with any of the other presentation media. For example, the facility model presentation would be more persuasive if accompanied by a handout including word descriptions, blueprints or layouts, maps, and photographs. Handouts are valuable to provide information during the presentation or as a resource for participants later.

Advantages

The advantages of handouts are numerous. A need for extensive note-taking by the audience is eliminated. People not able to attend can get the handouts and catch up on what they missed.

In the development stage, artwork or photography may be adapted to the printed page. The presenter can easily re-sequence the content. Revisions or updates of the materials are easy to make using a word-processing or desktop-publishing program. The materials can be produced economically, distributed easily, updated or revised periodically, and used to display still visuals.

Limitations

An audience looking at handouts during a presentation may become too involved with the printed materials and may not focus on what the speaker is saying. The sound of pages turning may be distracting both to the speaker and the audience. The audience may decide that attendance during the presentation is unnecessary, take a handout, and leave.

Preparation

Written words and the way they are presented on paper give the audience an impression of a speaker similar to the impression spoken words make. Therefore, the preparation and presentation of handouts is important. For example, if the pages are unattractively arranged and presented, the reader forms a negative impression similar to the impression formed by watching a speaker who may be untidy or "sloppy" in appearance.

Desktop-publishing software

Material today can look like published material instead of typewritten material. The page-layout capabilities of desktop-publishing software have glamorized the written page. Although desktop-publishing software has many sophisticated features over word-processing software, the distinction between them has merged. The final printed output may show very little difference.

In both cases, a page may contain type in different fonts, sizes, and styles. Lines, boxes, and shading may be included. Also, clip art, photographs, charts, and graphs may be imported from other programs. Design ideas that can make handouts attractive and more readable are important.

Design ideas

The first design idea to consider is the effective use of space. Pages should not be cluttered. Fifty percent of the page should contain blank (or "white") space, which is spread out over the page. Centered, side, and subheadings break the monotony of text reading and serve as "road signs" to direct and focus the reader's attention. Font sizes and styles can be varied when a distinction is needed. Fonts are available in a wide variety of typefaces; however, be careful that a different font serves a purpose, such as to emphasize or differentiate. A page with too many different font changes will be distracting.

Illustrations such as charts, graphs, or pictures create visual interest and may serve to tell the story better than written words. Cartoon figures can help to illustrate points. (More adults than children read newspaper cartoons.)

One effective way to provide a handout is to make miniatures of selected visuals from the presentation. Most desktop presentation software provides a feature allowing two, three, four, or six miniatures to be placed on the page. Titles and footnotes can be added to the sheet if desired. Placing three visuals vertically on the left of a page allows the listener to make notes in the column on the right.

Reproducing all of the visuals from a presentation may be overkill; however, it is effective to include carefully selected visuals the audience may want to refer to later. Then the audience members will not try to re-create the visuals in their notes.

Production

The production of handouts is also important. Considerations are the paper, the reproduction method, and the type of binding.

Paper. Handouts are probably best duplicated on normal 8 ½ x 11-inch paper, although other sizes may be used if a purpose is served. (For instance, a spreadsheet often won't fit on standard-sized paper and requires 8 ½ x 14-inch paper.) Although the visuals used for projection may be in full color, it is probably not economical to have the handouts in full color. However, using a variety of paper colors can be effective as a coding device. For instance, a speaker can refer to the yellow sheet or the blue sheet.

Paper is available in many new colors and textures. The paper you select can make your handouts unique—and help to set any tone, from flamboyant to conservative to distinguished.

Reproduction methods. Handouts may be reproduced using a copier or other printing process. Good quality reproduction is needed for readability purposes as well as for creating a positive impression on an audience.

Binding. Handouts may be several loose sheets, or they may be arranged in a particular sequence and bound as a package. They may be stapled together or inserted into a notebook of some type. A notebook increases the cost but is effective in organizing several materials and providing a personalized "take-home" booklet that serves as a reference.

Distribution

When you provide handouts for the audience, be sure to prepare enough for everyone. If a larger than expected audience shows up for a conference presentation, you can get a list of names and addresses and mail handouts to those who don't receive them. With the high cost of postage and the extra effort of addressing and mailing involved, it is usually easier to prepare more handouts than needed rather than run the risk of not having enough. An audience will generally want the handouts immediately, not next week.

Appropriateness. A speaker should consider the appropriateness of materials and when they should be distributed. Members of an audience may feel they have gained more if they can take away tangible evidence (such as handouts or a booklet) for future use or reference. On the other hand, only material that will be useful to the majority of the audience should be distributed. If materials are found in a trash can outside the door, you have a strong hint for the next time around, that the handouts probably did not really serve a purpose.

If members of the audience show an interest in an item not available during the presentation, you may want to follow up by getting a list of names and addresses or by collecting business cards from those who want the additional information. Caution should be taken, however, to promise only what you will deliver.

Timing. Authorities disagree on when to distribute handouts. Some say handouts are distracting and take the audience's attention away from the speaker. Therefore, they prefer to wait and distribute them after the presentation.

If audience members are to refer to the handouts, they will need them at the beginning of the presentation. Then they can see what is in them and know whether they need to take notes. However, to keep control of an audience's attention, you need to tell listeners specifically what they should be looking at in the handouts and when they should be listening to you.

Handouts can be distributed before the presentation begins by placing them on the desks or chairs before people enter the room. A helper can distribute handouts to the audience as they come into the room or at some other point during the presentation.

If a helper is not available to distribute handouts, an audience member can be drafted. A speaker distributing handouts from the front of the room can give the stack to a person on the side of the first row and ask that person to count out the number needed for the row, then pass the rest of the stack back to the next row. Usually, the end persons all catch on and will do the same. This technique speeds up the distribution considerably compared to the whole stack being passed to each person. You may want to hold your remarks until all materials are distributed.

In any event, distributing a collated package of handouts is less confusing than distributing numerous pieces of additional information. Caution should be taken, however, to promise only what you will deliver.

If handouts are used for resource materials only, place them on a table at the back of the room for participants to pick up as they exit. This is convenient for the participants because of traffic flow; however, a similar stack could be placed at the front of the room for those individuals who wish to come forward to talk with you.

Models or replicas

Models or replicas are excellent for demonstration purposes. If you are trying to motivate workers about moving to a new location several hundred miles away, you may want to give them an idea of how the new facility, presently under construction, will look when it is completed. A realistic miniature model of the facility and its community would be far more appealing than an engineering blueprint of the new facility and surrounding area.

Models can be a product shown in actual size, such as a speaker demonstrating to a small group an ergonomically designed chair using an actual chair. *Miniatures or reduced sizes* would be more appropriate if the chair was a part of the facility scenario mentioned before. If the chair controls were being demonstrated to a large group, an *enlarged* chair would allow the audience to view the demonstration better. A less expensive *replication* of the chair could serve effectively as a demonstration tool.

Advantages

Models are very realistic in either full-size or scaled versions. In the case of viewing the planned company facilities and the surrounding area, the audience members have the advantage of almost being there—even though they are not physically at the facility. Thus, a model can prepare a person for the actual event. An existing model may be more convenient to acquire than making actual visuals requiring overhead or computer projection.

Limitations

Making a realistic model can be expensive. A model must be the proper size to be visible to the entire audience.

Posters and flipcharts

Posters and flipcharts can be made in a wide variety of sizes. Posters can be displayed throughout the presentation as they are usually made on a stiff paper-board. You can have a stack of posters and reveal them one by one or display them around the room so that all posters are in view at all times. Flipcharts usually consist of thinner paper attached to a pad and placed on an easel board.

Posters are frequently thought of as a presentation media more appropriate for elementary schools, and flipcharts as a device used in training sessions. These stereotyped uses are not the only uses. Similar to other presentation media, both posters and flipcharts have distinct advantages as well as limitations.

Advantages

Posters or flipcharts can be made before the presentation and carried into the presentation for use. No special equipment is needed other than a place to show the materials. Flipcharts also can be developed during the presentation. By using marking pens, the presenter or a member of the audience can use the flipcharts for recording key points. This procedure is effective during brainstorming sessions.

As a flipchart is completed, it can be torn from the pad and attached to the wall with masking tape (assuming this is allowed in the meeting facility). Thus, a chronological record of the presentation is shown on the wall to aid discussion. Late arrivals have a quick view of what has occurred before their arrival.

Limitations

Posters and flipcharts are appropriate for audiences with a dozen or so participants. If care is taken to make the writing large, they may work successfully for an audience of 15 or 20. The presenter's back must be to the audience while writing on the flipchart, whereas an already-made poster or flipchart allows the presenter to use a pointer and face the audience. Writing or printing must be large to be legible from a distance.

Preparation

To determine if print is large enough, try to read the poster or flipchart from a distance equal to the farthest distance viewers will be seated. Because many people write on a board unevenly, light-blue lines can serve as a guide and will not be seen by the audience. You can purchase poster paper with light-blue grid lines, or you can lightly draw the lines before the presentation.

Three or four colored markers can help highlight points as well as add variety. To avoid "see-through writing," some presenters use only every other page in a flipchart pad when they are developing flipcharts in advance. The pages can be taped or stapled together for easy turning.

Too much writing on a poster or flipchart can reduce its impact. The design principles given in Chapter 16 apply to both posters and flipcharts, as well as overhead transparencies and slides.

The preparation of posters or flipcharts has traditionally been a manual method. However, computers and other equipment can now be used to prepare more appealing products.

Manual preparation. The traditional way of preparing posters or flipcharts is by using marking pens in a variety of colors. Illustrations or pictures also can be pasted on.

Electronic preparation. Text layout can be prepared using computers to take advantage of typography capabilities for a variety of fonts, sizes, and styles. Computer programs such as TypeStyler can provide special effects, such as stretching the type into interesting shapes. Illustrations can be added with draw programs or by importing clip art or scanned photographs. After a master copy is printed on standard 8 ½ x 11–inch paper, special equipment, such as a ChartPrinter, can produce easelpad-sized flipcharts.

Notetakers/copyboards

Notetakers/copyboards are available to aid in meetings for recording the notes and interaction of the group by writing on a board and then making copies of the board for members of the audience. The board looks like a regular write-on board, but a device is attached to produce a paper copy of the words and illustrations written, drawn, or even taped to the board surface. Copies are produced from the board by scanning the image to make a copy. Several companies manufacture these products, and they vary in how they operate and in the quality of output.

Overhead transparencies

Overhead transparencies are also called view graphs or foils. An overhead projector needed to project the transparencies is relatively inexpensive and commonly found in both meeting rooms and classrooms.

The use of overhead transparencies has many advantages as well as a few limitations for users.

Advantages

Unlike writing on a flipchart or a board, the speaker or presenter can face the audience throughout the presentation when using overhead transparencies. Because a speaker needs to maintain eye contact with the audience as much as possible, doing so while showing a visual is helpful. The audience does not feel left out, and discussion and participation are easier.

Overhead transparencies can be made spontaneously by writing on acetate film with special markers in a variety of colors. Materials also can be prepared before the presentation by hand or, more professionally, by computer. Word-processing or desktop-publishing programs can be used to make transparencies; however, presentation software offers many benefits.

A distinct advantage of overhead transparencies over 35mm slides is that changes (deletions or adjustments to the sequencing order) can be made minutes before the presentation or even during the presentation itself. For instance, if your presentation is taking longer than anticipated, you may need to avoid showing a few of the visuals in order to keep on a time schedule. Also, overhead transparencies can be viewed in fully lighted rooms.

Limitations

Overhead transparencies may not be appropriate for large rooms and auditoriums. Experiment to see if the projected visual can be easily read from any seat in the room (note that you may not always be able to do this in advance). The print of typewritten visuals is far too small for distance viewing and will strain the audience. Visuals simply typewritten with no enlargement should not be used. Transparencies look much better in frames, but these take up considerably more room than slides in a briefcase or suitcase.

Placing the visuals on the projector and removing them can become distracting as well as time consuming. You must stand right by the projector to change the visuals. If you are on a platform using a microphone, a helper can sit near the overhead projector and change the visuals at the appropriate times. This process should be rehearsed so that the helper develops the proper timing sequence of changing the visuals. If you have to nod or ask for the visual to be changed repeatedly, thought patterns can be broken—for both the speaker and the audience.

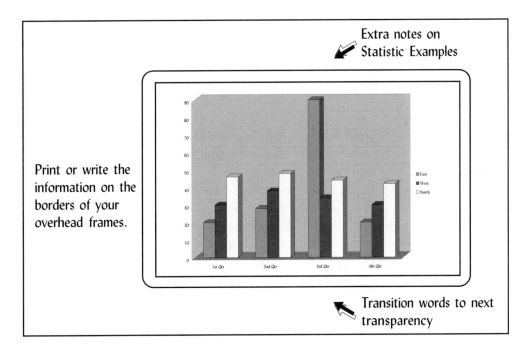

Preparation

Preparing overhead transparencies involves gathering the right type of products for use as well as following good design techniques. Chapter 16 covers design techniques appropriate for all types of media; however, a few special design techniques for transparencies are mentioned in this section.

Write-on method. Overhead-projection marker pens (available in a variety of colors with fine or broad tips) are available for use in preparing transparencies. The handmade look can be an effective delivery method because it is spontaneous. Preparation can be accomplished minutes before the presentation when a computer and a printer are unavailable. The effect of using such visuals can be that of "I made these a few minutes ago especially for you" versus "my secretary made this canned presentation several speeches back."

Color. In addition to using colored markers, a presenter can bring the audience out of the monochrome world by using colored transparencies. A rainbow package, for instance, includes blue, pink, yellow, and green overheads. This tinted background can be more stimulating than using clear transparencies and can reduce glare.

Transparencies are also available that, when reproduced by a thermofax (heat process), will develop with a colored image on clear acetate, such as red, blue, or green on clear. Another type produces yellow images on a dark blue, red, or green background.

Color highlight film is a special write-on film coated with a vivid blue emulsion. When you use special, colored highlight pens (red, green, or orange), the emulsion disappears and color from the marker remains, making a dramatic, sparkling image right before the audience's eyes. An overlay of this color film sheet can be placed over a prepared visual and the highlight marker used to circle, underline, or highlight important points. A special eraser allows you to erase the markings for use in your next presentation.

Full-color images can be produced with ink-jet, thermal-transfer, or laser printers. Color technology has made full-color visuals for overhead transparencies a reality. With the necessary equipment, the beautiful, vivid color of slides can be printed on overhead transparencies.

Production

Even though it is possible to produce overhead transparencies through photographic methods, overhead transparencies are normally produced by thermofax, photocopiers, laser printers, or color printers.

Thermofax. The thermofax is a machine that serves as a popular means to develop the transparencies. An original master is placed behind the transparency and then fed into the machine. The imaged transparency and the master emerge from the machine. Because the thermofax works on a heat process, the transparency may curl, making the use of a frame mount more important.

Photocopiers. Many users today prefer to use their copying machine for making transparencies. Transparencies specially made for copiers are available in several different weights or thicknesses. (Transparencies made for the thermofax are not of the right weight and may melt on the copier drum, causing serious damage.) When transparency sheets are fed through the copier instead of paper, toner adheres to each sheet.

Laser printers. Overhead transparencies also can be made by placing transparency sheets in the paper tray of a laser printer. As you can with a copier, be careful to use the right type of transparency. They are heavier than thermofax transparencies. Special overheads for laser printers can be purchased, although overheads for copiers can be used. Caution should be followed, however, as transparency film that is not heavy enough can melt and ruin the printer drum.

Color printers. Technology uses several other different techniques to print in full color. Laser printers use colored toners, ink-jet printers apply the colors in a spraying process, and thermal-transfer printers use layers of color film to transfer the color to paper or an overhead transparency.

35-millimeter slides

A sophisticated type of presentation media is 35mm slides. Although the preparation of the original is similar to that of overheads, the production techniques are different. Colors are very sharp and clear, and slides are associated as a tool for the very professional presenter. The technology of today makes production easier and faster than in the past.

Advantages

Slides are small, convenient to use, and relatively inexpensive. You could add slides or rearrange them as needed as you prepare the presentation.

Actual camera shots may be included in addition to computer-generated visuals. Because you can change slides with a handheld (possibly cordless) remote control, a large number of slides can be viewed quickly and smoothly, in contrast to having to change transparencies on an overhead projector.

Limitations

For slides, the room needs to be darkened for effective viewing. Thus, the audience may not be able to see you and vice versa. As a result, interaction with the audience may be reduced or completely eliminated.

Film must be shot and processed, which requires you to allow sufficient preparation time. One-hour developing is available in metropolitan areas. Because slides are arranged in a tray, you cannot rearrange or eliminate a few slides to meet audience needs or time restraints during your presentation.

Production

You can produce 35mm slides in several ways. The first method has been available for years and involves the traditional focus-and-shoot technique. The second method is a more recent technology development and involves the use of a film recorder. In either case, the exposed film must be processed. Another method creates a slide from your hard copy using a slide-maker.

Computer to camera. Shooting directly from the computer to a camera involves taking a picture of the computer display. Slides produced in this matter may show a loss in quality when compared to the original.

Computer to film recorder. A film recorder is a peripheral device that allows computer images to become 35mm slides. It contains a lightproof box with a back (photographic jargon for camera) aimed at a tiny cathode-ray tube that displays the image to be recorded on film.

The camera on a film recorder is normally a 35mm camera, but it can be substituted by an instamatic camera to create 4x5 transparencies. The original purpose of these small transparencies was to shoot a test slide; however, enlargers are available that allow users to project these miniature overheads on the screen. In addition, overhead projectors are available that enlarge the projected image for the audience. Much less space is required to store these miniatures.

The process of creating slides is as easy as telling the computer to print a laser copy. A slide is created by opening the image file from within the film recorder software and giving the print command. Depending upon the particular film recorder and the resolution desired, the imaging of each slide may take between two and 10 minutes. Therefore, the shooting of a roll of film (24 or 36 slides) can require between six and eight hours. Because this process ties up the computer, many companies will batch the slides to the film recorder for shooting during the night hours.

Hard copy to slide-maker. A slide-maker enables you to make slides directly from your hard copy. This device is convenient if you have a photo or other camera-ready material and have no need to generate the material for the slide from your computer.

Computer-based media

A computer-based show eliminates the need for overhead transparencies and 35mm slides because computer-generated shows are displayed directly on a computer screen or projected for viewing by larger groups. The projection methods for this newly developing area of computer-based shows are classified as LCD (liquid crystal display) panels, projection units, videoshow devices, or videotape.

LCD panels or pads are flat-panel units connected to a computer and placed on an overhead projector. The devices allow you to project information displayed on the computer screen. Most units presently in use are monochrome, although more expensive units are available that will project in color. A mouse-controlled pointer on the computer screen will project to focus audience attention on a specific point on the screen.

Projection units represent a direct computer-to-projector system of creating an on-screen presentation. Units can be permanently mounted on the ceiling or a high wall. As with the projection panel, a mouse-controlled pointer is useful to highlight or emphasize various points on the screen. Such units fall into a higher price range; however, clear and colorful projections are possible.

Other types of video presentation devices are coming to the forefront in the rapidly developing technical world. For instance, you can create a presentation on a computer in your office and then go to the presentation and use a videoshow device. This device uses random-access technology to retrieve images from your disk.

Another alternative is to convert computer images to videotape by use of a special card in the computer and a connected video recorder. Announcements or voiceovers can be edited into the final production.

Advantages

The advantages of computer-based shows are many. Very professional shows in full color are possible. Many of the specialized software programs have a screen or slide-show option that allows you to program how the images will advance. The user might key in the number of seconds between visuals, advance to the next image by clicking any key on the computer, or go to a specific slide by simply keying in its number. Information can be modified spontaneously to reflect new information or audience input.

Many presentation programs include dramatic special effects or transition possibilities that are used when the screens change to the next image. These special effects can be fades, wipes, or dissolves similar to those used in a television studio.

Limitations

The main limitation of a computer-based show is high cost—or, stated in another way, the expense of hardware/software/peripherals. Because this technology is advancing so rapidly, equipment will become obsolete rapidly. The equipment may not be available in the right place at the right time. For instance, visuals carried to a meeting on a disk are useless if compatible equipment is not available to project the contents of the disk. Presenters also may find their presentations are relatively inflexible.

Preparation and production

Preparation for a computer show is very similar—using the same software—to making computer-generated visuals for overhead transparencies or slides. However, additional software can be used to create multimedia productions (as described in Chapter 17).

Bulletproof advice

➤ **Selecting and making the visual aids are only part of a Bulletproof Presentation.**

  ▪ Make sure visual aids are appropriate and have the right impact.

➤ **Decide whether your presentation requires handouts.**

  ▪ If it does, decide when you will distribute handouts as you prepare your presentation.

➤ **Use overhead transparencies in small group presentations.**

➤ **Use computer-based presentations if you have the equipment or don't mind the expense.**

CHAPTER 16

DESIGNING VISUAL AIDS FOR YOUR PRESENTATION

In the area of visual skills, these are the areas we'll examine:

➤ Guidelines for use.

➤ Graphic enhancements.

➤ Clip art.

➤ General design principles.

➤ Use of color.

The 3M Corporation conducted a series of studies to determine the effectiveness of visuals. What the studies revealed was that the effective use of visuals can make the speaker appear more professional, better prepared, more credible, and more interesting than those who do not use visuals effectively.

People remember:

- **10 percent of what they read.**

- **20 percent of what they hear.**

- **30 percent of what they see.**

- **60 percent of what they see, hear, and read!**

Guidelines for use

**When using visuals, remember that the most
powerful effect they will have will be to reinforce the
key points of your presentation.**

That is the key reason why I suggest you not even worry about what visuals to have until after you have developed and refined your content. After you have written and edited your presentation several times, you are ready to prepare the visuals that will accompany the ideas. Choose visuals that will help your listeners remember your key points and ideas. They are also useful in aiding your audience with terms, definitions, or topics that are difficult to understand. They should include more than just words; add graphs and charts, pictures and even photographs if necessary.

Audiences are very visual. The more visual you can make the presentation the better—as long as the visuals do not overpower the central message. If you overdue it, then the audience will believe you had little substance and tried to cover it up with pizzazz.

All AV materials will require significant preparation, but some require more time than others. For example, preparing flip-chart sheets can be set up relatively quickly, but a multimedia presentation will take considerably longer. (However, the multimedia presentation can be used over and over again.)

Generally speaking, the higher the complexity of the audio-visual materials, the longer it will take you to prepare them. If you do not have the time or talent to create high-impact visuals, enlist the support of someone else, whether that be support staff, a colleague, or even an external agency. Make sure whomever you choose knows what you want and need and that you guide his or her efforts carefully. **Make sure to keep your audience clearly in mind when you decide what visuals to use.**

Go back to your audience analysis and remind yourself about who will be there. Just as you tailor the content to the people in the audience, you will tailor the media you use as well. Different AV aids will suit the audience in both size and style. However, you are limited in the number of ways you can adapt various media. For example, if you wanted to use computer graphics but discovered that the resolution is poor for the size of the room, you might opt to project onto multiple screens or you may want to choose a different media altogether.

Structuring your visuals

Your presentation can be enhanced by using graphic elements within the design of the visuals. Traditionally, professional graphic artists and typesetters were required to produce a visual including anything other than ordinary typewritten material. Today's computer-software packages allow presenters to incorporate a wide variety of visual enhancements without hiring typesetters and artists to do the work. Even though it is impossible to quickly absorb the knowledge artists and typographers possess, it is possible to follow sound principles of design.

General Design Principles
◈ Use the landscape layout.
◈ Keep alignment consistent throughout.
▪ Usually left justify.
▪ Sometimes center justify.
▪ Almost never right justify.
◈ Balance all the elements.

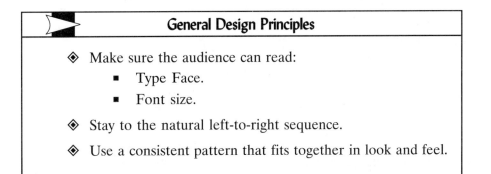

Word-processing and desktop-publishing programs offer the advantages of large, bold fonts along with the incorporation of graphics. However, presentation software makes the visual preparation task much easier. For instance, the programs may include a dialog box asking whether a slide or an overhead size is desired. The size will then automatically adjust for your selection. Other helpful features include the capability of producing miniature visuals for handouts, making notes pages, and running computer-based slide shows.

Graphic enhancements

Rules (lines), boxes and circles, and borders and frames add interest to a visual and make it both eye-catching and pleasing to view. The designer has complete control over colors used for each enhancement. Effective use of blank space is also important.

Rules (lines)

Rules come with a variety of choices and can be scaled (expanded or contracted) from very thin lines to very thick lines. They can be used to divide the visual into sections by placing a horizontal line between the title and the text or using vertical lines to divide the text into two or three columns.

Boxes and circles

Presentation software allows the user to draw squares, rectangles, or circles, using lines of different widths. A box is useful for enclosing either the title, the charts, or both. For an effective 3-D look, boxes and circles can be made with a shadow box.

Borders and frames

Using borders or frames around the entire visual is an alternative to include on a master template design. You can work logos, titles, and subtitles skillfully into the design of the border to keep this identification in front of the audience at all times. However, because slides are automatically inserted into a mount, and transparencies can be mounted, a frame or border around the edge is not essential. Thus, you can have more space available for designing the visual contents. If a frame is not used, identifying information should still be placed attractively in some way at the top or bottom of the visual.

Blank space

The effective use of blank space is an important part of all visuals. Too much information clutters a visual until the viewers either ignore the visual—because it is too complicated—or read it vigorously and forget to listen to the speaker. For the printed page, a desktop-publishing rule of thumb is that a page should have at least 50-percent blank space, which includes all margins and spacing between the various elements on the page. Visuals for projection should probably have as much as 60 or 70 percent blank space. This blank space should be evenly distributed unless your design purposely has an informal balance plan.

Shading and backgrounds

Boxes, circles, or even whole visuals can be filled in by using a shading or screening effect (a gray shading). Most desktop-presentation, graphic, and drawing software can be screened from zero to 100 percent to allow you to get the desired shade. In addition to a normal dot screening, most programs will have a variety of screening patterns from which you can choose.

Background designs are also available that can be imported. A company named Artbeats (*www.artbeats.com*) has a wide selection of designs, ranging from bricks, tiles, and line drawings to natural images, such as water drops or flowers. These backgrounds can help set a theme. For instance, if you were displaying information about a spring fashion show, a flower or raindrop background might be appropriate. However, be careful to keep the background blends from overpowering the visual.

Typography

Individual letters, numbers, and symbols are type. With today's software, you have an enormous variety of options available to you in how you arrange and emphasize words with the use of type. You will need to make choices about many considerations, among them:

→ Typefaces/fonts.

→ Type families.

→ Type styles.

→ Type size.

Typefaces/fonts. The terms *typeface* and *font* are often used interchangeably. However, a *font* is a complete alphabet of uppercase and lowercase letters plus all related symbols, special characters, and punctuation marks. A *typeface* is the style of a particular font.

The entire appearance of a visual can be affected by the selection of typefaces. Characteristics such as formality and informality are expressed by typeface choices.

Two major categories of typefaces are serif and sans serif. *Serifi* are the short cross-strokes that project from the top or bottom of the main stroke of a letter. Type without the serifs are called *sans serif (sans* means without). An example of a sans serif type is Helvetica, which has a very clean appearance.

Some designers of visuals prefer the crisp, clean look of sans serif letters; others believe the serifs, particularly within the modern category, are more distinctive and thus more readable when they are projected.

Try out different fonts to get the readability and look you need. You may want to get opinions and reactions from several people before making your final selection. As a final caution on type fonts, be consistent and restrict yourself to one or two fonts within a single presentation.

Type families. A type family is a variation of a typeface that shows a marked resemblance but has individual design variations in weight, proportion, angle, and surface texture. Though members of a typeface family may use varied and diverse type styles—such as bold, italics, or shadow—they all maintain the basic characteristics of the parent design. A type family can have as few as two members or as many as 40.

As in the case of typeface, restrict your use to two or three variations on a visual. Otherwise, your visual will look cluttered and will be confusing.

Type styles. Frequently used type styles are plain, bold, italic, underscore, shadow, and outline. However, many software programs have a variety of other selections, such as word underline (versus all underline), strikethrough, small caps, all caps, superscript, subscript, and superior.

Type-style variations of a typeface should be used with care to serve their intended purpose. Too much variety on a visual can be distracting and confusing.

Type size. Point size is the smallest typographic unit of measurement. One inch contains 72 points. A 12-point typeface measures 12 points from the top of the highest ascender (letters such as h or l) to the end of the lowest descender (letters such as p or y). Line widths are also measured by points; thus, if you want a thin line, you might use 1 point; for a medium-sized line, 4 points; and for a thick line, 12 points.

Use large, bold type on visuals so information can be easily read. Use a hierarchy of sizes, with headings larger than the other text items in the visual. Appropriate typeface or font sizes for headings is between 24 and 36 points. Other text on the visual could appropriately be 18 to 24 points. Rarely should a font size less than 14 points be used because it will not be visible from a distance.

(Note: Some presentation programs may use other measurements, such as centimeters. When using other measuring systems, be sure to follow the same idea of making headings and subheadings larger than the text in the body.)

Spacing. Both horizontal and vertical spacing should be considered when designing visuals for presentations. Vertical spacing is called either leading (or line spacing), and horizontal spacing is called word spacing.

Leading (or line spacing). Leading, commonly called line spacing, is the vertical space between lines. The term originated in the early days of typesetting when strips of lead were placed between rows of typeset letters on printing plates. This spreads the lines apart vertically for easier reading when printed.

Leading is measured from one baseline (the bottom of letters such as e or a) to the next line. If you are familiar with the typewriting term of *single spacing,* the equivalent publishing term would be 12-point type on 12-point leading (12 on 12).

Software provides automatic leading based on the size of the typeface being used. To increase the space between lines for easier reading, 12-point type could be adjusted with 13- or 14-point leading. Opening up lines is especially important when designing visuals for projection. The additional space really improves readability.

Too much leading, however, may make items appear unrelated. Test out your visuals for their readability when projected.

Word spacing. Word spacing refers to the space between words; it is automatically set in relation to the typeface and size selected. On a printed page, the closer words are to each other, the easier they are to read—within reason. On a visual, words that are too close together may become harder to read. When you are using larger letters, you can add an extra space between letters in words.

An additional variation to horizontal spacing is *kerning,* which is adjusting the distance between individual letters in a word. The letters are usually brought closer together to make a better fit, such as with an A and a V. Some software packages also use the term *tracking,* meaning the compressing or expanding of the space between the letters to make words easier to read.

Kerning and tracking procedures may help with readability as well as allow you flexibility in determining line lengths. Experiment to find the best combination for your selected typeface, size, and family.

Lowercase versus uppercase

As with many of today's publishing words, the terms *lowercase* and *uppercase* originated long ago when typesetters kept their capital letters in the upper case and small letters in the lower case. They would remove letters individually and set them in sequence to form words.

People often believe that using all caps makes a sign more readable or visible. One reason for this assumption is a carryover from typewriter days, when the only way to emphasize print was to make it appear larger with all-capital (uppercase) letters.

Actually, more than 95 percent of all reading material is in lowercase. Thus, people have not had as much practice reading uppercase letters as they have lowercase letters. The lack of descenders and ascenders in capital letters reduces readability, because capital letters are less distinctive at a quick glance.

Therefore, consider using lowercase with initial caps on your visuals—even on the titles. For emphasis, make titles large and bold. You want viewers to read the visual quickly and easily.

Enhancements

Interesting visual effects of stretching, distorting, and rotating text are possible. Software is available that will stretch words into a variety of unique shapes. Some draw programs can rotate or distort text also. Many draw and desktop-publishing programs can wrap blocks of text around irregular objects.

Though these interesting effects may be eye-catching, use them with caution to be sure they add interest without too great a loss of readability. Try for an appealing combination.

Art as design elements

Have you ever picked up a book and thought about how boring it looked—though you had not read a single paragraph? People form judgments very quickly. The use of art can make your visuals draw the attention of your viewers much more readily. However, you should be extremely careful that the image your visuals portray will generate the type of emotional reaction you want.

Art for visuals can be obtained by three different methods: clip art (purchasing commercial art called clip art); scanned art (scanning artwork or photographs by using a scanner to digitize—that is, read into a computer—the images); or user-created art (using draw software to create your own art).

Clip art

An abundance of clip art, frequently called *canned* art or symbols, is available for computer users. Most presentation software is packaged with some clip art. Clip art can be purchased separately by computer users. This canned art is typically delivered on disks with a hard-copy booklet of the images and their file names. Users buy the disk but, in effect, are paying for the right to use the clip art as many times as they wish.

Clip art may be regular commercial software or either public domain or shareware. Regular commercial software is more expensive because the developers are trying to make a profit. They must pay artists for creating the work and also pay their company operating expenses.

Public-domain software is not copyrighted and is free to the public, although the supplier may charge a small fee to cover the costs of disks, mailing, and labor. Shareware has been donated or is shared by the creator rather than sold by a company. As with public-domain software, charges are needed to cover the administrative costs of copying and distributing the clip art. Shareware authors frequently include a message requesting that a small fee be sent if you find the software useful (an honor system).

Due to their larger storage capacity, compact disks and optical disks are used for clip art. Because of the large memory storage required for color line art and photography, the CD-ROM (read-only memory) and optical disks are valuable peripheral devices to use.

Online services through a modem are another method of obtaining clip art. Try *www.clipart.com* and *www.barrysclipart.com.* Companies providing this service charge for each piece of clip art you request for your use. Clip art acquired on this basis from a commercial vendor can cost from $5 to $20 plus an annual subscription price for the service.

Scanned art

Using a scanner and special scanner software, you can digitize artwork, photographs, or text into computer-readable code. Most scanner software has functions that will allow you to manipulate, touch up, or alter the image. You also can import the digitized images into paint software for editing before transferring the images into presentation software for your presentation. With good editing features, you can produce a scanned image that is equal to and sometimes better than the original. In addition, you can lighten or darken color shades, scale an image to the desired size, and even change a color.

Scanners are either gray-scale or color scanners; they are available in either sheet-fed or flatbed units. Scanned images have an upper resolution of 300 dots per inch—the same as most laser printers. Because scanner images rake up to one megabyte of memory for one picture, a hard disk or removable cartridge is necessary.

The applications for scanned art are endless. A company logo, a photograph of a building or the company president, and drawings of a company's product line are all uses that could be made of a scanner. However, using art or photographs for scanning has legal considerations: You may not own the copyright to the image you are scanning. The following paragraphs explain what you can copy and what you cannot.

What's legal?

The licensing agreement on most clip-art packages entitles you to use the art on one computer at a time and as part of any document or publication you choose to distribute. You don't normally have to identify the source of the art in a caption or print a copyright notice. Vendors understandably do, however, object to the sharing of clip art via a network in offices that haven't purchased a site license. As with any single-user program, clip-art disks should only be copied to make a backup or to transfer them to your hard disk.

"Piracy is a significant concern to clip-art manufacturers," says George Riddick, president of Marketing Graphics, Inc. "We want to give people the most flexibility in using images for what they do, but they should live up to the licensing agreement. We offer LAN and site-license agreements. Early on, we had a copyright notice on our images, but it proved impractical. It's not our job to disrupt our customers' presentations."

J. Paul Grayson, chairman and CEO of Micrografx, is also trying to encourage licenses: "That way you can authorize a whole company to use it, and it can be placed on the hard-disk server."

User-created art

Rather than purchasing clip art or scanning images from artwork or photographs, some people like to create their own art using paint, draw, or some presentation software. Then they do not have to worry about another speaker using the same piece of clip art or about violating copyright laws.

A variety of programs is available for creating original art with the computer. Such programs come equipped with tool boxes containing items commonly found on an artist's workstation: pens, paintbrushes, paint buckets, spray cans, color palettes, line/box/circle tools, and so on. Textured patterns and color templates allow interesting effects to be added. Original production of art can be very rewarding for artistically inclined people. It can be quite time-consuming, also.

General design principles

After examining graphic design devices, type, and art, a few general design principles are important to obtain an effective overall look to your visuals.

Landscape vs. portrait

Basic design principles involved in page layout for desktop publishing apply to designing visuals—with one major difference. Visuals for transparencies and 35mm slides should be designed using *landscape* (horizontal) versus *portrait* (vertical) placement.

Most people automatically begin to make their visuals using portrait arrangement simply because that is how text is usually printed on paper for word processing and desktop publishing. Yet, as a general design principle, a landscape arrangement should be used for three reasons.

First, the eye finds it more pleasing to look across rather than down and up. Second, longer lines are available for bullet lists and pictures when the visual is wider. Third, the bottom of a vertically designed visual may not be clearly viewed in most room arrangements.

Alignment

Alignment refers to how the text lines up on the margins or within the center. Consistent alignment throughout the presentation contributes to unity and continuity. Alignments options are left, right, centered, and justified.

Left. Alignment of text for a flush left and ragged right edge will result in varying line lengths. Effort should be made to space the words so a minimum amount of variation occurs. Hyphenation may be used on occasion if absolutely necessary, but it should be used with extreme care to assure readability.

A slight difference in line length gives copy a distinctive and perhaps less formal look. It can even increase legibility by anchoring the eye movement from line to line. Therefore, left alignment is frequently a good choice to use in making visuals.

Right. In right alignment, the lines are uneven on the left but align flush on the right margin. This arrangement is appropriate with only a few lines of type and when you may want to draw interest to the material on the end of the lines.

Centered. A formal and conservative alignment method is centering each line. Both the left and right margins will be ragged. Even though the visual may have a look of dignity, viewers may have trouble reading centered lines as easily, because the viewer must find the beginning of each new line. Therefore, limit your use of centered lines to visuals with no more than two or three lines.

Justified. When all lines are the same length and begin and end at the same positions, text is justified. Justification should not be used if there are wide gaps between words or if the type appears to become smaller or larger when justified. Because justification works better with long lines than short lines, it may not be a good choice for visuals when large font sizes are used.

Balance

Balance is created by placing all the elements on a visual to achieve a general sense of equilibrium, so that visuals do not appear lopsided. Formal balance involves placing the art and type in a centered manner and reflects formality and dignity. For informal balance, images are placed at random (but with an informal balance plan) on the visual. This type of balance is generally more interesting and eye-catching than formal balance and provides much more flexibility in design.

Proportion

As noted previously, blank space improves readability. However, this blank space should be arranged into pleasing proportions. Space around the edges and within the visual itself is extremely important.

Artwork and text should be sized or scaled appropriately to fit the allocated space. Most presentation programs can adjust image and text dimensions for a pleasing appearance.

Sequence

One method of sequencing a design capitalizes on the natural eye movement when reading. Through habit, the eye moves from left to right and from top to bottom in a "Z" pattern when first scanning a page. Therefore, the first area a viewer will see is the upper left-hand corner of the visual. Placing the presentation title in this corner would give the viewer a constant reminder of what the presentation topic is; or, you might want your company logo in that position to remind the audience what company you represent. Because the last area to be viewed is the lower right-hand corner, you might prefer to place your name there.

Emphasis

One element of the visual should dominate all others. This dominating element could be the title, the art, or the message itself. Both color and size are effective tools to use in creating the dominant feature of the visual. How to use color effectively will be discussed in Chapter 17.

Unity

A unifying design, shape, and pattern should hold the visuals together within a presentation. Therefore, the design of the master template is very important. You should follow a theme within a presentation rather than giving an audience the feeling of, *Wow, what will the speaker show next?* As important as the design is, it should almost be considered transparent and should blend in with the talk rather than steal the show.

Refer to the section later in this chapter on the use of color in presentations. Color can add a whole new dimension to your presentation—whether the color consideration is your room, the visuals, or even your handouts.

Always make your opening slide a title slide that includes the title or topic of the presentation, your name and position, your company logo, and any additional information that's appropriate, such as the date.

Opening slide example.

Often your key points can be illustrated in bullet form and will allow your audience to follow along with you. Clip art can add to the ideas, but only if it is appropriate. Computer-generated slides will allow you to use animation techniques to reveal bullets as you go and can be useful in focusing your audience on the key points for each slide.

Simple charts and graphs are also useful; just don't make them too busy! If the audience members are working hard to just understand what they are looking at, they will miss whatever point you are making. Examples of charts or graphs include:

➤ Pie charts to show proportional relationships.

➤ Bar charts to show relationships among sets of data.

➤ Line charts to show trends.

Here are some examples of charts and graphs that explain the information well and poor for a variety of reasons.

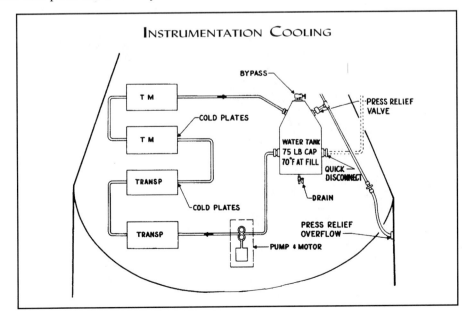

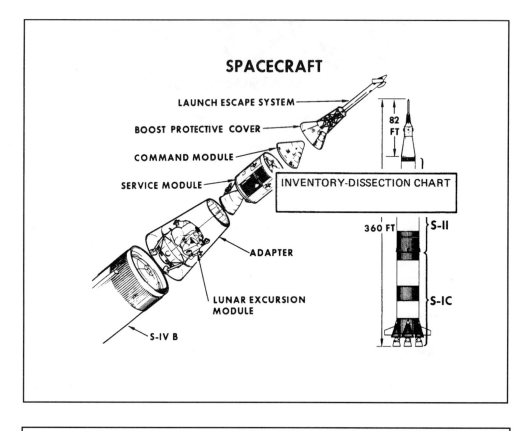

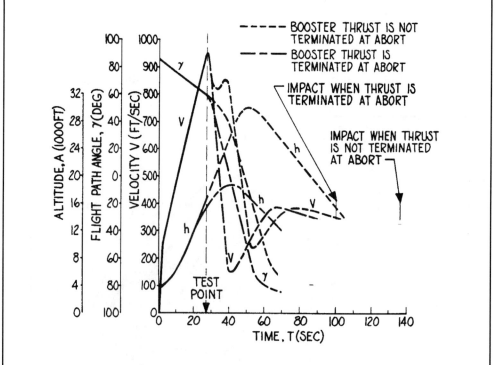

Example of a poor line graph.

Also, I recommend never doing a cut-and-paste of a spreadsheet into a presentation. If you must display numbers, pull out the key numbers and present them. If the source of the numbers is essential, then only show the spreadsheet for a short time, with the applicable numbers highlighted for emphasis. Then move to the next slide with the key numbers alone.

Diagrams and charts are very helpful if they are not too confusing. Examples of useful charts or diagrams might be:

Organizational charts

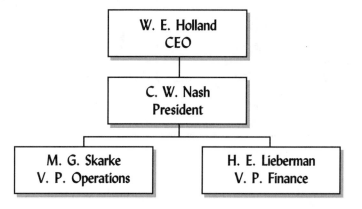

PERT charts

A PERT chart will assist you in illustrating the critical paths in completing a project efficiently.

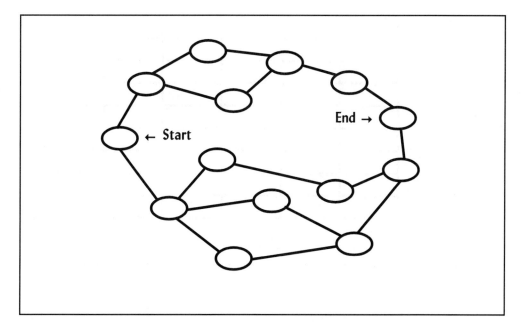

Flowcharts

Flowcharts can help illustrate the steps and decision points involved to complete a process.

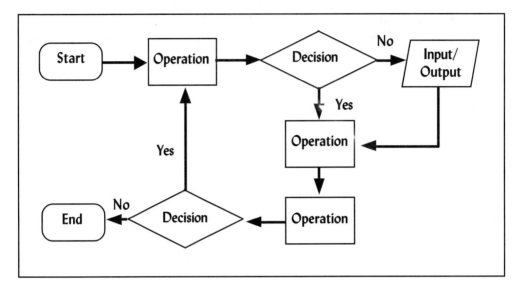

Growth charts

Growth charts will help you illustrate the time various project activities will take to complete.

Case Study Team Project						
Define subject						
Set objectives and strategies						
Project plan						
Research						
Project status						
Interview						
Rough draft						
Rewrite						
Final paper						
Weeks	1	2	3	4	5	6

Week for case study to be completed

Pie charts

Pie charts help you show relationships by dividing the whole into representative parts. Programs such as Excel will aid you by adding colors and generally using numbers that are rounded off for convenience.

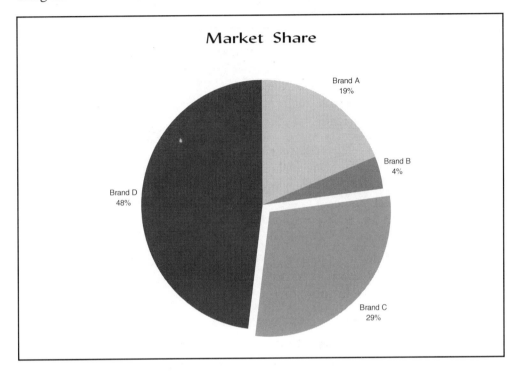

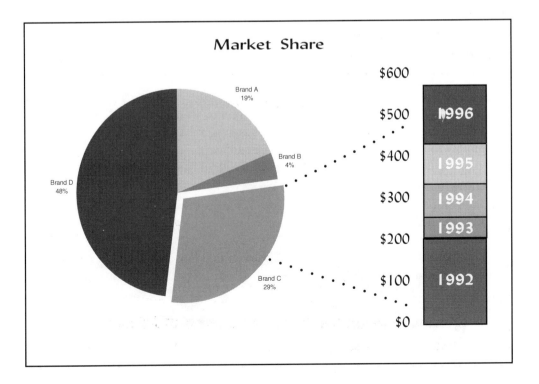

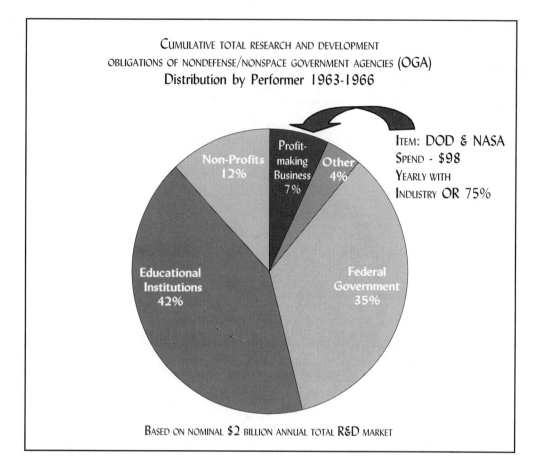

CUMULATIVE TOTAL RESEARCH AND DEVELOPMENT
OBLIGATIONS OF NONDEFENSE/NONSPACE GOVERNMENT AGENCIES (OGA)
Distribution by Performer 1963-1966

ITEM: DOD & NASA
SPEND - $98
YEARLY WITH
INDUSTRY OR 75%

Non-Profits 12%
Profit-making Business 7%
Other 4%
Educational Institutions 42%
Federal Government 35%

BASED ON NOMINAL $2 BILLION ANNUAL TOTAL R&D MARKET

Area charts

Area charts are filled-in line graphs. They can help you compare relationships between volume or quantities.

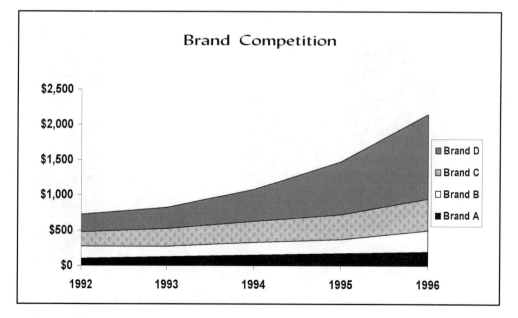

Brand Competition

Brand D
Brand C
Brand B
Brand A

Line charts

Line charts are similar to bar charts, but they can help you show trends over a series of time periods.

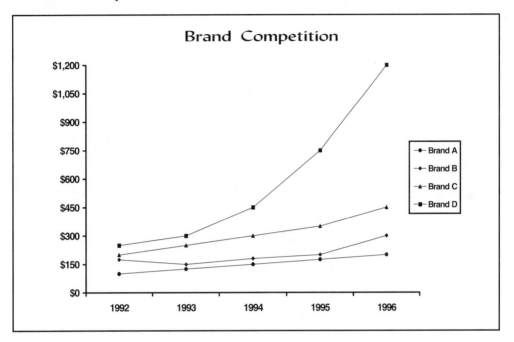

Bar charts

Vertical bar charts are very useful in showing how things have changed over time. Keep these types of charts simple.

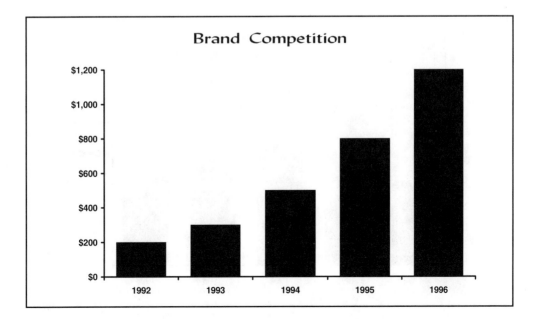

Clustered bar charts are effective in making comparisons as long as you don't make them too complex.

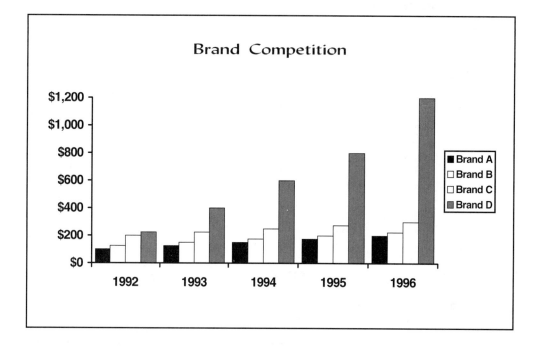

Stacked bar charts will help you make comparisons while emphasizing the total. Hint: Use the darker color at the bottom and make them lighter at the top.

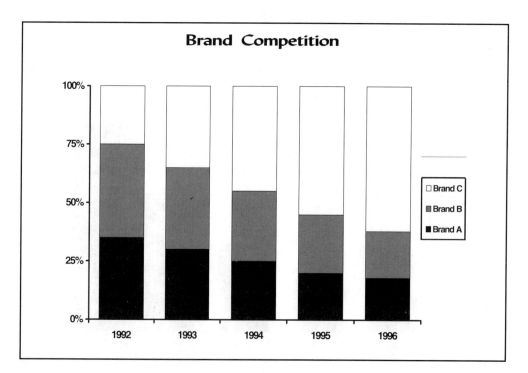

Here is another way to illustrate a comparison. Hint: You should use either an ascending or descending order.

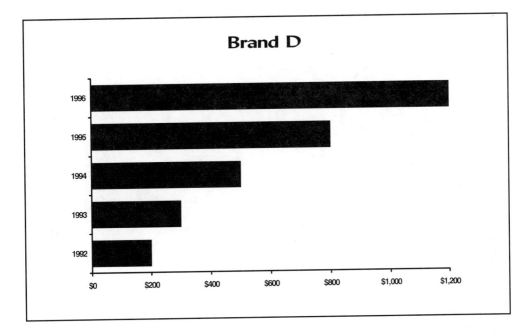

Paired horizontal bar charts are useful if you need to compare positive and negative data.

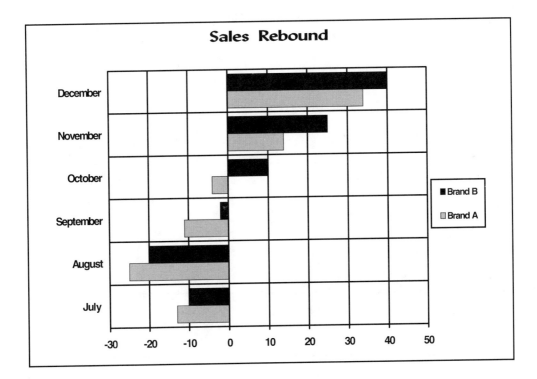

Pictograph

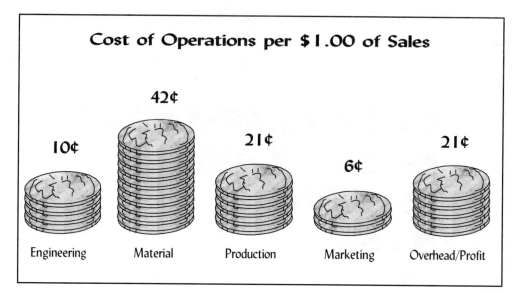

Scattergram

Scattergrams are quite useful in correlating sets of data. The only caution is that it may be too technical as a visual unless you work hard to keep it simple.

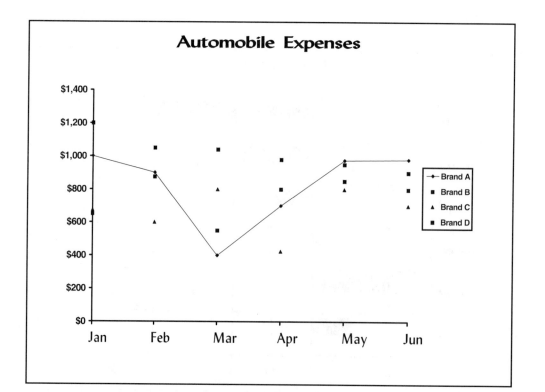

Again, try to keep any diagrams or charts as simple as possible—even if it means leaving out some information.

If you must use spreadsheets or complex diagrams, use a laser pointer or old-fashioned accordion pointer to direct your audience to the pertinent information. Also, it would probably be a good idea to give listeners a hard copy that they can use to follow along. **Be sure to practice with whatever visuals you decide to use.**

You may find that some just do not work. Get rid of them! Remember to use the visuals while you are making the point, but then turn off the projector, cover the flipchart, or put away the prop when you are finished.

Also remember to become familiar with any equipment you will use during the presentation. Check out the equipment before the presentation and find the focus and the power switches. This is especially important if the equipment you will use for the presentation is different from the equipment you practiced with in your preparation. **Whatever you do, don't read the visuals.**

Nothing is more distracting to an audience than having the presenter read the visuals to them. Audiences can read much faster than you can speak, so don't read to them. Remember: These are highly educated, professional people; they can read! Use visuals to reinforce key points and then move on.

Designing your visual aids

When designing your visual aids, refer to your audience analysis so that you make them audience-appropriate. Next, review your situation analysis and confirm that these visual aids will work best in your setting. Then use the design principles that follow.

Low Complexity	High Complexity
Flip Chart	Computer Graphics
Handouts	Video
Overhead Projector	Multimedia
Slide Projector	

Low-complexity audio-visuals

The advantage of low-complexity audio-visual materials lies in their simplicity. They need only a power outlet in the wall (or none at all) and they can be prepared easily in advance. However, these different types of materials are usually best for smaller audiences.

Overhead transparencies

**Overhead transparencies are the
most popular type of visual used in presentations.**

Overhead transparency examples.

They are also called view graphs and foils in some places. They offer the advantages of being very portable and easy to use. There are several software packages on the market today that can help you prepare overheads very inexpensively. Unlike flipcharts, which require you to look away from the audience, overheads allow you to face the audience as you make a point.

This is an excellent way to present charts and graphs. You can use a pointer to draw attention to particular information, such as numbers, without blocking the audience's view. Another successful tip is to take a pen or pencil and lay it on the overhead, with the shadow pointing to the information you wish to highlight. You can do that without standing there pointing at it. I have also seen people use the little hors d'oeuvre "swords" very effectively for the same purpose.

When you begin to build these overheads, the best route is to follow the basics for construction that come with the various software packages. These software packages, such as Microsoft Power Point, have templates that you can use to develop the presentation slides quite effectively. I know that many times it seems so obvious that a presenter has used the basic Microsoft templates, but I would rather see that than a series of slides or overheads that are all bold-faced and capital letters. I have seen enough of those to know that presentation will never be Bulletproof!

General design principles

➤ Most overheads will probably be in the landscape layout. There may be times when portrait layout is the best, but they're the exception rather than the rule.

➤ Alignment of the text lines should be consistent throughout the presentation, whether you elect left-justified or center-justified. Rarely will right-justified make sense except for a few lines to draw attention to them.

➤ Balance of all the elements will provide interest and not make the overhead appear "lopsided."

➤ Readability is important. Make sure the audience will be able to read the type from the most distant part of the room. Increase the font size if you think there could be a problem.

➤ Stay within the natural left-to-right sequencing that most people are accustomed to seeing.

➤ Unify the design of the slides so that the various overheads or slides have a consistent pattern and look as though they fit together.

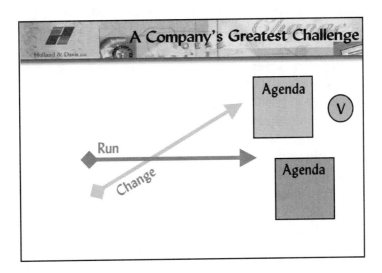

Balance the elements to provide interest.

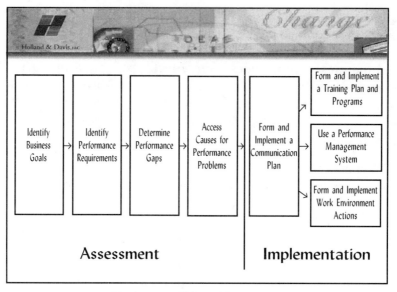

Use the natural left-to-right sequence.

Use of color

Research has shown that color enhances the communication process. It accelerates what people remember and increases their comprehension. That is why colors are used in advertising so often. Colors can be very effective in drawing attention to specific points, particularly red. However, use red sparingly or it will not only lose the effect you want, but it will actually irritate the audience. (Not only does red have a negative connotation in most people's minds, but the color will "bleed" in most people's vision, making it harder to focus.) Yellow can be used in a way similar to a highlighter pen on visuals, as long as it is easy to see.

Working with color

Today's technology makes it possible to use color in designing presentations—with the potential of selecting 16.8 million colors. Of course, color output devices (printers, projection units, or film recorders) are needed to make use of these colors in your presentation.

Because using color can greatly increase your production costs, you may need justification for this added expenditure. A summary of research findings on the effectiveness of color is given later in this chapter.

Within visuals, color can be used for coding/signaling purposes, for mood effects/color psychology, and for improving readability. Certain combinations work better than others.

Coding/signaling. Color is a useful coding or signaling tool to show either association or differentiation. It can show emphasis or hierarchies, too.

Association or differentiation. Colors create identity. For instance, the color green means money or go; yellow says caution; red means stop or danger. Developing an effective color scheme for a presentation can establish a similar identity, although the associations may be different from those just mentioned. For instance, if you are developing a motivational speech, you might want to use red in your background theme throughout the presentation to show a high level of intensity—with the interpretation of *go for it* rather than stop. In contrast, a yellow background would give a cheery light touch to the presentation, not caution.

Color is useful in distinguishing between elements. Handouts using different colors of paper can help the audience to find a particular sheet quickly; you can say, for instance, "On the blue sheet...." Illustrations on the visuals (and handouts, if a color printer is available) can be done in color to distinguish different classes, elements, or levels.

Emphasis or hierarchies. You can draw attention to type or graphics in your visual by using a dark, vivid color on a light background or a light color on a dark background. For example, in using a dark blue background, white can be the most dominating color (useful for the title), followed by a bright yellow for a bullet list. Both white and yellow stand out; because white contrasts more, the reader's eye will travel to the white title because it will dominate over the yellow list.

Hierarchies, showing either a logical progression or level of importance, can be indicated by using colors going from either light to dark or gray to bright. In contrast, a rainbow progression gives equal importance to all items.

Mood effects/color psychology. Color plays a role in how we think, feel, and act. There has been a great deal of research on how color affects people. Dr. Stephen Mason, a psychologist in Irvine, California, has done some work that you should consider in selecting colors for your presentation visuals. As you prepare for a presentation, use these color theories to help you set the mood you wish to establish within the audience.

In Bulletproof Presentations, the trick is to use colors to enhance the impact of your ideas. Variety is important. Don't use the same old template of bullet points in black all the way through the presentation. Mix colors for emphasis or to affect mood.

Red seems to be a color that demands attention. Red says, "This is important, so pay attention." However, be careful in using red. This color has a negative connotation for some groups. For example, "red ink" equals bad news to financial types. Also, if you use too much red, it has a tendency to "bleed" and that makes it hard to read. My suggestion is to use red sparingly—that is, to command attention or as an accent only.

Yellow will get an audience's attention, too, but the mood will be slightly different. Yellow is often easier to spot than red (note that fire engines are almost universally yellow now). Yellow is an optimistic color that draws attention because it is seen as cheerful and sunny. During a presentation, save yellow for important information that you want to be received in a positive way. However, be careful with yellow, as it can be hard to see at times in a large room.

The use of pink might seem strange because it is not seen as a "business color." However, research by law-enforcement officials found that pink had a calming effect on prisoners. Even the most agitated prisoners began to calm down when placed in a pink room. In a Bulletproof Presentation, then, if you simply want to present a message and then get away with an absolute minimum of resistance from the audience, consider using pink!

Blue and green are cool colors that put people in a quiet and tranquil mood. If you are expecting a problem with a particularly controversial topic or recommendation, you might use a pale blue or green background, which will cause the group to be more subdued and could assist you in keeping the temperature down.

Finally, violet has a remarkable effect on people if used wisely. For some reason, this color has the ability to make otherwise conservative business people become suddenly very creative and innovative. If you want to bring out some creative interaction during your presentation, consider using violet. Violet is one of the most popular colors among teenagers, so if I discovered a large group of teenagers in my audience analysis, violet would be a color I would want to use. However, too much violet can create a problem. When used in excess, violet can cause people to become drowsy and you could find yourself fighting to keep the audience awake.

Improving readability

For the psychology of color to be effective, however, visuals must be legible. Poor color choices and combinations can hinder rather than help. Try out color visuals to see if they are readable, especially from a distance.

As a word of caution in selecting color combinations, remember that approximately 10 percent of the male population and almost .5 percent of the female population is colorblind and may have trouble distinguishing between colors such as red and green. Therefore, they would have trouble interpreting a graph using red and green side by side. They might see one large area rather than two different areas.

Color definitions. Color is fundamental to virtually every facet of life. Yet, the way one individual perceives a color may be different from another individual's perception.

If colored lights in the light primaries of red, green, and blue are projected in overlapping circles, they mix to form the secondary colors of yellow, magenta, and cyan. Where all three primaries overlap, the result is the color white. This system is called additive color and is used in computer graphics and color television.

Colors seen on objects operate in a different system than the system seen in beams of light. In this type of system, the result of the three primary colors overlapping is the color black. This method is the one used in printing processes.

Other elements useful in understanding color are hue, saturation, lightness, and brightness. In computer graphics, another element is graduated color.

Graduated colors

Many computer programs using color can produce special effects—called graduated, gradient, or ramped—within colors dissolving into interesting blends. One color, two colors, or a whole range of colors can be selected. Color ramping may be specified as vertical, horizontal, diagonal right, diagonal left, from corner, or from title.

The use of graduated colors can provide an interesting, appealing background for your master template. Some programs will allow objects or text to be filled with graduated color. However, be sure the colors do not distract or reduce readability.

Color research

Research has shown that color enhances the communication process. Ronald Green concluded in an article titled "The Persuasive Properties of Color," which appeared in the October 1984 issue of *Marketing Communications,* that color:

1. Accelerates learning, retention, and recall by 55 to 78 percent.

2. Improves and increases comprehension up to 73 percent.

3. Increases willingness to read up to 80 percent.

4. Increases recognition up to 78 percent.

5. Increases motivation and participation up to 80 percent.

6. Reduces error count from 55 to 35 percent.

7. Sells (products and ideas) more effectively by 50 to 85 percent.

The effects of color also apply to more than the presentation media. Many color theories can also be applied to the presentation environment. Do not forget to consider the colors when you are doing your situation analysis.

One additional note regarding color: If you use a company logo, get the exact logo from the company communications department so you can reproduce the colors exactly. Many companies are very fussy about the colors of their logo and are not amused when someone, even within the company, does not reproduce it correctly.

Software packages allow you to print paper copies for your notes as well, so you never need to look at the screen to know what is there. An additional advantage of using overheads is the ability to put your presentation notes on the borders of the boards that hold the transparencies, if you choose that approach. (See the section on software packages in the next chapter for more details.) Finally, remember to practice with your overheads. They are a little more difficult to manage during a presentation than they may look, because experienced presenters make it look easy. The time spent practicing and moving smoothly between overheads will mark you as a confident, qualified presenter!

A helpful hint here is to place your overhead on the glass of the projector and check it on the screen to make sure it is straight and square. Then take two pieces of masking tape and place them on one of the upper corners and the same side to form a right angle. Bump the overhead up against the tape a couple of times to create an edge. You now have a frame in which to slide your overheads and you can be certain that they are placed correctly on the screen without even looking.

Sometimes you may want to use a blank acetate sheet and write on it as you present. This can be very helpful to the audience particularly if you are spontaneously answering questions, for example.

Creating overheads and using an overhead projector limit the size of the audience to smaller groups of less than 50 people. If your audience is much larger than that, audience members will have trouble reading the screen. However, by projecting the overheads using a computer and a projector allows you to use those same overheads for very large audiences.

Screen position

One of the problems with projecting on a screen in a fairly large room is the "Keystone effect" that occurs. It is called that because the angle of the light from the projector, whether it is an overhead or a computer projector, causes the light to hit the screen at an angle that resembles a keystone. As a result, presenters can sometimes have a difficult time adjusting the focus. You get the bottom of the screen in focus only to discover that the top of the screen is now out of focus!

Keystone effect

The best way to correct the problem is to arrange the screen so that the top of the screen is closer to the projector than the bottom of the screen. Most portable screens will have a bar at the top of the frame that folds out and allows you to project the top of the screen a few inches away from the frame toward the audience. In rooms where the screen comes down from the ceiling, if you can use tape or rubber bands to hold the bottom of the screen back against the wall, it will provide the same results. Either way, you will have really improved the problem caused by the keystone effect.

Handouts

Sometimes the audience will need to follow along with you as you make your presentation. In that case, you must give them a written copy of appropriate material before you begin speaking. However, if they do not require that information, *do not give it out!*

Handouts can be valuable for a presentation, but do not pass anything to the audience members while you are speaking.

They will begin to look through the handouts and totally ignore what you are saying. It's better to use them at the end of the presentation as a way for the audience to remember what you said.

Some of you may be thinking right now, *Right! Like I could not hand the management committee the handouts until after the presentation!* I do understand that situation and I would never suggest you make listeners mad by not giving them a handout. However, **I suggest that you use your audience analysis to give you clues as to what these people will want to see and put that very early in the presentation.**

If you wait too long, they will either interrupt you or begin shuffling through the papers and ignore your presentation. That is not a Bulletproof approach!

Also, consider the appropriateness of the materials. Many audiences will feel they have gained more from your presentation if they can take something tangible away with them. It could be a booklet of your overheads or slides as future reference or copies of white papers or position papers that have been written on your topic.

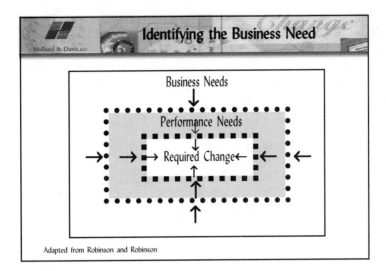

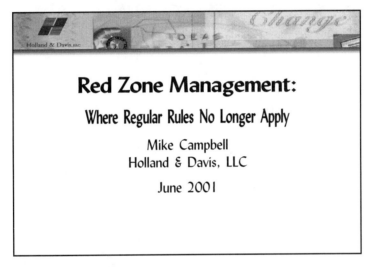

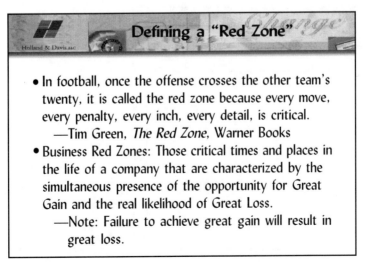

Notice the difference when too many words are on the slide.

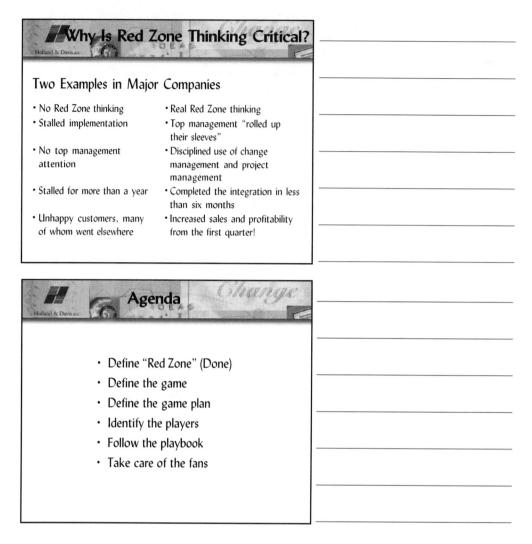

Example of a notes page with 3 slides.

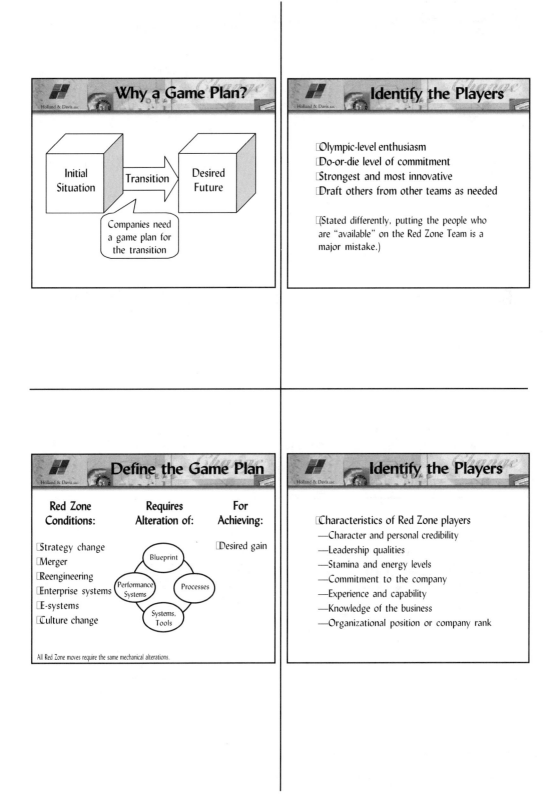

Example of a notes page with 4 slides.

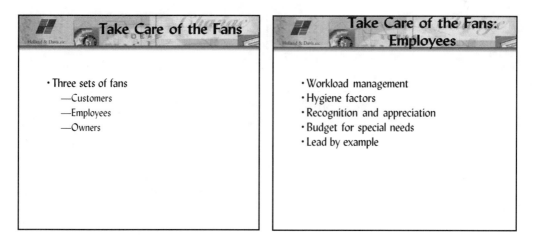

Take Care of the Fans

- Three sets of fans
  - —Customers
  - —Employees
  - —Owners

Take Care of the Fans: Employees

- Workload management
- Hygiene factors
- Recognition and appreciation
- Budget for special needs
- Lead by example

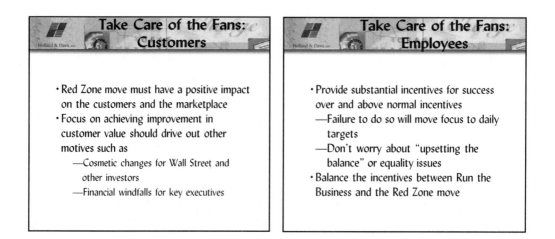

Take Care of the Fans: Customers

- Red Zone move must have a positive impact on the customers and the marketplace
- Focus on achieving improvement in customer value should drive out other motives such as
  - —Cosmetic changes for Wall Street and other investors
  - —Financial windfalls for key executives

Take Care of the Fans: Employees

- Provide substantial incentives for success over and above normal incentives
  - —Failure to do so will move focus to daily targets
  - —Don't worry about "upsetting the balance" or equality issues
- Balance the incentives between Run the Business and the Red Zone move

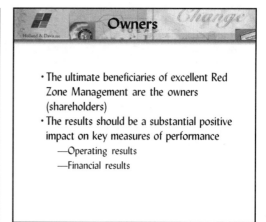

Take Care of the Fans: Red Zone Customer Scorecard

Customer		Present Position				Desired Position				Needed Action	
Value	Attributes	Our	C1	C2	C3	Our	C1	C2	C3	Advance	Hold
Convenience	Location	+		+		+		+			√
	Access	+	+			+	+				√
Need Fulfillment	Price		+	-		+	+			√	
	Quality	+	-			+	+	+		√	
	Service	-		+		+	+	+		√	

Owners

- The ultimate beneficiaries of excellent Red Zone Management are the owners (shareholders)
- The results should be a substantial positive impact on key measures of performance
  - —Operating results
  - —Financial results

Example of a notes page with 6 slides.

If people ask you for copies of materials you referenced and did not bring, be sure to get a business card from them and send them the material as a follow-up. However, be certain that you *do* follow up!

Your personal and professional reputation
can be either enhanced or diminished
by how well and how timely you respond to requests.

Flipcharts

You can prepare any number of sheets on the flipchart in advance and use them very effectively to highlight information during your presentation. **Use a variety of colors for each point so it stands out clearly, and make sure everyone can see the flipchart.** Be careful with your writing! You must write so the audience can read it.

Don't be concerned if you don't have the greatest handwriting ability. As long as people can read it, they will give you the benefit of not having the most stylish handwriting. If you are capturing ideas during your presentation, obviously try to spell correctly, but most people will be forgiving of a few errors. If you are unsure of either of these, perhaps another audio-visual aid would be better.

Posters are not often used in business presentations, but they can be very valuable if you are going to repeat your presentation several times at different locations. You will be able to prepare them in advance and they are quite portable. Any charts you make in advance should have every word spelled correctly.

The limitation on both flipcharts and posters is the size of the audience. To be effective, you probably cannot have an audience of more than 20 people. Otherwise, they will be difficult to read and they will only irritate your audience. With small groups they can be very helpful.

Slides

Slides can add various dimensions to a presentation, particularly when you need sharp, clear colors or images. You can use the same software programs to produce slides that are available for creating overhead viewgraphs. When you decide to use slides, you need to prepare your slides in a carousel well in advance of the presentation. Slides are an excellent choice when the room is too large for an overhead projector. They are also great for illustration purposes when pictures will help convey the message.

The major disadvantage to slides, in my opinion, is the need to turn the lights down to see them. Too often, I have seen audiences struggle to keep their eyes open when the room was darkened. (This is particularly true just after lunch.)

However, if you believe slides are best for your audience and your presentation, be sure to practice operating the projector before you give your presentation so you can become familiar with the controls.

Props

Anytime you can use a model or prop effectively, do it!

They are excellent at helping the audience to understand your main points. However, they must add to the presentation, not become the presentation. Again, the key is allowing your audience to see the prop. It is terrific to make a point about using your Palm Pilot effectively, but if the audience members cannot see the one you have in your hand, they will become frustrated.

High-complexity audio-visual aids

The impact of using high-complexity AV aids can be striking and well worth the effort. These aids involve a higher level of technical complexity and may require a specialized team to set them up. Remember there is a higher chance of breakdown or failure and you will need to make contingency plans just in case. Always take along a series of low-complexity materials with you as backup and make sure there will be someone at the presentation who can help you if things go badly.

Computer-based media

A computer-based presentation eliminates the need to produce overhead transparencies and slides because you are driving the presentation right off a computer. The newest projection equipment is becoming smaller and cheaper every day. At the time this book went to press, you could buy a very powerful computer projector weighing less than six pounds for less than $3,000.

There are obvious advantages to this system. First of all, you can modify slides almost literally right up to the time you begin to present. Although I don't recommend doing that, sometimes circumstances require those types of changes— for example, if you just received some new financial figures that need to replace the figures you originally had in your presentation. A mouse-controlled pointer will allow you to emphasize or highlight certain points as you speak.

The major limitation to this presentation technology is the cost of laptop computers. This presentation approach is very difficult to do with a standard PC. You need a laptop to be effective, and laptops can be expensive relative to desktop PCs. Try to borrow or rent equipment if you do not have it available. Because the technology changes so rapidly the equipment could become obsolete very rapidly.

Videos and CD-ROMs

Use video to show short, live action images or a taped message from a speaker who is not able to attend in person. You can use CD-ROM packages with moving images and an audio track with a large monitor with speakers. Again, in either case, be sure the monitor is large enough for the entire audience to see without straining.

Computer graphics and animation

Software can be used to display various types of graphs, charts, or three-dimensional images onto a screen. You can use moving graphics to show how data can change over time quite effectively. (We will explore more about this technology in the next chapter.) There is an abundance of clip art on the market these days that can be used for a variety of different presentations. Most presentation-software packages will have clip art as part of the package; however, the images have been used so often that it might be wise to purchase another package "off the shelf." These images can be relatively inexpensive, and most clip art packages will let you reproduce the images as many times as you wish.

Scanning images into your computer and then pasting them into a presentation is another matter altogether. I am not a legal expert, but there are copyright considerations involved with scanning images into your presentation. If you work for a company, using the company logo for a presentation is probably no problem. However, if you conduct training programs and are going to use the company logo on your material as a way to "customize" the materials for your client, you should obtain permission to use the logo. If you are at all unsure about using an image, even one copied off the Internet, it is best to consult an attorney to be safe.

Service bureaus

For many of these complex visual aids, I would highly recommend that you consider using service bureaus for production. These people specialize in the types of highly complex visual aids discussed in this chapter and will undoubtedly do a better job than you can as an amateur. Please consider that you are devoting a great deal of time and effort to develop a Bulletproof Presentation and that all that effort can be washed away if your visuals come across as amateurish.

You will need to sort out the advantages and disadvantages of these various media and pick the one that will best meet your objectives and situation for the presentation. **If you have not done so, look back over the situation analysis you did earlier to remind yourself of the various elements to consider.**

Visual aids will add the "sparkle" you want in any presentation.

Think carefully about which additional items you might need to make a Bulletproof Presentation. Here are some ideas:

- ➤ Sets of magic markers for writing on flipcharts.

- ➤ Spare flipchart pads.

- ➤ Blank acetate sheets for writing on an overhead projector.

- ➤ A laser pointer for a distant screen.

- ➤ Backup disks or CDs for multimedia presentations.

- ➤ Extension cords for power.

- ➤ Adapters if you are going overseas for your presentation.

Taking the time to prepare the logistics of your presentation will provide tremendous rewards during the presentation. Just remember: Don't begin working on visuals until after you have done everything else first!

Practice

The best advice any presentation coach can give you is to practice, practice, practice.

The more practice you have done, the more comfortable you will feel, and the more confident you will appear to the members of the audience. Practice with the content and the visuals you will use. Try to duplicate the setting as closely as you can while you rehearse.

Rehearsal is a vital part of preparing for any Bulletproof Presentation. It offers an ideal opportunity to become comfortable with your material and to smooth out any rough spots in your delivery. **Remember: You cannot practice too much!**

Each time you practice, you should be able to rely less on your notes. Also practice handling any questions you are sure will be asked during the presentation.

Be sure to practice *aloud*. The main point of practicing is to learn your material. It is your best opportunity to fine tune the presentation. Practice by speaking clearly and with the tone and volume you anticipate to use during the presentation.

Invite a colleague or friend to listen to your presentation and give you feedback and criticism. Ask for an honest evaluation of the presentation and look for suggestions for improvement. Remember to let your friend or colleague know the audience's background, as that may help him or her not only listen, but also give you constructive criticism. Ask him or her about any distracting mannerisms and whether you body language is appropriate.

Bulletproof advice

➤ **People remember 60 percent of what they read, hear, *and* see.**

- Powerful visuals will reinforce the key points of your presentation and should include more than just words.

➤ **Keep any diagrams and charts as simple as possible.**

- It may mean that you have to leave out some information, but they will be more useful and more compelling as complements to your words.

➤ **Whether you choose high-complexity or low-complexity visuals, use the general design principles.**

- Make sure you unify the design of the visuals so they have a consistent pattern and look like they fit together.

CHAPTER 17

CREATING "COOL"
VISUALS USING
SOFTWARE PACKAGES

Because many companies, as well as smaller engineering and computer firms, no longer have a graphics department to produce visuals, this chapter suggests various software packages that are available for the personal computer. Because new packages are continually released, it is not meant to be an exhaustive listing, but rather to reinforce that there are several different options available.

All of these packages include blueprints that allow the creation of quality visuals that will have the look and feel of the professionally produced visuals of the past.

Match visuals to your audience using the audience analysis, but remember: **The visuals should not become the presentation**. They add sparkle and "pizzazz," but they cannot carry an entire presentation.

Windows versions of the top three presentation graphics packages are Microsoft PowerPoint, Lotus Freelance Graphics, and Software Publishing Corp.'s Harvard Graphics.

To provide the ease of understanding, I've divided the software packages into preparation and presentation.

Preparing the content

After you have done the hard work of analyzing your audience and situation, developed your overriding theme, and chosen a strategy, one of the great features of these software packages is to allow you to pick from templates and select the scenario that best fits your presentation situation.

> **Be careful when using the templates or your presentations will
> start to look too "canned."**

They even offer a suggested outline, which walks you through the creation of your message.

Of the three packages, Lotus Freelance offers the most content rich masters. Freelance provides more than 30 SmartMaster Content topics based on the advice of such notable business experts as Philip Kotler, Trout and Ries, and Zig Ziglar.

When you start a new presentation in Freelance, you are first asked to select the Content and Look of the presentation.

As you browse through the topics, a brief description tells you what each SmartMaster Content Topic is designed for. Below the content topics is a list of "Looks" and a thumbnail image of each. Specific Looks have been preselected for each SmartMaster, but you also have the option of replacing them with one of the 125 Looks included with the program.

Once you select the Content and Look, a list of pages for that topic appears. You now have the option of selecting any or all of the pages to include in your presentation. As you browse through the list, you once again receive a written description of what is included on each page. You also get to view a thumbnail image depicting the page's design. **What really sets Freelance's SmartMaster Content pages apart from the other programs is the level of detail.**

Not only does it suggest textual content, but it also includes suggested clip art, diagrams, and data charts, which make it easy to break free of the word chart doldrums.

PowerPoint's key head-start feature is the AutoContent Wizard.

Introduced in PowerPoint 4.0, the AutoContent Wizard in the Windows 2000 version has incorporated more presentation topics to choose from, as well as more criteria for structuring your presentation. This tool is particularly helpful for the novice presenter. When you create a presentation using the Wizard, you are asked to select the type of presentation you intend to give from a list of six topics or to select "Other" to see a more detailed list of content templates, including Creativity Session, Employee Orientation and Financial Report. Later versions can be modified, either by the user or by the systems administrator in your company (if you have one), who can also add (or restrict) additional templates including those that contain your company logo.

Once you select the topic of your presentation, the Wizard asks you to select a style (professional, contemporary, or default); the length of your presentation (30 minutes or less, more than 30 minutes or undecided); and the type of output you intend to use (black-and-white overheads, color overheads, on-screen, or 35mm slides). It even asks if you intend to print handouts. Once you answer all of these questions, the AutoContent Wizard structures your presentation. However, you can chose to simply choose a type and click "Finish" without tailoring the template with additional inquiries.

Unlike with Freelance, however, the suggested content is primarily limited to textual directions for what you should include on each slide.

Microsoft could really improve the value of this tool by helping users with better clip art, not just help with the words. SPC's Harvard Graphics was actually the first program to incorporate content-based master templates with its Quick Presentations feature.

SPC has enhanced this feature in the Windows version by adding more topics. With Quick Presentations, you select from a list of presentation subjects, such as

Brainstorming, Sales Presentation, or Marketing Plan. As you browse through the list, the program provides a brief description of each, as well as thumbnail previews, which you can scroll through to see the design and layout for each slide. You are also asked to select the output medium: screen, black-and-white printer, color printer, film recorder, or plotter (a specialized printer that produces maps, large posters, and so forth).

From this information, Harvard creates a structure for your presentation. Its approach is a bit different than the other two packages in that it actually creates specific content for a model company.

The templates provide suggestions for creating a variety of chart types throughout the presentation to make it more visual, as well as tips for tasks such as hyperlinking to slides based on your audience's response.

The downside to using content masters from popular presentation packages, of course, is that you may walk in with a presentation nearly identical to the one just delivered by someone else.

Whether you decide to use content masters to create your presentation, an integral feature for organizing your thoughts and honing your message is the outliner. Most outliners are pretty standard: You type in or edit your text topic by topic, just as you learned to do in elementary school when you tackled your first report. Although the outliners are pretty standard, Freelance 96 has brought some life, yet added functionality to its outliner, by including pictures of your presentation pages next to the text.

The pictures aren't just for looks, either. As you add or edit text on the yellow legal pad outliner, the picture changes to provide you with immediate visual feedback. If you don't want these visual cues, you have the option to turn off the page display. Additional features in the outliner include the ability to edit text attributes and rearrange your presentation content by dragging and dropping, just like in the slide sorter view.

What about existing material?

In today's busy work environment, there isn't time to reinvent the wheel every time you set out to create a presentation. If you have existing content out there somewhere, you want to be able to find and incorporate it into your presentation as seamlessly as possible.

All three programs offer some nice features for working with existing data.

Freelance, for example, has a feature called the Presentation Page Browser, which is designed to guide you through the process of copying pages from an existing presentation into a new presentation. With the Browser, you can either click and add, or drag and drop pages into your presentation. The added pages automatically inherit the look of the current presentation.

Similarly, PowerPoint features File Finder which allows you to access and preview information in other presentations or documents that you may want to include in your presentation.

All three programs support allowing you to drag and drop information between applications. Harvard Graphics is particularly strong in this area. You can drag and drop graphic images from another application into the Slide Editor;

drag and drop a presentation or style file from Windows Explorer into the Editor, Slide Sorter, or Top Window; drag and drop a chart or graphic object from the Slide Editor to another application; drag and drop within the data form; drag and drop slides between presentations in the slide sorter; and drag and drop text into a text edit tool.

Embellishing your presentation

Everyone likes to add a little pizzazz to his or her presentations, whether it's a nice drop-shadow text effect, a really cool textured background, or some whiz-bang multimedia.

For many business users, however, these kinds of embellishments require more time and effort than they are able, or willing, to invest. With the Windows 98 versions of PowerPoint, Freelance, and Harvard Graphics, it's now much faster and easier to spruce up your presentations.

PowerPoint and Freelance, in particular, have enhanced their multimedia capabilities greatly over previous versions. In PowerPoint, for example, you can now add animated builds and sound effects to clip art. You can animate text and objects through the Animation Effects toolbar or from the Animation Settings dialog box in the Tools menu. The Animation Effects toolbar pops up to build effects, such as Animate Title, which makes the title fly across the page into position; Build Slide Text, which flies each bullet point onto the slide from the left side of the page; or the bolder Drive-in Effect, which flies each bullet point in from the right accompanied by the sound of screeching brakes.

You can also add animated builds easily with Powerlink's Animation Effects toolbar. Within Animation Settings, you can specify how to build the object, which effect to apply, when to build the object, and whether you want the object to dim after the build is completed.

Freelance 96 also allows you to add animated effects to objects, as well as text and slides. Because Freelance's tools are organized by tasks, you need to highlight the object that you wish to animate to bring up the appropriate tool set. When you want to add effects to an object, go to the Screen Show Effects dialog box in the Group menu. This dialog box allows you to display the object either as the page appears or after the page appears. If you choose the second option, you can bring the object up with a click of the mouse or set it to appear after a specified number of seconds. To see how this works out with the other items on your slide, there is a Sequence button that allows you to see a list of everything on the page and the order in which it is set to play. You can also rearrange this order by dragging and dropping items in the list. In addition to setting the sequence for transitions to take place, the Screen Show Effects dialog box allows you to select the effect you want to apply; attach a sound; or even attach an action, such as jump to another slide, run an application, or play a movie.

Both Freelance's and PowerPoint's approaches produce the same end result: quick and easy builds that can add life to your screen presentations.

In addition to screenshow embellishments, all three programs feature a number of enhancements to help you create more graphically appealing presentations. Freelance, for example, provides more than 100 professionally designed diagrams, including flowcharts, Venn diagrams, pyramid charts, and time lines, which help you transform boring words into graphic content that is both more interesting and more understandable to your audience. Adding one of these ready-made charts is as easy as adding clip art. You can also create custom diagrams from the wide selection of text shapes and connectors included with Freelance's drawing tools.

For more advanced users, PowerPoint has beefed up its fill options, offering texture fills, multicolor gradient fills, and semi-transparent fills. The program comes with 12 built-in texture fills, including wood grains, marble, sand, granite, cloth, and even crumpled paper. You can also add your own textures and your own bitmaps as fills. Multicolor gradient fills include Fire, Early Sunset, and Rainbow. And with semi-transparent fills you can create semi-transparent shadows and see-through screens.

The most important way Harvard Graphics helps you to enhance your presentation is through its highly integrated Advisor system. As you work on your presentation, Advisor offers a three-tiered system to help you create a more effective presentation. The first tier is Quick Tips, which provides advice for carrying out actions specific to the content of the slide you're working on, such as "To text, double-click it."

The second tier is Design Tips, which offers style guidance. Once again, the advice is dependent on the content of your slide, so if you choose to add a pie chart to your slide, Advisor will tell you what a pie chart is best used for and give you tips on how to use it most effectively.

The third tier is Check Design, which works similar to a spell check, combing through your presentation looking for style errors, such as text that is too small to read. A particularly nice addition to version 4.0 is Fixer Mode. If the program finds a design problem, you can click on the Fix button to automatically go to the problem area. Advisor then guides you through correcting the problem.

Collaborating with others

In today's business environment, few presentations represent the effort of a single individual anymore.

More often than not, several individuals collaborate on a presentation, each offering their own perspective. Sometimes the creation process is broken down between multiple team members. At other times, one author takes on the primary task of creating a presentation, while the other team members offer their feedback as the project progresses. Coming from Lotus, the king of groupware, it should be no surprise that Freelance Graphics offers the most innovative approach to collaborating on presentation creation.

Freelance 96 provides two new key features designed to aid this collaboration: TeamMail and TeamReview. Using any VIM or MAPI e-mail system, TeamMail enables you to send a presentation file, or selected pages from a presentation file, to your fellow team members.

You can choose to broadcast the presentation to several individuals at once or route it to a list of people one by one, for editing, commenting or creating.

When routing a presentation, you can track its progress as it moves from one person to the next on the list. All of the comments, edits, and creative work are saved in a single file, which is passed on to the final person on the list. In addition, you can choose to include a copy of Freelance's screenshow player for those who don't have a version of the software on their computer. **TeamReview takes the collaborative effort a step further.**

A fully automated online tool, TeamReview allows you to send your presentation to a group of reviewers, other team members, your supervisor, or whomever you want feedback from. You can distribute the presentation by floppy disk, a local area network, e-mail, or posting it in a Notes database. Once reviewers receive the presentation, they can choose from a variety of tools. Quick Comments are ready-made electronic "sticky notes," with messages such as "misspelling" or "punctuation error" that reviewers can add quickly and easily as needed. They can also type in their own messages on blank electronic sticky notes with the Add a Comment feature. If they want to add visual edits to the presentation, they can choose from four mark-up tools: a straight line marker, a circle tool, a Freehand tool, and an arrow tool. All of the tools are color-coded by the reviewer, and reviewers can choose to see others' comments so they don't all say the same things. There's even online help to walk the reviewers through the process.

Once all of the reviewers have made their comments, they are consolidated into a single file for you. This process works slightly differently, depending on how you choose to send your file. For example, if you send your presentation to the reviewers via floppy disk or e-mail as an attachment, Freelance automates the process of retrieving the comments and consolidating them into the original presentation document. If you post the presentation for review over Lotus Notes, you just open your presentation file, and all of the reviewers' comments will be right there, ready for your perusal. You can then check out all of the comments and make the necessary changes in your final presentation.

For their parts, both Harvard Graphics and PowerPoint allow you to access e-mail directly from their File menus. With PowerPoint, you can also choose to route your presentation to multiple individuals via the e-mail system.

Preparing and rehearsing

Once you've finished creating the bulk of your presentation, you have to start thinking about those minor details, such as, *How do I get this multi-megabyte presentation to fit on a few floppies to take with me to Detroit tomorrow?; I wonder if I'm going to be able to make all these points in 20 minutes*; and, of course, *Oh my God, I forgot to make handouts!*

Fortunately, PowerPoint, Freelance and Harvard Graphics each have a little something to offer for these critical details. PowerPoint, for example, offers a Pack and Go Wizard, which walks you through the process of compressing and saving your presentation across multiple disks, automatically saving all of your linked files and multimedia files. Harvard Graphics also allows you the option of preserving your data links when copying your slides. To make more effective handouts, Freelance provides several different options.

You can print handouts with two, four, or six slides per page or you can print audience notes, which offer the option of including one, two, or three slides per page plus notes for added guidance. You can also select from 10 different border styles to add a professional look to your handouts.

To create handouts with greater impact in PowerPoint, there's a new feature under the File menu that allows you to send the information to Microsoft Word. This feature allows you to choose from all the different layouts, all of which include one or two slides and accompanying notes. Using OfficeLinks and OLE, your slides and speaker notes are then sent to Microsoft Word, where they are formatted.

PowerPoint also finally includes a black-and-white view, so you can preview your full-color slides in black (and white) before printing them out and finding that your beautiful charts have all blended into a dull gray color. The feature allows you to make a variety of adjustments to ensure attractive and readable black-and-white printouts.

If you want some automated help rehearsing your presentation and ensuring that it falls within your time requirements, Freelance includes a Rehearse mode bar. This feature allows you to pause and resume your presentation, activate a timer, or bring up your speaker notes. The time display shows your elapsed time, both on a per slide basis as well as the total run time of your presentation.

Presenting

With the globalization of business, it's becoming increasingly important to go beyond the telephone conference call to communicate with employees and clients scattered throughout the world. To support the growing need, all three packages provide presentation conferencing to remote sites via modem or local area network.

Built on the Remote Access Services technology integrated into Windows, Freelance's TeamShow feature allows presentations to be delivered to computers connected via a local area network (LAN), modem, or even a serial or parallel cable. During a TeamShow presentation, the presenter's screen features a status bar that enables him or her to advance the screen show to the next page or return to the previous page, as well as view or edit speaker notes or capture additional information and viewer feedback from the discussion.

PowerPoint's Presentation Conferencing feature also allows you to display your presentation to several virtual meeting attendees via a network.

An interesting feature in PowerPoint is Stage Manager, which helps you deliver your presentation more effectively by providing previews of upcoming slides, a slide meter for monitoring progress, and access to PowerPoint's unique Meeting Minder feature. There are some nifty new features in PowerPoint. It will allow users to View on two screens and Powerpoint2000 will support Windows 98's multi-monitor configurations. See your system administrator if you want to use these features.

SPC was the first to integrate such capabilities into its program. Although Harvard Graphics 4.0 provides no new enhancement in this area, the program does continue to allow you to display your presentation on up to 64 computers simultaneously during a conference call. To participate, each attendee logs into the server of a local area network. The conference leader has tools for advancing the screenshow, as well as a chalk tool for highlighting key points. The leader can also pass control of the conference to other attendees. With a messaging system, attendees can send messages to each other without interfering with the conference call.

If you have a burning desire to show your presentation to the universe of Internet users, Freelance offers a way to do that, too.

You can either publish your presentation to the Internet in World Wide Web format for users to browse through live on the Internet or you can post native Freelance files, which users can download and view as multimedia screenshows. When published in Web format, your Freelance presentation includes a Table of Contents browser that allows users to go directly to the pages of interest to them. If you post a presentation in native Freelance file format, you can include a link to the Lotus home page, where users can download and install the Freelance Graphics Mobile Screen Show player and then view your presentation, whether or not they have Freelance Graphics installed on their computer.

Follow-up

The critical follow-up stage after a presentation is an area that has always been ignored by presentation programs—until now. PowerPoint for Windows features an innovative tool called Meeting Minder, which is designed to improve follow-up after a business meeting. During a meeting, you can choose to bring up the Meeting Minder screen, which provides an electronic notepad for recording meeting minutes, notes, and action items. At the end of the meeting, Meeting Minder automatically creates an Action Item slide for everyone to review. You can also quickly and easily print out your meeting minutes for distribution to the other meeting attendees.

Bulletproof advice

➤ **Software packages will allow you to create quality visuals that look and feel like professionally produced visuals.**

- Although the packages will put sparkle into your presentation, remember that they should not *become* the presentation.

➤ **Software packages allow collaboration with others.**

- Key features of the various software packages allow a team to collaborate on building a presentation. Be sure to take advantage of those features.

➤ **Many packages even allow you to rehearse at a distance.**

- Even with those features, be sure to come together for a dress rehearsal before the actual presentation.

Part V

Handling
Special
Situations

CHAPTER 18

ORGANIZING TEAM PRESENTATIONS

More and more, organizations are turning to teams to improve their products and services. As a result, more presentations are being done by teams rather than individuals. This chapter will help you adapt the information you have already learned to a team presentation, and it will introduce ideas that are unique to team presentations.

Organization

Consider this

I was in the offices of an aerospace company in Houston, within a stone's throw of NASA's Johnson Space Center, coaching a team of rocket scientists (yes, they really were rocket scientists!) on a presentation they were preparing for NASA. It was a very important presentation on a project worth more than $100 million, and all of the people were quite nervous.

As I listened to them give their presentations on the space mission (prior to any coaching), I commented that what they were saying was "really Greek" to me. One of the senior people, who had been in the space program since the days of John Glenn, said, "And what you do is Greek to us!"

However, I was able to take them through this process of developing a team presentation, and within three days the difference was enormous. Moreover, their fear of the presentation turned to excitement and confidence.

Later, when I contacted them after their scheduled presentation, the leader of the team nearly shouted into the phone: "We knocked their socks off!" They had come to believe in the process and to believe in themselves. I doubt any of them will approach a presentation with the same fear and foreboding again.

They had used the process to create a Bulletproof Presentation.

You can create Bulletproof Presentations as a team, too! Team presentations are very common today and the stakes are usually high. With all the downsizing in companies today, you may find yourself giving an important presentation that a few years ago would have been handled by your manager or the salespeople. This seems particularly true in the technical fields of engineering, computers, and accounting.

**Just because there are more people in front
of the room doesn't mean you can't get
shot down collectively just as easily as individually.**

Remember what Benjamin Franklin said upon signing the Declaration of Independence; "We must all hang together or we shall surely hang separately!" In team presentations, you must *really* hang together!

Consider this

One client of mine, a CPA, told me how difficult his firm found giving presentations to attract new business. As he said, "That was *not* what we were taught in school!" And they were not.

In such a competitive environment, people who never before had to sell their services find these kinds of presentations really nerve-wracking. However, there aren't very many people I can think of who don't have to worry about the competition.

Before you lament on the fact that you will be required to give a presentation as a team, remember that the potential rewards for good team presentations are significant in terms of dollars and opportunity. The exposure you could receive not only within your company, but also to others outside, could be invaluable to you as your career progresses during the next merger, acquisition, or downsizing.

My experience, which many of my customers confirm, is that you will rarely win a project or proposal due only to a terrific presentation. There are too many other factors that are part of the decision process. However, many projects and proposals have been lost *because* of a poor presentation. So although it may not win you any business by itself, it can certainly cause you to lose some important business.

I cannot tell you the number of times companies have come to me after losing a project or contract and not known why. They were sure they had the best price or bid, and they had all the experience and personnel. When I asked them how they prepared for the proposal presentation, they often say, "Well, we just got together for an hour the day before to go over our bid."

Consider this

When you get ready to practice your team presentation, my guess is you may hear comments such as:

"I'll just walk you through my part. I am still fixing it up"; or "Let me just tell you the main points of my part. I don't have time to go through it word by word"; or "I'll be a lot more enthusiastic when I give the real presentation."

The problem is that a team practice is just that: a team practice. Everyone is expected to practice and rehearse, or the team will not be Bulletproof during the presentation. If you hear these types of comments, you should consider whether that member should continue on the team.

I had one executive tell me that he watched two team members get into a heated fight, during the presentation, *in front of him—the prospective client!* I am sure that happened because they had not prepared some of the important details in advance. Needless to say, the executive did not give them the contract. If they were not clear on what they were proposing, he was not about to let them experiment in his company.

In talking with companies that request a team presentation, they say they want to get a real sense of the members of the team and their styles and attitudes.

Put yourself in the client's shoes. You are picking a company for an important piece of your business. It could have a major impact on the company for several years to come. Would the presentation be important to you? Of course!

First and foremost, the client needs to be sold on the individuals who will handle his or her company's business. That would be true whether we are discussing projects, products, or services. The way the team presents their ideas and solutions to the audience is viewed by the audience as a measure of how well their business would be managed by this team.

If the presentation looks boring, haphazard, disorganized, and unprofessional, the client may fear that is how its business will be handled.

Team presentations are unique

Team presentations demand careful planning. You will need to consider these questions:

➤ Who will begin the presentation?

➤ Who needs to present which information?

➤ How will you "handoff" from one presenter to the next?

➤ Where will the rest of the presenters stand or sit while one is speaking?

➤ Who will manage the questions and answers that will come up during the presentation?

➤ Who will create the visual aids so that they are consistent and are prepared in time for rehearsals?

It is more difficult to organize and execute a Bulletproof Team Presentation than an individual presentation.

Having coached both teams and individuals over the years, I have seen people make the mistake of thinking that if they just string a series of good, individual presentations together, the whole team presentation will turn out fine.

However, there are several potential problems that are not a concern during an individual presentation. They include:

➤ Conflict between team members.

➤ Inconsistencies in the message or facts.

➤ Communication problems between team members.

➤ Duplication of efforts that waste time.

➤ Agenda logistics.

The points that follow will help you avoid these problems.

Developing the Bulletproof Team Presentation

The first task any team must address is to name one person as a team leader. The team leader will take the responsibility of ensuring that the team puts together an effective presentation outline (and then follows it!).

The team leader does not need to be part of the team. In some companies where I have worked, the team leader was the project manager, but in others, it was someone completely different. However, if you choose someone outside the team, make sure he or she has some stake in the outcome of the presentation.

Team roles

The team leader. This person is responsible for coordinating the team's activities and making sure that tasks are completed on time. Here are some other responsibilities:

➤ Encourage everyone to participate.

➤ Keep the channels of communication open.

➤ Prepare the team blueprint.

➤ Make sure the team follows the blueprint.

The team leader should make sure that each member wants to participate. If any team member does not wish to participate, then you need to see the project manager immediately. Don't leave someone on the team who is half-hearted. However, don't eliminate someone because he or she is uncomfortable giving presentations. The process that you will be using to develop and deliver the presentation should help anyone who is nervous. I am talking about someone who, for whatever reason, might end up hurting the efforts of the team simply because he or she *won't* participate fully.

> **Just as we do with individual presentations, the first area of focus for team presentations is content organization.**

The team leader can use the Presentation Planning/Preparation Worksheet (in the Appendix) to organize the content. There are two ways the team leader can use the tool and organize the presentation.

First of all, as the team leader, you can assume the sole responsibility for filling out the form and then giving the assignments to other team members. This is the quickest way and usually results in a fairly cohesive presentation. However, some members of the team may resent the fact that they had no voice in the construction of the presentation. (In fact, my experience says that this scenario will happen more often than not.)

The second way would be for you, as the team leader, to work with the team in completing the form. This can yield buy-in from the team and increased team spirit, along with clarity of purpose and direction. However, the downside to this approach is the additional time required. This will require careful planning on your part, because you will need to allocate the proper amount of time not only for yourself, but also for all the members of the team.

Weigh time vs. buy-in in completing the blueprint.

It is really important to keep the channels of communication open. One of the surest ways to develop problems is to leave someone out of the loop on what the team is doing.

Two of the ways you can keep everyone informed are by maintaining or sending checklists, time lines, and the like to everyone and by being responsible for all the logistics, including organizing and conducting the dress rehearsal.

Finally, be sure that all the members of your team are contributing to the team blueprint in their portion of the presentation.

**Remember: If one team member fails to
plan and follow the outline and blueprint,
the presentation effect will probably be lost.**

The team member. Each team member is responsible for his or her portion of the presentation. He or she must:

1. Prepare thoroughly.

2. Encourage other team members.

3. Remain enthusiastic.

The success of the team presentation depends upon many other considerations, including enthusiasm. If the team is not convinced, the audience will not be either!

Very often team members believe that their only role is to prepare their part of the agenda thoroughly.

Presentations will rarely win an agreement by themselves. There are many other factors that come into play during the entire process. However, a poor presentation will definitely hurt any chance you have of succeeding. Contrary to what most people think, the client really wants you to succeed! No one enjoys sitting through a boring, unprepared presentation. They are pulling for you; don't disappoint them!

Follow the process for Bulletproof Team Presentations and you will be amazed at the quality of both your presentation and those of your teammates.

Overriding theme

One of the best examples of tying everything together in a team presentation was demonstrated while I was working with a marketing services group. They chose "Building a Bridge to the Future" as their overriding theme.

Every member of the team explained *how* he or she would help the client build a bridge to the future in the presentation. And for their visuals, they had a picture of a large suspension bridge superimposed in the background of each overhead. It made a terrific impact on the audience, and they achieved their goal of making a sale.

The first order of business, regardless of your approach, will be to establish your overriding theme (OT).

Remember the concept of the OT. If audience members don't remember anything else, they will remember this. You must do this first because it forms the foundation for everything that follows.

The real key to a Bulletproof Team Presentation is establishing the OT and then building the various pieces of each member's presentation around it. Just as in an individual presentation, every piece of information, topic, or visual must support the overriding theme. Supporting the OT is what will ensure that the audience will not be able to poke holes in your ideas. Listeners might not agree with what you have to say, but they will not be able to discredit it. That's what makes your presentation Bulletproof!

Brainstorming

I can't tell you how many times teams have told me, "We can't get anything done in our meetings!' It is usually this tendency to get sidetracked on details. In fact, a recent survey conducted nationwide suggested that the greatest stress associated with belonging to a team was team meetings.

However, in order to best tap the collective experiences and knowledge of the team, as the team leader, you may wish to conduct a meeting to complete certain portions of the outline. Brainstorming may be used to identify the topics the team thinks will support the overriding theme, or possible objections and concerns.

If you are the team leader, or volunteer to lead the session, remember these brainstorming guidelines:

1. Generate as many ideas as possible. Aim for quantity, not quality.
2. Have everyone write their ideas down on sticky notes first, and then begin the discussion.
3. Keep focused on the problem or opportunity in mind.
4. Post *everyone's* ideas on a board or flip chart. (Having them on sticky notes saves you from rewriting them.)
5. Do not judge any ideas as good or bad; they are just ideas.
6. Ask each team member to share his or her ideas *one at a time* until all ideas are exhausted.

As I have facilitated these types of sessions for teams, I have noticed that there will be a tendency during these meetings to get sidetracked onto specific issues. Don't let the team debate *any* of the ideas until *all* the ideas are on the board or flipchart.

Using this brainstorming process can help ensure that your team is well pre-pared. The individuals will start functioning as a team with a clear overriding theme understood by all.

The overriding theme will help team members tremendously in building their individual presentations.

Having every team member participate gives you, the team leader, an oppor-tunity to make sure everyone is "singing from the same hymnal," so to speak, and to ensure that each presentation supports the overriding theme.

Plan a smooth, unified presentation that appears as one presentation given by several people instead of a series of individual presentations that may or may not tie together.

Strategy

Too often, the strategy for team presentations is topical. Although there is nothing wrong with the strategy, my experience has been that it is usually pretty boring! The idea of just going from one topic to another is logical, just not very appealing.

Refer back to Chapter 8 on choosing a strategy. Team presentations should have a strategy that allows the listeners to follow the logic of the ideas easily, just as an individual presentation should.

It has to make sense to the audience; you already know it!

Using the ideas that you generated during the brainstorming session, experi-ment with various strategies and notice how you would group or select the many ideas using each strategy.

Don't just pick the first strategy that comes to mind; play with a variety of approaches.

I recommend that the team try about three different strategies to see which one you like the best. I am confident that one will appear to the group as the clear "winner." Remember: You want to choose a strategy that will not only support your overriding theme, but will also allow all the team members to appear at their best.

In choosing the strategy, you will also need to keep in mind the various strengths (and weaknesses) of your team. Then you can assign the various parts to the appropriate people, and everyone will feel good about their contribution, and the team as a whole.

Agenda

The agenda for the presentation should follow the strategy with sufficient details to allow everyone to do their part well.

The agenda should include the:

1. Presenters' names.

2. Time allotted to each speaker.

3. Topics for each speaker.

4. AV equipment everyone needs for their presentation.

Each member of the team should have copy of this agenda. Obviously, the audience will not have such a detailed agenda, but the team needs it to feel comfortable and prepared.

With a team presentation, there is more of a chance for the audience to get lost. The first speaker's "roadmap" will be very important to help the audience follow the presentation. Use a visual "moving agenda" to help the audience follow the presentation.

This could be in the form of a checklist that is checked off as each presenter proceeds. It could also be something as simple as a flipchart with the agenda printed on it. The key point is to keep the moving agenda in front of the audience at all times. For obvious reasons, that means you cannot use an overhead or slide.

Introducing the team members

I usually recommend that the team leader give a brief introduction of each of the team members as part of the introduction. You are generally not trying to give all the details on each member, but just enough information to give the audience members confidence that this team is qualified to speak to them.

During the presentation, have each team member introduce the following speaker after concluding his or her portion of the presentation. It eliminates the need for each speaker to begin by saying, "Hi. I'm Mike Campbell, and today I'm going to talk about shared services." Each successive speaker can begin his or her presentation with his or her own grabber to catch the audience's attention.

Handling questions

I would strongly encourage the team leader to field all the questions posed during the presentation. The one exception to this is obviously when a question is directed to a particular member of the team (of course, that team member should handle it!). Otherwise, the team leader should field the questions and direct them to the appropriate team member. This approach has two advantages:

1. It gives the team member a chance to gather his or her thoughts before responding to the question.

2. It casts the team as well-coordinated and organized in handling situations.

Both approaches are positive influences on the audience.

Planning visuals

When you are planning a Bulletproof Team Presentation, the team should work to format each presenter's visuals so that they look the same. There are many ways to use visuals to present a unified theme.

For example, each visual could have a logo that reflects the overriding theme. (Remember the group building a bridge to the future?) In any case, the visuals should have consistent backgrounds and the same typeset. It is very important to title the visuals boldly so that the audience can follow them clearly. Also, the titles must be consistent with the agenda presented. One method that has worked very well for groups I have coached has everyone submit their drafts to the team leader. The leader then has all the visuals made up at one time.

Connecting over distances

The technology available today comes from:

➤ Lotus.

➤ Microsoft PowerPoint.

➤ Harvard Graphics.

In today's corporate environment, it is very possible that members of the presentation team may not even be in the same geographic location.

In the past that has provided a serious challenge to teams. However, technology has come up with some answers.

These software packages allow you to:

➤ Distribute the information easily.

➤ Add comments and suggestions.

➤ See what others have written.

➤ Track who has seen the file.

➤ Save the presentation in one file.

Lotus, one of the leaders in groupware, offers the most interesting approach to helping teams work on their presentations with Freelance Graphics.

Freelance provides two new features designed to help a team put together a presentation long distance: TeamMail and TeamReview. **Using most common e-mail systems, TeamMail enables you to send a presentation file, or selected pages from your team presentation file, to all your fellow team members.**

You can choose to broadcast the presentation to each individual or route it to the entire team. This is a great feature for editing, commenting, or even creating the visuals for your presentation. The system allows you to track the file as it moves from one person to the next on the team. Best of all, the comments, editing, and any other work are saved on a single file. That way everyone can look at the comments and suggestions the other team members made. Another great feature allows you to use Freelance's screenshow for those who do not have a copy of the software.

TeamReview takes the presentation development even further. Using an online tool, TeamReview allows you to send your presentation to other team members for their feedback. You can distribute the presentation by floppy disk, using a LAN (local area network) or e-mail or by posting it in a Notes database.

Both Harvard Graphics and PowerPoint also allow you to access e-mail directly from their File menus. With PowerPoint, you can also choose to route your presentation to multiple individuals using the e-mail system.

E-mail is a critical component
for preparing at a distance.

After your team members receive the presentation, they can choose from a variety of tools to make their comments. Quick Comments are ready-made electronic "sticky tabs," with messages such as "misspelling" or "punctuation error" that reviewers can add quickly and easily where they see errors. They can also type in their own comments on blank electronic sticky tabs with the "Add a Comment" feature.

If they want to suggest adding a visual to the presentation, they can choose from four mark-up tools: a straight-line marker, a circle tool, a Freehand tool, and an arrow tool. All of the tools can be color-coded by team members so that all the team members can see each other's comments. That way they won't end up repeating the same things. There's even an online help function to walk your team through the process. Once everyone has made their comments, they are consolidated into a single file for the team leader.

This process works slightly differently, depending on how you choose to send your file. For example, if you send your presentation to team members using a floppy disk or e-mail as an attachment, Freelance simplifies the process of reviewing the comments by putting them together into the original presentation document. If you send the presentation for review through Lotus Notes, you just open your presentation file, and everyone's comments will be right there. That allows you to check out all of the comments and make any necessary changes in your final presentation.

All of these suggestions will help you
build the presentation at great distances,
but the team must still prepare with a dress rehearsal.

Sometimes teams will believe that technology has eliminated the need for the dress rehearsal and not pay enough attention to this important step.

Dress rehearsal

One insurance executive related a story to me about a presentation he and his colleagues had not coordinated through a dress rehearsal. He was overseas and the executive team was making a major presentation that meant a very lucrative opportunity for his company.

As he began to listen to the first of his associates, he noticed his teammate began using some of the same ideas he had prepared for his presentation. He even used one of the jokes he had prepared! You can imagine how he felt, knowing he was expected to talk for 30 minutes—to this very important group—and the previous speaker had used most of his material! A dress rehearsal would have prevented that very embarrassing situation from ever happening.

**A dress rehearsal is essential to
uncover and strengthen any areas of weakness.**

Communication and coordination can be very difficult. This is particularly true if some members of the team (or perhaps the entire team) are not in the same physical location. It also prevents one speaker from overlapping into the content of another, and "stealing their thunder." Even after you have used the strategy and assigned people to specific portions of the presentation, you would be amazed at how often people will use the same information or data in different points. There is nothing wrong with duplication of information, if you know it in advance, and it fits both the individual presentations and the overall team presentation.

When all the team members know when they are presenting and how their topics are related to other topics and presenters, they will see how the entire presentation fits together.

Knowing what each person on the team is saying in advance will help tremendously when it comes to the difficult question period that often follows these types of presentations.

However, as I suggested in the section for developing individual presentations, leave the "grabber" until the rest of the presentation is either complete or nearly complete.

After you have had a successful planning session and dress rehearsal, you can address the grabber.

Ask for suggestions from the team now that everyone has heard the entire presentation. Good ideas will flow. Sometimes the team may want to use a quote or a statistic that one of the individual presenters used in their presentation. That can be just the right thing to do, but be prepared for some resistance from that individual. They may feel it leaves a hole in their presentation. The team may need to work and find a suitable replacement for that information if they want to use it as the grabber.

Transitions. Transitions are what will give the team presentation the professional "feel" of one presentation given by one team.

The team needs to be sure there is a smooth transition between each presenter and topic. This is an area where preparation and planning are critical. You want the transitions to flow smoothly. It should be easy for the audience members to recognize that they are attending a unified presentation, not several disjointed solos. The transitions need to be planned in advance and practiced in the dress rehearsal until they are easy and clear.

Resources. Resource requirements are usually more extensive (and expensive) with a team presentation. You need to consider the commitment of money, personnel, and time that are required for successful team presentations.

Management backing is crucial to any successful team presentation. Try to get this commitment in advance in case there are questions later on, either from your team members or from another person in management.

Sometimes managers are reluctant to give people the time they need to prepare. Perhaps they feel it should not take so long. The only advice I can offer in this area is to guarantee you that there are no shortcuts to a Bulletproof Team Presentation. If you don't spend the proper time getting ready, you will look unprepared.

Room set-up. The team should diagram the room layout so that all the presenters know where they will be standing (and sitting!) during the presentation.

The team needs to know where they will be in relation to the audience at all times. Put yourself in the best position to watch your colleagues and the audience. You will learn a lot by noticing the expressions and body language displayed by the audience during a presentation. You need to look at and listen to each of your teammates as he or she is presenting. The audience will focus on the whole team, not just the presenter!

Find a place that is as similar in size and layout as possible to conduct your dress rehearsal. If you know that you will be using a lavaliere mike, for example, practice with one. You would be surprised at how clumsy you will feel clipping and unclipping the mike during the transitions. However, with a little practice, you will begin to feel comfortable. And with that will come confidence.

Sometimes it is not always possible to duplicate the room or setting, but the closer you can come to simulating the actual situation, the less nervous everyone will be. Again, it comes down to anticipating all the possible contingencies and addressing them.

Potential risks

Because the stakes are greater in a team presentation, the risks are, too. Potential risks should be discussed along with how the team will solve those problems if they come up.

This is usually most appropriate during the dress rehearsal, but any time the team uncovers a potential disaster in the making, everyone should be made aware of it, and plans should be made to eliminate or minimize the risk.

**Covering and/or eliminating potential risks
are key elements to creating the Bulletproof Team Presentation.**

Many of these potential problems are included on the Team Presentation Worksheet in the Appendix.

Conclusion

In conclusion, team presentations offer some exciting challenges—and terrific rewards. Using the process described in this chapter, and combining it with the information we have already covered in earlier chapters, you and your team can make a Bulletproof Team Presentation!

Bulletproof advice

➤ **Be sure you organize your presentation team correctly.**

- Remember that team presentations are more difficult to organize and execute than individual presentations. A good team presentation requires more than a series of good individual presentations.

➤ **Clarify all team roles before you begin planning the rest of the elements of your Bulletproof Presentation.**

- First choose your team leader and make sure he or she is committed to the successful outcome of the presentation. Then make sure all the team members understand and agree to their roles.

➤ **Choose the overriding theme that will create that special memory for your audience.**

- Build all the necessary pieces of the presentation around the overriding theme, and make sure all the team members will contribute their portion to supporting the overriding theme. That is what makes for Bulletproof Team Presentations.

➤ **Brainstorm all your ideas and then chose a strategy that will fit the audience.**

- Lay out at least three approaches on the strategy after you brainstorm all the ideas that need to be included. Let the strategy and the overriding theme dictate what to leave in and what to take out.

➤ **Pay attention to all the logistics involved in your presentation.**

- Choose your agenda and time everything. Don't forget important elements such as the agenda, transitions, dress rehearsal, audiovisual equipment, and room set-up. Be as prepared as possible for all potential problems.

➤ **Use technology wisely if your team is scattered geographically.**

- Computers and networks can allow a team to do much of the work now without being in the same room together. Even though you will not be able to do everything this way, it sure beats the alternative!

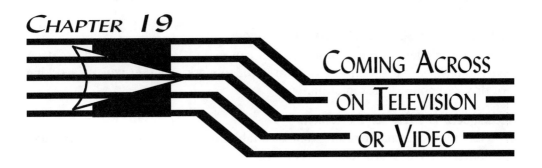

COMING ACROSS
ON TELEVISION
OR VIDEO

TV and video require special techniques

All of the techniques you have learned for developing your Bulletproof Presentation apply equally to recording a video or appearing on television. However, some of the delivery techniques are different. Video and television record images and sounds that are largely ignored by the audience during a live presentation. Here are some examples:

➤ **Video cameras are deadly in their sensitivity to detail.** With strong lighting, powerful lenses, and tracking, they capture every detail.

➤ **Studio microphones amplify every flaw.** If you get a frog in your throat on stage, you can turn your head and clear your throat. But television microphones record every noise you make.

➤ **The bright lights play tricks on you.** If you tend to perspire, lights will make you sweat. Also lights do things to colors, so they can make you look washed out or almost ghastly.

➤ **The impersonality and confusion of the studio is different from a live, responsive audience.** A talk that appears lively on stage can look dead on TV. Cameras don't show any response; you never know how you're coming across.

➤ **The hectic pace of TV eats up time.** Points you can spend five minutes making on stage have to be made in 30 seconds or less on television.

➤ **Audiences expect network quality, regardless of your budget.** TV viewers are accustomed to network quality. They expect you to look like a network news anchor and all your supportive videos to look like professional news footage.

➤ **Audiences aren't as courteous or attentive to television presenters as they are to stage speakers.** If they get bored, they'll flip channels or turn off the video recorder.

➤ 227 ≪

Have I frightened you into reconsidering your decision? I hope not, because video not only enables you to reach more people than any other medium, but often you can reach more people in one local news interview than in a lifetime of speaking to audiences. Once you learn some basics, video can even be fun.

Techniques to survive and thrive on video

Let's consider simple techniques you can use to look and sound great on television. These work well in any form of video work, whether you are working live or videotaping a presentation.

Technique #1: Dress for the camera.

Generally speaking, clothing that is suitable for business wear is also suitable for television. There are some exceptions.

Do:

➤ Wear mid-tone, soft, and warm colors. Subdued shades of blue, gray, brown, green, lavender, or burgundy are good colors for suits, ties, scarves, and dresses; pastels are good for shirts and blouses.

➤ Wear solid colors or muted patterns.

➤ If you are seated:
  - Men: Unbutton your coat and pull it together in the front, straighten the bottom, tie your tie shorter than normal so it won't hang down between your legs, and wear over-the-calf socks.
  - Women: Make sure your skirt covers your knees.

➤ Wear lightweight fabrics (even in the winter) that keep you cool under the bright lights.

Don't:

➤ Wear whites, yellows, reds, or drab grays.

➤ Wear bold patterns such as plaids, stripes, polka dots, checks, herringbones, or hound's-tooth.

➤ Wear vests or other tight-fitting clothes that make you look squeezed.

➤ Dress too casually or faddishly.

Technique #2: Use makeup.

Don't be afraid of makeup, but test in advance. A camera balances all the shades, hues, and intensities of color and lighting on the set. That means your face may look washed out, lines emphasized, and dark spots under your eyes exaggerated. Don't count on studio people to make you up; they may say you look fine.

Do your own makeup. For women, it's mainly a matter of putting on more foundation and highlighters than for street wear. Use less eye shadow than normal.

Men can buy pancake makeup to enrich their natural skin tones and apply it in the restroom before they go on the set. The important thing is not to use plenty of it, but to cover all visible parts of your skin. If you have thin or light-colored eyebrows and lashes, you might want to wear mascara. If you are balding, a little powder on the head can soften the glare.

If you have a chance, experiment beforehand with similar lighting and cameras. In any case, ask for a videotape copy and assess how good your makeup looks before your next appearance.

Technique #3: Control your expressions and movements.

Much of the time you're on camera, all the audience will see is your face, so your expressions are emphasized. A frown can look like a scowl. Try to look pleasant always, even while discussing a serious subject. Let your face convey strong emotions and sincerity. Smile at every opportunity, but avoid wrinkling your forehead. Never tighten up your eyebrows.

Assume you are always on camera. You can't tell when the camera is in close, so you need to control your movements at all times. Keep your chin up and minimize head movements. Don't fidget with your clothes or touch your face during filming. If you sweat, ask to be "mopped" during a break.

Technique #4: Use your gestures to good advantage.

Gestures can enliven your appearance on TV. A small gesture goes a long way. Use controlled gestures and make them fit what you are saying. Keep your hands above your waist any time you want to make a special gesture. Shoulder height is better. Be careful that you don't let your hands come between your face and the camera.

Tailor gestures to the camera.

Technique #5: Exude energy and enthusiasm.

It may seem like an impossible mission with all that's going on around you, but energy can do wonders to make you more interesting to watch. You don't have to emote like a ham actor. Just show your excitement and conviction for what you are saying.

Energize yourself. The best places to let your energy and enthusiasm show are in your face and your voice. Raise your eyebrows, let intensity show in your eyes, and slightly exaggerate your normal expressions. Put warmth and conviction in the tone of your voice, and vary your volume to emphasize certain points. Most of all, be warm, friendly, and sincere. Let viewers know you care.

Technique #6: Look into the camera.

Consider the camera an audience of one. Maintain flawless eye contact with it. Nothing destroys credibility the way failing to look into a camera does. **Remember that your audience is behind the camera.**

When you are being interviewed, glance briefly at your questioner, then look back into the camera. You are talking to the people on the other side of the television set, not to those in the studio.

Never assume that the camera and the microphone are turned off, even if someone signals "cut." Keep looking at the camera until a studio person steps on the set or your host stands up.

Technique #7: Compact and enliven everything you say.

On tape, every word, noise, and grunt comes through. What sounds like interesting banter in private conversation sounds like rambling and stumbling around on video.

It is vital to make every word pay off. Know precisely what you will say and how you will say it. That is not always easy, but you can prepare for any kind of questions. Practicing on audiotape is a good way. Practice saying things concisely and getting to the point quickly. Practice making every word count and using short, crisp sentences.

On the set, speak distinctly. Enunciate clearly. Avoid stalling tactics such as "uh" and "you know." **Be both concise and precise.**

Make your comments come alive by using active verbs and descriptive nouns. Stay away from adjectives and adverbs. Give a complete response to questions you are asked, and avoid the temptation to answer with a simple yes or no or by merely nodding your head.

The greatest challenge can be to keep the flow moving. A cardinal sin in any broadcast medium is excessive dead time (silence for 10 or more seconds). Respond quickly when someone throws the conversation your way. Never pause more than five seconds mid-sentence.

Special strategies for videotaped presentations

More and more executives and professionals are using closed-circuit networks or pre-recorded videotapes or videodisks to send messages.

The board chairmen of the big three automakers recently took to closed circuit networks to announce their latest employee profit-sharing payouts. As executives with other major companies do, they often appear on video to speak to workers, stockholders, and even customers. It's a good way for a busy executive to add a personal touch in far-flung organizations.

Making a professional-grade video can be expensive and time-consuming. Here are some strategies for videotaping presentations.

Strategy #1: Work from a prepared script.

In many live-audience situations, it is best not to use a word-for-word script, but videotaping is a special circumstance. It's the one place I recommend working from a prepared text. A video presentation has to be twice as smooth as a live presentation to look half as good. Your audience's expectations are based on the delivery of TV-network professionals, who all work from scripts. Subconsciously, your audience will judge you against network standards.

Your script must be tightly written and flow smoothly. I suggest you get professional help in the writing. You might want to prepare a rough draft, then call in a pro to smooth it out. Once you get it back, read it aloud (preferably before a small video camera) to be sure you can say each word and phrase comfortably and that there are no tongue twisters.

Keep it trim and smooth. Cut the presentation to the bone. Take out all superfluous words. Change all passive verbs to active words. Replace weak words with strong ones.

Strategy #2: Use a TelePrompTer.

The TelePrompTer displays your printed text on a screen beside the camera lens. As you read, an operator moves the text scroll up (on a "crawl") so that the line you are reading is near the center of the screen.

You can prepare your final text in ways that make it easier to read. One method is to type all letters as capitals. Another is to use a punctuation mark at each logical pause, then to allow an extra white space between all in-sentence punctuation and two extra spaces between sentences. That way, you can easily see where the breaks are.

TelePrompTers are simply computers linked to a screen that you can read while looking into the camera. Work with the technician, who will man the TelePrompTer, to provide you with the breaks and patterns in the text. Then work on the speed you want as you deliver your presentation.

Strategy #3: Practice, practice, practice.

Practice reading with full expression and energy. The more natural it sounds to you, the easier it is for an audience to follow. Practice with a TelePrompTer, if possible.

Shoot for a conversational tone in your voice, not the typical reading tone. If you read it through enough times, you can almost speak it, with only an occasional glance at the text.

As you practice, look for places to pause for emphasis. Pauses should last three or four seconds. That may seem too long to you, but it will add impact to your presentation. Winston Churchill used this technique in his radio speeches. Brits would sit up and lean toward the "wireless" to hear what was coming next.

The key to making pauses work on video is to look directly into the camera lens during each pause. Your audience will know that you are doing it intentionally and catch your emphasis.

While rehearsing, practice reading a little faster than you normally talk. Slow talk on video sounds halting and tentative. It is almost impossible for most people to talk too fast for video, if they enunciate clearly.

Strategy #4: Build in cues.

Write or draw in cues to remind yourself of special things to do to add life to your presentation. These include smiling, raising your eyebrows, and deepening your voice for effect. These make you look more real and add variety to your delivery.

Use verbal cues if they work best for you. One famous orator used to write at various points in the margin of speeches, "Shout! Weak point!"

Some speakers find it easier to use symbols they devise themselves. Samples include:

A slash (/)	=	Pause.
Three slashes (///)	=	Long pause.
Underline (_)	=	Verbal emphasis.
Double underline (=) =		Strong emphasis.
Asterisk (*)	=	Smile.

Whatever works best for you, cues help you remember to add variety to your delivery.

Strategy #5: Talk to one person.

When the taping begins, visualize yourself talking to a stranger. Imagine you are telling the stranger something you feel strongly about and that the person is responding positively.

By doing this, you will maintain a more conversational tone, which is very important for video. It's important to think of the person as a stranger because you tend to be a little less energetic and enthusiastic with a friend.

Video is a very personal and involving medium. It requires a personal touch. On the other hand, it can easily make you look lifeless, so it requires a great deal of energy. The balance between talking to one person, but thinking of that person as a stranger you want to impress, gives you the right mixture of credibility and energy.

Strategy #6: Use a natural setting.

If you have the option, aim for a more natural setting than a lectern, which creates a barrier and robs you of the advantage of intimacy with your audience.

This brings up the question of setting. You could use a desk, but that's a little stilted. Some speakers sit on the front of their desks. It's hard to look natural that way, because most people don't sit on desks.

One good option is a room setting with a sectional sofa. It can be colorful and it creates the feeling that a member of your audience could be sitting down with you for a chat.

One caution: Don't sit so far back in a huge plush sofa that it looks as if the sofa is swallowing you. Sit on the edge as if you are vitally interested in the conversation.

Another option is an on-location setting, which requires taking the camera into a plant, a showroom, or other natural setting. Location shooting has the disadvantage of extraneous noise and poor acoustics. But it offers so many advantages that it is often worth a sacrifice in sound quality. The major advantages are that it boosts your credibility and it makes for interesting and comfortable viewing by the audience.

Strategy #7: Provide visual interest.

People are used to watching TV, where action is the norm. To stand and talk for more than a few minutes can make viewers subconsciously expect a commercial break and tune you out.

There are many ways to get around this problem. One is to tape part of the program in the studio and the rest at various locations. This works if you do it right. If you choose this option make sure you use transitional statements to explain why you are jumping around. Always give a reason for being in each location.

Another option is to have a camera crew shoot some shots (this is called "wild footage") to splice in during the editing process. They simply take pictures of various locations, then electronically edit you out and the pictures in at designated points in the tape. Network and local news use this tactic.

An expensive, but effective, combination of quality ideas is to use a "chroma-key" system to electronically put you on location. The technical people tape the wild footage, then superimpose you over the pictures. This requires special equipment.

Titles also can be used to provide visual interest. You can make these from slides, or get special effects and titles from computer genographics. The latter work better, but can be more expensive and take longer to produce.

Bulletproof advice

➤ **Review and use one or more of the techniques for preparing for television.**

- Watch how you dress.

- Use the seven techniques!

➤ **Choose a strategy for preparing a videotape.**

- Pick one of the seven strategies and prepare accordingly.

➤ **Use the key elements to develop a Bulletproof Presentation.**

APPENDIX

WORKSHEETS FOR
PRESENTATION
PREPARATION

Presentation Planning

Purpose of presentation:

What do I want the audience to know?

What do I want the audience to do?

What do I want the audience to feel?

Is it realistic, achievable, measurable?

Have I taken a positive approach?

The purpose of my presentation is:_____

_____

_____

_____

My overriding theme (something they won't forget) is:

_____

_____

_____

_____

Audience Analysis

KEY INDIVIDUALS	RELATIONSHIP	LEVEL (1-5)	CREDIBILITY	QUESTIONS/CONCERNS

Information or techniques to gain acceptance:

Audience benefits from presentation:

Situation Analysis

ENVIRONMENTAL FACTORS			
ENVIRONMENTAL CONDITIONS			
INSIDER/OUTSIDER CONSIDERATIONS			

Size of group: _____   Time of day: _____

Allocated time: _____   Location: _____

Audience Checklist

❑ Who plans to attend?

_____

_____

_____

_____

_____

_____

_____

❑ Who really cares about the topic I am presenting?

_____

_____

_____

_____

❑ What are their responsibilities?

_____

_____

_____

_____

❑ Who will be attending that really understands the topic I am presenting?

_____

_____

Can I preview my presentation with that person? _____

❑ What is their relationship to the ideas I am presenting?

_____

_____

❑ Who created things the way they are today?

_____

_____

Audience Checklist (continued)

❑ Who has won a promotion as a result of the way things are today?

_____

_____

_____

❑ Who might look bad if things change from the way they are now?

_____

_____

_____

❑ Why are they attending?

_____

_____

_____

❑ Who will dislike my ideas? What will they dislike about them?

_____

_____

_____

_____

❑ Who loses power if things change?

_____

_____

❑ Who loses access to power if things change?

_____

_____

❑ Who is most affected by my ideas? How will they be hurt/helped? If I assume they will be hurt, how will they be hurt? If they will be helped, how will they be helped?

_____

_____

_____

_____

_____

Presentation Checklist

❑ Confirm the date and number of people.

❑ Confirm seating arrangement.

❑ Ensure everyone can see the screen.

❑ Get directions to the location.

❑ Confirm set-up time.

❑ Confirm name of AV person.

❑ Confirm table for handouts.

❑ Confirm size of room.

❑ Confirm chair for presenter.

❑ Confirm lectern with light.

❑ Confirm table for refreshments.

❑ Confirm breakout room(s).

❑ Request water pitcher and glass (easy to reach).

❑ Locate temperature control for room.

❑ Locate light switches or dimmer switches.

❑ Provide name tags and/or tents.

❑ Provide masking tape.

❑ Pack business cards (if needed).

❑ Confirm proper dress for occasion.

Audio/visual Checklist

❑ LCD panel (and know how to use it!)

❑ Computer.

❑ Remote mouse.

❑ Note cards.

❑ Backup overheads.

❑ Extra transparencies.

❑ Overhead projector (with masking tape for squaring image).

❑ Spare projector bulb.

❑ Stand for projector.

❑ Pointer (if needed).

❑ Flip chart ads and easels.

❑ Markers for flip charts.

❑ VCR monitor and video.

❑ Type of microphone.

❑ Workbooks and/or handouts.

❑ Models or props.

❑ Video cameras and tripods.

❑ Blank video cassettes.

❑ Extension cord.

❑ Screen (with extension to prevent keystoning effect).

❑ Podium.

Presentation preparation

Introduction

➤ Establish rapport.

➤ Grabber.

➤ Purpose.

➤ Benefits.

➤ Roadmap.

Remember:

- Simplicity.
- Timeliness.
- Association.
- Perspective.

Strategy

Select the right strategy for this presentation.

- ❑ Chronological.
- ❑ Topical.
- ❑ Problem/solution.
- ❑ Most critical to least critical.

- ❑ Procedural.
- ❑ Big picture/little picture.
- ❑ Motivated sequence.
- ❑ Spatial.

Body of the presentation

Strategy:

_____

_____

_____

Use three to five main points.

1. _____
2. _____
3. _____
4. _____
5. _____

Main Points	Examples	Visuals
1.		
2.		
3.		
4.		
5.		

Questions I need answered:

➤ What new information does it need?

_____

➤ Do I need to ask for commitment at the end of the presentation?

_____

➤ Do I need any information about someone's attitude?

_____

➤ Do I know enough about the audience's level of commitment?

_____

➤ Have I done enough to pre-sell my ideas?

_____

Team Presentation Worksheet

Presentation Date: _____   Strategy: _____

Team Leader: _____   Dress Rehearsal Date: _____

Resources Required: _____   Risks and Solutions: _____

_____   _____

_____   _____

_____   _____

_____   _____

AGENDA

Time	Topic	Presenter	Transition	AV Required

GLOSSARY

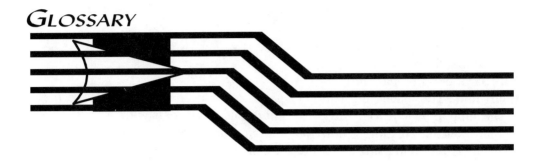

Accent lighting. Directional lighting to provide a focus on one area of a room.

Acoustics. The structural and decorative features of a room that determine how well sound can be heard.

Agenda. Detailed information about a scheduled meeting, such as beginning/ending times, date, place, topics, and responsibilities.

Alignment. Arrangement or positioning of type elements with respect to left and right margins (flush left, centered, flush right, or justified).

Ambient lighting. The general, overall illumination in a room.

Animation. The capability of presentation and multimedia software to create illusions of movement.

Articulation. The act of saying words distinctly and clearly.

Audio-visual presentation. A presentation in which a speaker uses visual images of some type to help convey the presentation message.

Balance. A sense of equilibrium in the design. Balance can be formal (where all images and/or text are arranged symmetrically) or informal (where images and/or text are arranged asymmetrically). Informal balance provides the greatest design flexibility.

Bar chart. A single-scale graph drawn with parallel bars used to compare quantities at a specific time or to show the quantity variance of something over time.

Baseline. The imaginary line on which the bottom of letters rest.

Bit. The basic unit of numbering in a binary numbering system (binary digit).

Bit-mapped. Images (pictures or fonts) made up of individual dots, as opposed to lines or other shapes.

Borders. A line or pattern used around the edge of a visual to add a consistent look to a series of visuals in a presentation.

Build series. A variation of a bullet list in which each item is highlighted as discussion progresses. Usually the completed items remain on the visual in a dimmed color and the current item is highlighted in a brighter color.

Bullet list. A vertical list with items introduced by small graphic symbols (such as a bullet, arrow, box, and so on) that set them apart from each other.

Business presentation. A form of heightened conversation. If the business presentation is effective, the listeners know, think, or do what you wanted them to know, think, or do. At a minimum, they have understood what you wanted and refused after giving you a fair hearing.

Camcorder. A camera that records video.

Canned art. See *Clip art.*

CD-ROM. See *Compact disk.*

Chart junk. Too much information or graphic enhancements, which cause the meaning of a chart to be distorted and difficult to understand.

Climate control. Heating, ventilation, and air conditioning systems (HVAC) combined to help control the interior climate for the comfort of the people in a room.

Clip art. Illustrations available commercially; now available on computer disk for easy retrieval of black-and-white or full-color images. Most vendors usually provide a hard copy of the illustrations. The term *clip art* is a carryover from the days when these illustrations were available only on paper and designers literally cut out the illustrations with scissors and pasted them on their page layouts. Today, graphic file formats for the illustrations must be compatible with desktop publishing, word processing, or presentation software being used.

Cluster seating. A seating arrangement suitable for small-group discussion, usually with four to six people in a cluster.

Clustered bar chart. A group of bars that represent similar items from different data sets. These charts are effective for making comparisons.

Color. The reflection or absorption of light by a particular surface.

Column bar chart. See *Vertical bar chart.*

Compact disk (CD). A plastic disk that uses optical storage technology to store digital data as microscopic pits and smooth areas that reflect light differently. Most disks presently in use provide read-only memory; they are referred to as CD-ROM disks.

Computer conference. An electronic meeting between people sending messages via a computer network (computers cabled together or connected through telephone lines).

Context. The background of the message; the reason you are making a presentation. It helps the listeners understand why they are listening to you.

Copyboard. A board used to record, display, and reproduce whatever is written upon it. This is an excellent meeting management device to capture participants' ideas in brainstorming and planning sessions.

Critical listener. The listener whose needs govern the choices you make as you prepare the presentation. The person who will make the decision about what to do with your ideas and who will determine whether what you want to have the listeners know, think, or do gets known, thought, or done.

Critical path method chart. A process diagram showing the chronological succession of project activities.

Deliverable. Something tangible that you produce. It can be a report, a product sample, or a written procedure; always something that can physically be given to someone else.

Decibel. A measure of sound intensity.

Desktop presentations. Visual presentations prepared on a desktop computer system (computer, laser printer or other output devices, and presentation software). Presentation software provides automatic sizing for slides or overheads, word-processing capabilities, drawing and graphic features, and development and projection of computer-based screen shows.

Desktop publishing. The process of producing publication-quality materials, such as brochures, catalogs, books, and so forth, with a desktop computer system (computer, laser printer, and page-layout software); allows a level of printing sophistication formerly possible only by professional typesetting and graphic design artists.

Desktop video. Video production using low-cost video equipment and desktop computers.

Deviation bar chart. A chart with bars to the left or right of the reference axis indicating the area of standard deviation. Used to emphasize differences from an expected value.

Diagrams. Images showing either spatial relationships or process paths.

Dialog box. An on-screen message box used in some software to convey or request information from the user.

Diaphragm. The area in your lower chest that acts as an air valve: It rises and falls to let air in and push air out.

Digital sound. Sound created using a computer.

Digitize. To turn an image (artwork, photographs, text) into a format usable by a computer system through a process that scans the image into digital bits.

Dingbat. A decorative character or symbol (such as a star, flower, or pointing hand) used for bulleted lists, borders, or decoration.

Dissolve effect. A transition technique in computer-based presentations for changing one computer visual to another by having the existing visual appear to dissolve on the screen.

Energy. The sense of power a speaker communicates when he or she uses a full voice, gestures, and expressions that match the topic.

Enunciation. The act of saying words that are complete and easy to understand; achieved by avoiding mumbling and slurring of your words.

Evaluation feedback. Audience reaction to a presentation; can be obtained informally by observing responses and attitudes of the audience or formally by using an evaluation form.

Exploding pie chart. A pie chart with emphasis added to one segment by visually pulling it away from the whole. Also see *Pie chart.*

Fade effect. A transition technique in computer-based presentations to change one computer visual to another by having the existing visual appear to fade off the screen.

Film recorder. A device with a camera used to expose film to make slides of computer images for a presentation. When using presentation software, a film recorder is one available output device.

Flatbed scanner. A type of scanner with a glass plate similar to a photocopy machine on which the image to be scanned is placed. Also see *Scanner*.

Flip chart. A large paper tablet, usually placed on an easel, suitable for use in presenting to small groups; may be prepared during a presentation or created in advance using a computer, software, and printing devices to make professional-looking visuals.

Floor plan. A diagram showing drawings prepared for a room to show the seating arrangements. Can be developed using computer-aided software.

Font. A set of characters (the full alphabet, numbers, and symbols) in one weight and style of a typeface. Also see *Typeface*.

Footcandle. A unit of measurement used to determine light density.

Formal balance. A centered pattern of images on a page or visual arranged to be symmetrical.

Frame. A perspective or a viewpoint that you put on a fact or issue; for example, business professionals tend to frame situations as opportunities, not as problems.

Frame. An individual slide, overhead transparencies, or film image.

Frame grabber. A device used to capture one or more video images.

Front projection. The capability of equipment within a room (such as a slide projector or ceiling-mounted unit) that projects presentation visuals on a large screen for audience viewing.

Gantt chart. A process diagram representing activities occurring either sequentially or concurrently along a time line.

Glass-beaded surface. A projection screen surface that provides superior brightness, greater picture depth, richer detail, and excellent tone gradation in a normally darkened room; suitable for slide or movie projections.

Grabber. The way a presenter uses a story, anecdote, or statistic to grab the attention of the audience at the beginning of the presentation.

Gradient color. The gradual change of one color to another with no discernible break.

Graphics. Image enhancements such as lines, boxes, backgrounds, art, clip art, scanned images, and so on, used to create interesting and appealing visuals.

Gray-scale scanner. A type of scanner that uses variable values for different shades of gray. Also see *Scanner*.

Grid. A pattern of evenly spaced, intersecting lines on a chart showing scale and reference values; may also be used like graph paper on a screen as an aid for alignment while developing visuals.

Group decision support system. Computer systems and software designed to facilitate group input and decision-making.

Group, large. An audience of more than 30. If the presenter has a difficult time seeing each person in the audience, it is probably a large audience.

Group, small. An audience of one up to 30 people.

Handouts. Printed materials used during a presentation. Appearance is very important. Distribution timing depends on the purpose and desired audience interaction.

Heckler. Someone in the audience who interrupts, harasses, and annoys you; usually has a specific concern he wants to make and makes it in ways that interrupt the flow of your presentation, prevent other listeners from asking questions, and intimidate you.

Herringbone pattern. A seating arrangement where tables and chairs for participants are arranged in V shapes with tables angled.

Hidden agenda. A purpose someone has that he doesn't let anyone know about. Hidden agendas are dangerous for presenters because people who have them tend to argue about points that don't seem significant or seem irrelevant. If the presenter knows about a hidden agenda, the arguments make a great deal of sense and the presenter can respond more directly to answer the concern and keep the presentation on target.

Horizontal bar chart. A chart with one scale used to show relationships or a single point in time. Usually ranked by size with the largest bar on top.

Hue. The actual name used for the color of an object (such as red or blue); however, the perception of hue is affected by background or surrounding colors.

Import. To transfer a single image or a complete file from one document to another using one or more computer programs.

Influencers. People the critical listener trusts and believes have his or her best interests at heart.

Justified. Text aligned on both left and right margins (flush-left or flush-right alignment) with spacing between the words and letters adjusted so that all lines begin and end in the same positions; gives printed lines a blocked look.

Kerning. The adjustment of space between paired letters. Most software provides automatic kerning, but sometimes an adjustment may be necessary to improve the appearance and readability of the text.

Keystone effect. The distortion of the image from a projector onto a screen so that the top section of the image is wider than the bottom section of the image.

Landscape. Page orientation where printing is aligned horizontally on the long edge of the paper (for standard-sized paper, the 11-inch side). Also see *Portrait.*

Laser optical disk. A device used for the storage and retrieval of still pictures or video pictures and sound.

Lavaliere-type microphone. A small microphone that can be clipped to clothing; usually equipped with a long cord to allow mobility when speaking.

LCD panel. A liquid crystal display, flat-panel unit connected to a computer and placed on an overhead projector. The projector light shines through the LCD panel to show the computer's screen image. These units can project in black and white or in full color.

Lead time. The time before a presentation that is available for planning and production of needed materials.

Leading. The vertical spacing between lines of text, measured in points.

Lectern. The stand you put your notes on; often huge, wooden furniture with lights for the notes and buttons for controlling the machinery for visual aids. Sometimes lightweight, portable, and easily collapsable if leaned up; other times are half-height that sit on tables.

Left alignment. Text that is aligned at the left margin but ragged (uneven) at the right margin.

Legend. A caption or notation explaining the meaning of colors or patterns used in a chart.

Lightness. A quality of color determined by how much white, gray, or black is in the hue.

Line chart. A chart used to illustrate trends (usually over time) by connecting data points with curved or straight lines; may show a comparison of several trends by using multiple lines differentiated by color or line styles.

Map. A place diagram showing a map.

Master. See *Template.*

Matte surface. An all-purpose surface for projection screens that is less expensive than glass-beaded or pearlescent surfaces.

Media. Communication devices used to support and help convey a presentation message. Media may take the simple form of overhead transparencies or a handout to complex forms such as computer-based or multimedia presentations.

Model. An actual product or miniature scaled mock-up that closely resembles the real product.

Modified classroom. A seating arrangement where tables and chairs for participants are arranged in a semicircular arrangement. Tables are often connected with trapezoid pieces for a smooth, continuous appearance. Rooms may be tiered for maximum visibility.

Modulation. A change in the tone or pitch of the voice.

Multimedia presentations. Visual presentations that integrate text, graphics, sound, animation, video, and interactivity to communicate information and express imagination to an audience.

Nonverbal communication. Body language, including mannerisms and gestures, that conveys messages.

Numeric chart. A chart used to convey information and concepts to audiences by showing the relative proportions of data sets; shows frequency distributions, time-related events, comparisons, or correlations.

Optical disk. See *Compact disk.*

Organizational chart. A diagram used in presentations to illustrate hierarchical relationships, such as a company structure.

Overhead transparency. A plastic sheet printed with text, graphics, or pictures that allows an image to be projected to a screen by means of an overhead projector. (Also referred to as a viewgraph, foil, or overhead.)

Overriding theme. The information that remains in the mind of the audience after the presentation is finished.

Paint program. Software that enables the user to draw. Drawing tools represented by various paint object icons (such as a brush or spray can) are used to color the on-screen pixels in different colors. Images are treated as a collection of pixels rather than objects or shapes.

Paired horizontal bars. Bars in a chart used to compare negative/positive sets of data. Usually negative values are placed on the left of a reference point and positive values are placed on the right.

Pearlescent surface. A projection screen surface that has excellent reflectivity and brilliance. This surface is useful for video and liquid crystal display projection.

PERT chart. A type of chart used for management planning, showing the correct order of events and activities in a particular project.

Pictorial symbols. Images used to represent the value or exact size of a bar. May include pictures, symbols, or other objects.

Pie chart. A type of chart that contains a single-scaled, circular graphic that shows proportions in relation to a whole.

Pixels. Tiny dots of light (picture elements) that form characters and objects on a computer monitor; clarity of the monitor is determined by the pixel resolution (the density of the pixels).

Place diagram. A diagram that displays spatial relationships.

Podium. The wooden structure you stand on top of; can be solid or flimsy, can permit you to stand still, or can make your every minor movement look like big motion to listeners. Helps you stand above the listeners so that it is easier for a large group to see you.

Point. The smallest typographic unit of measurement for typefaces and lines. One inch contains 72 points.

Portrait. Page orientation where printing is aligned vertically on the short edge of the paper (for standard-sized paper, the 8 1/2-inch side). Also see *Landscape.*

Posters. Thick, oversized pieces of paper; can be prepared during a presentation or can be made in advance using a computer, software, and printing devices to make professional-looking printed visuals.

Presentation graphics. High-quality slides, overhead transparencies, or computer images for displaying information to an audience. The term may be used to represent specific programs that create graphs. Also see *Desktop presentations.*

Presentation media. The combination of written materials and projected visual images used in a presentation; a term coined by Apple Computer, Inc., to encompass both the areas of desktop publishing and desktop presentations.

Presentation strategy. A crucial part of presentation planning that includes audience analysis, time consideration, resource availability, objectives, research, and presentation organization.

Preview. The process of checking before a presentation to see that slides or other materials are arranged in proper sequence.

Process diagram. A diagram that shows sequential, branching, or concurrent steps in a procedure from its beginning to end.

Projection unit. A direct computer-to-projection system for displaying computer-based presentations that allows vivid, full color projection.

Rear projection. The capability of equipment to project images from behind the wall at the focal point of the presentation room. Only the visual, not the equipment, is visible for audience viewing.

Rehearse. To practice a presentation by actually going through the materials and giving the presentation.

Review. To go over notes before a presentation in order to study pertinent facts, figures, ideas, and transitions.

Right alignment. Text that is aligned at the right margin but ragged (uneven) at the left margin.

Roadmap. The sequence of topics you will explain to support the message; it is the facts, grouped by topic.

Rule. A horizontal or vertical line of varying width, texture, and color.

Sans serif. Typeface characters designed without serifs (small strokes on the ends of the main character stems).

Saturation. The brightness and vividness of a color.

Scale. Numbering on the axes of a chart. Should be in units easily understood by the readers/viewers.

Scale drawing. A place diagram representing the representative relational scale of an object or site.

Scanner. A device that digitizes an image (artwork, photographs, or text) and stores it as a computer file. The use of optical character-recognition software is necessary to interpret the scanned image as text.

Scattergram. A chart showing the correlation between two data sets. Points are plotted on two independent scales and tested statistically with regression analysis.

Screening. Various densities of black-and-white patterns used to create an illusion of different shades of gray.

Seating cone. The area of a room where seated participants can view a projection screen.

Serif. Fine cross-strokes or flares at the ends of the main stems of letters.

Stacked bar chart. A bar chart that combines related values into columns, and then compares columns representing different data sets; effective for comparing the total column values, but not effective for showing the related values that make up the columns.

Stance. Posture; how you stand.

Storyboard. A visual outline of a presentation showing sketched layouts of images (on paper or on note cards for easy rearranging) to be developed with the computer using presentation software. Some software allows the display of multiple images on the screen at one time in miniature form to aid in creating storyboards with a computer.

Task lighting. Illumination of a visual task area, such as a lectern, for improved visibility of notes.

Telephone conference. An audio conference between two or more people at potentially remote locations.

TelePrompTer. A computer linked to a screen that enables you to read your script from a glass square in front of the lectern.

Template. An image that serves as a background for computer-based presentations; adds consistency and continuity and may include such elements as the presentation title, a company logo, line art, or graphics; can easily be created, although presentation software provides many pre-designed templates, which also can be customized.

3-D. The three-dimensional illusion of depth for bar, pie, or line charts created by shading. Presentation software provides default values that can be easily modified to change the appearance of the bars or pie segments.

Time line. A line plotted in a diagram or graph designed to show historical progress.

Title visual. The opening visual in a presentation; serves the same purpose as a title page of a report and includes such things as title of the presentation, presenter's name, corporate logo, and so forth.

Tone. The mood of a presentation. Subdued colors may contribute to a conservative tone; bright, bold colors may convey a mood of excitement. Content, clip art, and other graphic enhancements will help to set the tone of visuals, and visuals will set the tone of the presentation.

Toolbox. A group of icons (miniature illustrations representing a function) that is visible on a computer screen with some presentation software.

Tracking. The overall spacing within text; often adjusted, especially for headlines and titles, when spacing between letters appears uneven.

Type. See *Typeface*.

Type family. All the variations of a basic type design in every weight and point size.

Type style. Individual variations of a typeface, such as plain, bold, italic, underscore, shadow, and outline.

Typeface. A specific type design, such as Times Roman or Garamond. Some people use the terms *typeface* and *font* interchangeably.

V-Shape pattern. A seating arrangement where tables and chairs for participants are arranged in a V shape with tables angled on both sides of a center aisle; also referred to as a chevron pattern.

Vertical bar chart. A chart with bars forming vertical columns to show quantity relationships or how something changes over time.

Video clip. A section of video tape.

Videoconference. A meeting in which people in two or more locations, usually distant, can see and hear each other.

Video digitizer. A device that captures images in digital form from videotape.

Video card. A special card in a computer connected to a video recorder that allows the conversion of computer images to videotape; used to edit sound or voiceovers into the production.

Video show device. Equipment that allows the projection of visuals prepared as a computer-based show without the computer.

Visuals. Objects or projected images containing text, graphs, and illustrations used to clarify a presentation message.

Voice, full. The result of deep breathing; allows you to project your voice to all members of the audience with full resonance and power.

Voiceover. The audio portion of a multimedia program when a graphic or video is displayed and the speaker can be heard but not seen.

Wipe effect. A transition technique in computer-based presentations for changing one computer visual to another by having an existing visual appear to be wiped off the screen.

Word spacing. Horizontal spacing between words created by the space bar on the keyboard; automatically set in relation to the typeface and size selected, but can be adjusted with some software.

X-axis. The horizontal line of a chart showing independent data classification; usually shows time stated in years, months, quarters, or weeks. (For a horizontal bar chart, see *Y-axis.*)

Y-axis. The vertical line of a chart showing the values of the dependent variable data set; usually the focus of the chart. (For a horizontal bar chart, see *X-axis.*)

INDEX

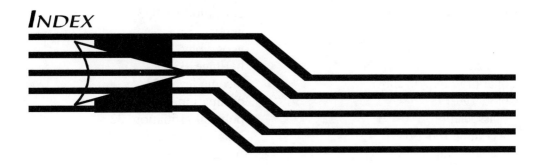

About the Author

G. Michael Campbell is a managing director with Holland & Davis, LLC, in Houston, Texas. He is a nationally recognized expert on performance consulting and shared services. He has been a featured speaker at numerous national conferences and has published several articles in a variety of national and international publications. As an outstanding speaker himself, Mike is sought by business groups looking for concrete results in an entertaining format. He has consulted with senior management groups on strategic and organizational issues, prepared management teams for organizational change and business development, and assisted major companies in training hundreds of employees in communication skills.